*f*P

Product
Creation

The Heart of the Enterprise
from Engineering to E-Commerce

Philip H. Francis

THE FREE PRESS

NEW YORK   LONDON   TORONTO   SYDNEY   SINGAPORE

THE FREE PRESS

A Division of Simon & Schuster, Inc.
1230 Avenue of the Americas
New York, NY 10020

THE FREE PRESS and colophon are trademarks of Simon & Schuster, Inc.

Designed by Stratford Publishing Services, Inc.

Manufactured in the United States of America

10   9   8   7   6   5   4   3   2   1

Library of Congress Cataloging-in-Publication Data

Francis, Philip H.
   Product creation: the heart of the enterprise: from engineering to e-commerce /
Philip H. Francis.
      p. cm.
   Includes bibliographical references and index.
   1. New products—Management.   2. Product management.   I. Title.

HF5415.153.F728   2000
658.5'75—dc21
                                                                00-060970
ISBN 13: 978-1-4165-7639-6   ISBN 10: 1-4165-7639-8

*To my mentors S. Rao Valluri, Royce Beckett, Kwan Rim
and Jerre Stead, with gratitude.*

Contents

In Gratitude

Three terrific women were most instrumental in helping me develop this book. First, grateful thanks to my dear wife, Diana, for her support of the time needed over the past several years to complete this project. Then there's Patricia Moody, accomplished author and editor in the manufacturing realm, who helped me enormously in shaping the book initially with its focus for working managers. And deep thanks also are owed to our talented friend Evelyn Forstadt, who edited the entire manuscript and provided invaluable advice for making it more cohesive.

Among many others who influenced me along the way is Dr. Joel Goldhar, professor of business at the Illinois Institute of Technology, who has for years helped form my thinking about the role of business strategy in manufacturing. Thanks go also to longtime friend Dr. Keith McKee, also of IIT, for his early review of the book and the helpful insight he offered for integrating the various chapters. And many thanks go to good friends Dr. Jim Ashton, CEO of Precision Partners, to Pat and Bill Wiggenhorn, both of Motorola, for their encouragement and advice in molding the book. I'd like also to thank Jerre Stead, CEO of Ingram Micro, for teaching me about unleashing the creative power of people in organizations and how customers *should* be treated.

I was lucky also to have the help of some real pros in developing the subject content of several of the chapters. Foremost among them are Scott Law, director of engineering at Schneider Electric, for our many discussions about product development processes, as reflected in Chapter 2, and Dr. Gerry Hoffman, professor at Northwestern University and information technology consultant, for his careful review of Chapter 4 on information systems. My son, Ed Francis, a Naval Academy graduate and a business leader himself with Andersen Consulting, critiqued Chapter 5 on leadership. Dr. Jim Hales, dean of the College of Applied Science & Technology at East Tennessee State University, helped with his critique on quality, Chapter 7. Chapter 9 on legal issues was greatly enriched by Larry Golden, senior patent attorney at Schneider Electric, and by our dear daughter, Mary Francis, an IP attorney with Thelen Reid & Priest, LLP.

My appreciation also goes to Walter Gillette, vice president of engineering for Boeing, for providing me with information on the 777 airplane, and to Prof. Eitan Zemel, then at Northwestern (now at NYU), for our many conversations about the role of total quality in new product development. Finally I want to thank Bob Wallace, senior editor at the Free Press, and his staff, particularly Anne-Marie Sheedy and Cornelia Faifar, for making this contribution possible.

Phil Francis

Preface

I've been fortunate to see the landscape of new product development (NPD) from many perspectives. I studied machine design in college and, early in my career, saw one aspect of NPD from my basic research in materials and mechanics. Next, I saw it while teaching design as a college professor and, later, by directing advanced manufacturing technology at Motorola. I saw it again at Schneider Electric (formerly the Square D Company) by having corporate responsibility for new product creation and, more recently, as a consultant helping others excel at it.

This journey has shown me that product creation is much more than design or production or any other single discipline. NPD has no organizational limits. Rather, it's a complex tapestry that comprises all the major processes found within any industrial or service organization. In short, it's an *enterprise* process. Certainly engineering and industrial design are core components—but so, too, is design's interface with manufacturing. Also essential is the customer's voice, quality commitments, technology, management, and leadership—and so on. The process of product creation should mirror the inner workings of the modern organization itself: fast, fluid, without hierarchies or internal boundaries, and knowledge-rich. Achieving this level of excellence requires good leadership and a good knowledge of processes.

During my own professional experience I've become a sort of missionary. I've preached the message that excellence in new product development can take place only in an environment where *all business processes* are focused upon NPD as the enterprise's basic business. From this premise follow many implications. For example, people should rotate through various areas and responsibilities in order to appreciate the "big picture." Also, senior managers—if they're to lead effectively—should understand in some depth the dimensions of NPD and its various requirements. The big decisions all across the organization must be made by people who have a modern understanding of production, R&D, technology, and of course, product strategy and how it's evolving in the modern era. Also, continuing education—lifetime learning—is now a requirement for successfully competing in business.

Another aspect of my mission is to bring this same message to our colleges of engineering, science, and business. With very few exceptions, our higher educational system—especially at the graduate level—breeds professionals who are narrow specialists. Education tends to be dispensed in information packets (courses) by professors who, because of their own narrow training, are limited in their ability to articulate the linkages among the many parts involved in new product development. Wouldn't it be wonderful if, say, engineering professors responsible for educating our future new product developers *themselves* had actual experience in creating new products—as professors of medicine do in their field? And shouldn't they be able to articulate the roles played by leadership, customer care, business strategy and operations, and customer intimacy? On the other hand, wouldn't it be equally good if our MBA programs could instill their students with appreciation of the roles of R&D and technology, quality, production systems, and leadership roles in running the modern enterprise? And how about both groups being able to address the vital roles played by processes, patents and related legal issues, and modern manufacturing methods? There are enormous pressures in the "real world" for new product developers to "get it right, the first time." I believe that competitive pressures ultimately will influence our colleges and universities to enrich their teaching approaches for engineers and businesspeople alike. It's simply the right thing to do. Witness the rapid emergence of corporate universities (now approaching 2,000 in the United States) chartered to educate employees in subjects that used to be the exclusive purview of academia.

I've written this book with a dual agenda. It's intended both for those trained in technology and for senior executive industrial managers. In doing this I've tried hard to sidestep technical jargon and details and focus instead on the conceptual material that is essential for practicing and leading new product creation. I've also tried to elevate the subject by making it the friend of the industrial manager who is (or wants to become) a leader in orchestrating the processes for product creation. The result, I believe, is an easy-to-read and rather thorough treatment of the subject. It's punctuated throughout with many practical specifics, and at the end of each chapter, I've included a list of "Ideas for Action" that are sure to be useful.

I hope you enjoy reading this—and refer to it along your journey—every bit as much as I enjoyed preparing it. *Bon appétit!*

P. H. Francis

A Briefing

The Landscape for Cultivating New Products

1.1: WHY MORE NEW PRODUCTS, PRODUCED BETTER AND FASTER, ARE IMPORTANT

If you want a peek at the future of how products will be developed and distributed, look no further than the Foot Locker, Athlete's Foot, or other athletic equipment retail outlets in your local mall. Not long ago if you wanted a sports shoe, you went to a department or discount store where you were fitted with a conventional shoe that would meet your needs.

Today the customer is greeted by a salesperson specializing in athletic shoes. This person does not ask you your shoe size. Rather, you are asked about your lifestyle! Do you run? Regularly or occasionally? Are you a competitive or a recreational runner? How about basketball or soccer or other sports? Might you wear them outside the athletic venue? Where and with what? What problems do you have with your feet? Are you under treatment, and do you use prescription insoles? What brand allegiances do you have, and why? Are you enough of a risk taker to experiment with a shoe that has different stiffness or friction characteristics? Are you perhaps interested in a custom-fitted shoe? Are you a fast runner? If you are, it's likely that you run on your toes, not heel to toe as slower joggers do. Apparently speed is a factor in selecting athletic shoes.

After completing this personal audit, you are shown a few candidates, and you narrow down your preferences based on price and the salesperson's recommendations. You are unlikely to buy a replacement for your old shoes, now well worn, because they've been obsolete for months. Product change—the universal constant—is inescapable. At this point your foot size is measured and you are fitted. The salesperson probably knows more about your recreational interests than your best buddy does.

This vignette illustrates how we are bombarded daily by a growing blitz of new products. Our culture accepts—indeed, pushes for—rapid product obsolescence. The forces of new technologies, media persuasion, and trendy lifestyles all conspire to influence us to buy more frequently.

Getting to Know You

This shoe-buying episode will become increasingly more sophisticated—and pervasive—as the future unfolds. Imagine an extension of the above scenario. Your spouse, who also is athletically inclined, is with you as you buy the shoes. The salesperson off-handedly asks if this is a special occasion or did you just "happen by." Your wife remarks that it's a birthday present for you.

The salesperson casually asks the birth date and remembers it as the transaction is completed. Just after you leave, that date—along with your name and address—is entered into an electronic file. It will now automatically generate and send you a "personalized" birthday card six weeks before your next birthday. Included with the card will be a coupon for a 15 percent discount on your next athletic shoe or accessory purchase if made at that or any other affiliated store.

The electronic file has behind it a database that allows the retailer to assemble all purchase information about you and your family members. This file allows the store to profile your particular family. The information system can target various customer groups by age, special interests, dates, and so forth and provide them with special promotional offerings as incentives to keep them shopping there. This is merchandising sophistication at its (current) best. It has enlightened, well-trained, and motivated employees backed by powerful information systems to please and to "hook" the customer. Customer loyalty is the goal and is indeed an integral component of product creation.

This scenario, of course, extends far beyond the shoe outlet. At no time in the history of the United States or other developed nations have we seen so much product diversity—and just plain product glut—as we see today. Not long ago manufacturers could sell virtually anything and everything they could produce to a young and growing economy thirsty for goods.

Products were pushed into our economy and we grabbed them. Quality wasn't really an issue, nor were consumers in a position to demand quick deliveries or special features. Henry Ford built his empire on the premise that customers would be content with a black car, and he was right. Land, labor, and capital were the essential ingredients then for a successful manufacturer. Variety mattered little.

But not so now. Many manufacturers, including such companies as Microsoft and Nike, and e-commerce companies simply have no traditional production facilities. They own little real estate. Their products are the result of intellectual prowess, not capital investment. They produce largely through outsourcing to independent production suppliers around the world. In short, they produce *differently* than manufacturers did in earlier times. And they market differently, via virtual malls and e-commerce.

This is today's manufacturing landscape—far removed from the industrial era of Henry Ford. As Larry Hollatz, group VP of Advanced Micro Devices puts it, "Intellectual, not physical capital fuels new growth industries. Communication between individuals and teams is more important than concentration of resources. Technical communication provides for integration of thought and planning. It has become impossible to avoid knowledge-spread. With so much data available, it is essential to demand that people use data competitively."

Product creation is the fuel that feeds today's growth and competitiveness. The very basis of the enterprise depends on placing a continuing stream of successful new products into the marketplace. All its purposes— profits and earnings, shareholder returns, service to customers, opportunity and fair treatment of employees, assistance to the communities in which it operates—directly depend upon the effectiveness of new product creation. Our capacity to produce in almost infinite quantities and varieties has shifted the balance of power and influence from the producer to the consumer. We used to pay lip service to the adage that the customer is sovereign. Today it is a literal fact; the consumer *is* in the driver's seat.

Staying on top of business opportunities in such a dynamic market requires leadership, the courage to take risks, and investment in new knowledge and intellectual property. As the adage goes, you can't save your way to prosperity. Leaders are sweeping away the obsolete notion of denominator management: companies boasting of gains that come from reducing expenses rather than increasing profitable growth. Sure, trimming waste, cycle times, and other process inefficiencies is important; you must attend to that. But it doesn't grow your company. That requires mastering new product creation and all its supporting cast. In the words of Samsung's chairman, Kun-hee Lee, "In the future, R&D, design, and product planning capabilities will determine 90% of a product/s competitiveness."

The Challenged Customer

The customer is the key determinant of new product success. The customer daily faces buying judgments that require decisions concerning finely divided choices: size/capacity, durability, convenience, value, after-sales service, financing alternatives, kinds of technology, and so on. But few of us have time and expertise enough to evaluate all these choices objectively. We therefore turn to other sources—friends, the manufacturer's reputation, brand loyalty, assessments from independent product evaluation sources—or the marketing media to help. Along with the privilege of having more buying choices, we find ourselves more challenged than ever in trying to make the right decisions.

The Diversity of Manufactured Goods

And the business of producing is much more sophisticated than it ever was. Even the very notion of what a manufactured product essentially *is* has changed. What exactly is a manufactured product? Is it a "thing"? What about a new home or natural gas distribution or an amusement park ride? Are these manufactured products?

I sometimes wonder what the general population thinks about the business of new product creation. As with art, the essence of "manufacturing" is in the eye of the beholder. It's easy to understand that assembled things are the result of manufacturing processes. But a product can also merge with service, as in the case of life insurance or dry cleaning. And what about software products, which are intellectual creations that are reproduced electronically?

Most people tend to think of manufacturing in terms of the production of tangible, discrete products: autos, electrical and electronic devices and computers, industrial machinery and tools, appliances, aircraft, and countless other kinds of widgets that go into these original equipment manufacturer (OEM) products. Discrete products, of course, have their own kinds of variety. Some are mass-produced; others—such as computers—are somewhat customized according to the buyer's particular option requirements. Still others are strictly built to order—such as large machine tools and buildings.

"Manufacturing" is indeed a big tent. It also includes producing substances, such as petroleum products, pharmaceuticals, rubber and plastics, chemicals, metals and alloys, and consumable foodstuffs such as beverages and related products. Some of these manufactured products are produced with continuous processes such as reactors and mixers and then delivered to the customer's site on demand, for example, electricity, telecommunications, and natural gas. Other continuous products are packaged in batches, in units of weight or volume. We, the end customers, buy a gallon of gas, a pound of salt, or a yard of fabric—convenient units of the product. Sometimes there isn't a clear line that separates discrete from continuous products. Consider microencapsulated medicines, beverage cans, or common carpentry nails. Anyone who has watched them being manufactured is struck that despite their "discreteness," because of their high speed of manufacture they appear to the eye as a blur of continuous product. Only when they are packaged for the convenience of the end customer do we notice their discreteness.

Whatever our notion of a manufactured product may be, anticipating what the customer will choose and pay for goods now drives many business decisions. Most kinds of products are available in various price tiers. Some products are driven by trend and fashion; others by utility and dependability. But in a marketplace rich with competitors ultimately it is *value*—the quality, dependability, and ease of service per dollar paid—that is most often the determinant of what a product will cost to manufacture. The manufacturer must take into account the price point for the product and then calculate the product cost that will deliver an acceptable return. Other product ingredients, like the appropriate design and technology, then become constrained by the allowable product cost.

Enter the E-Business Era

There's one more chapter to the athletic shoe story. As we'll see throughout this book e-business is rapidly changing the business landscape. The level of product and service business transacted over Web pages and through portals is skyrocketing.

Taking shoe shopping to the next level, suppose you get on your computer and surf to find the Web locations of a couple of athletic shoe producers you like. You call up a Web site of your choice, and a questionnaire pops up. It asks for your sex, age, body type, physical limitations, and the way you'll use your new shoes. It also asks for various measures of each of your feet and of any abnormalities or other problems that you suffer. It asks for styling preferences, colors, and the like. All these measurements create your "profile"; it defines your shoe requirements in detail. You gather this information and log on again and provide your vendor with the requested information. You provide your credit or debit card number and zap it back to your vendor of choice. When your shoe supplier instantly gets your order—*uniquely yours*—your shoes are manufactured (somewhere in the world) within 24 hours. Then your order is sent to you by regular or express post, according to your instructions.

Fantasy? Not at all. Toyota is rolling out a production process by which a car can be built to your own specifications within *five days* of order receipt. To put this in context, GM's benchmark is 17 to 18 days; DaimlerChrysler claims about 12. So the Toyota achievement, by comparison, is stunning! Now, if car companies can rapidly build "customized" products to order, why not sports shoes and, indeed, the entire market of manufactured goods? As we'll see throughout this book, there's little excuse for not dreaming the future, then implementing it.[1]

This vignette exemplifies the forces driving the new e-commerce era. You needn't "shop" in the conventional sense of driving to your nearest mall or discount outlet. You needn't choose among the available sizes or styles, for no matter how rich your vendor's inventory, it can't fully please even the majority of customers, let alone all. And by reducing the number of retail outlets, costs are reduced and some of that cost savings is passed on to you in the form of lower prices.

1.2: WHAT YOU'LL GET FROM THIS BOOK

Maybe you share my observation that different people usually see product creation differently. To the folks in the R&D lab, it means offering up new technologies and applications that will enable even better products. Their viewpoint is that innovation is the key to successful products. To engineers, it's product design and the design tools that can analyze the performance of a new concept or design. They see design as the centerpiece of product creation. To industrial designers, it's all about style and packaging—to catch the eye and imagination of the customer. Mark Dziersk of the Industrial Designers Society of America makes this point: "When industries are competing at equal price and functionality, design is the only differential that matters." To production, what counts is the means chosen to manufacture the product. Their pride comes from the fact that they *actually make* the item. To customers, it's the value offered by that product. They're really in the driver's seat; they're the arbiters of your future. And to management, what counts is quality and competitiveness. It's these leaders who must make the decisions and take the risks that will spell the success or failure of the business.

Different viewpoints; each is right in some sense. Yet these perspectives all need to be knitted together to achieve the goal of product creation. They require the active participation of all support functions—including information technology systems, operational systems, and the legal issues that govern commerce. After all, product creation is none of these; it's *all* of them working in harmony It can't be done with workers laboring in isolated functional silos. Product development must span them all and bring balance and harmony among the key themes we'll describe in this book. Employees must function as a collection of musicians, playing together harmoniously. When they can make beautiful music together, they'll put a lasting mark on your company's future. Success is yours.

I believe the way that most of us understand how to create valuable products is highly inefficient—if not essentially wrong. Each of us is schooled in one of the above viewpoints, and each of us sees our particular focus as the essential role. Those other functions are merely the supporting cast—important, to be sure, but secondary. As time goes by, some of us may widen our awareness about other functions through new assignments. But it's rare for us to come to understand fully the complexity of launching successful products. Just think of how much better we might do at bringing new products to market if only we had a better understanding of the whole picture. Meanwhile, the R&D folks continue to have little contact with customers; designers don't take real ownership of product liability issues; production people have little to do with sales and marketing, and so on. Too often our organizational systems perpetuate narrowness and isolation.

My objective for this book is to set out the entire score for product creation. We'll look at product creation as a process consisting of several integrated functions working collaboratively. You'll see how each chapter's issues are important and how they contribute to the overall achievement of producing new, valuable products. Sprinkled throughout are examples drawn from people and companies who've done it right—and occasionally wrong. At the end of each chapter, you'll find a list of "Ideas for Action" for you to consider as you strive to improve your product creation abilities. Debate them; enlarge upon them. But by all means *use* them.

PRODUCT DEVELOPMENT

BRIEFING

Chapter 2

How to Excel at Product Development

Since the beginning of the industrial age, land, labor, and capital have been the engines that drove economic progress. However, the role of these factors in new product and market creation has yet to be fully understood. For example, why is it that despite a slowdown in one or more of these three inputs, some economies still can accelerate?

Recently Stanford's Paul Romer, a developer of the "new growth" economic theory, shed some light. He's shown that *technology*, systems and software, is in fact a fourth ingredient of growth and is the factor responsible for economic acceleration. Technology can raise returns on investment and make these investments even more valuable because of legal monopolies such as patent and other forms of intellectual property. Technology has an immense effect on developed countries' economies. How much land, labor, or capital do you need to launch a new e-commerce business? Entrepreneurism mixed with a dash of technology now creates not just companies but markets and industries! We now see clearly that the process of innovation is essential to a nation's standard of living. And it leads inevitably to more innovation, more technology, and shorter product lives. Society's challenge today is to cope with and capitalize upon these four forces.[1]

We see abounding change as we get ever closer to our customers, divide our markets more finely, and exploit the enormous potential of Internet services and Web-based technologies. In fact, all signs point to more robust global markets, especially for research-intensive industries such as aerospace, computers, electronics, communications equipment, and pharmaceuticals. The National Science Foundation estimates that products from these sectors will grow at more than twice the rate of most other manufactured goods. These sectors in turn will pull through new products from their supplier chains. The winners will be those who can marshal innovation in their R&D, product concepts, and production processes.

At the enterprise level, the creation of new products and services is the fuel needed to feed our growth and competitive appetites. Such products and services are the very basis for any successful company. Shareholder returns, service to customers, opportunities for employees, contributions to the communities in which the enterprise operates—all depend upon serving the right markets with an ongoing stream of valuable new products and services.

You'll see my penchant for the term "product creation" throughout this book. Although this term is relatively new, it could as well have been used a century ago, when it would have been synonymous with "manufacturing." Back then, creating a new product simply meant coming up with a product idea that met someone's need, then designing it and producing it. Customers would come knocking at your door. Today such a primitive approach would likely be a path toward business failure.

Yes, product creation today is far more complex than in the days when all that was needed was to design it and make it. Now it consists of all the elements involved in bringing a product to market: R&D, customer inputs and market analysis, design, production, and all the supporting systems—such as information technology quality and intellectual property and after-sales product support—that are part of a new product launch. Taking a new product from conception to market involves many interconnected steps. It relies upon marketing and marketing intelligence, product definition, planning and approval, research and engineering development, process development, product launch, and of course, after-sales services. Rigorous design and product reviews need to be conducted at critical points in each project's development to ensure that all requirements are being properly met, on time. All these efforts need to orchestrated and managed with precision. Indeed, new product creation must not be looked upon so much as a series of steps but as an organic *process* of interconnected functions.

Customers, whether for internal use or for external sales, should inspire every new product. Therefore, step one must be to understand thoroughly the market dynamics. What opportunities lie within the market for products or services that will attract and keep your customers? Pay close attention to how you best can exploit these opportunities. The central idea is simply this: maintain and continuously improve the product creation process. If this is done properly, the products will take care of themselves in the marketplace!

In this chapter I'll use a couple of models that will help you in product creation. The first we'll see underscores the interconnectivity of the various stages of new product creation. We'll emphasize a process model that orchestrates events and information, resulting in superior, competitive new products. Then we'll look at using virtual teams for globally dispersed operations, developing some useful tools, and using some of these process ideas in the creation of software.

2.1: A Model for Competitive Product Creating

My objective in this book is to provide you with a road map for success in the rapidly changing, highly competitive arena of new product creation. Traditionally, this business subject has taken one of two paths: in the direction of product design (usually engineering-oriented) or in the direction of product strategy and the management thereof (usually business-oriented). I'll be the first to agree that these approaches are important—in fact, *vital* to anyone with leadership responsibility for new product creation. It's how we learned.

Yet today the subject is larger that that. New product creation is now being seen as the very heart of the enterprise—whether manufacturer or service provider. Creating excellence in new products/services means harnessing and integrating nearly all of a company's functions to work in lock step. The goal is *products via process.* I'll discuss throughout the book the importance of having a well-conceived process for new product realization—and also how to measure it and manage it. We'll see why the process involves more than just R&D, product design and testing, and production operations. Yes, these factors are key. But it takes close communication with information technology, with quality systems, customer care, operations management, legal support, and—yes, with effective leadership and a skilled and dedicated workforce—to make your mission really flourish.

A good product development process—PDP—is your engine for creating the products and services that you'll need to win in today's highly competitive environment. It's the creator of your future. To emphasize this point, let's reach back in history to the engine that is credited with creating the industrial age: the venerable waterwheel. There happen to be a number of analogies between our current and this ancestral development engine, as we'll see in subsequent chapters. They each consist of components having mutual dependencies. These ancient machines—like today's well-conceived and integrated product development processes—have enormous leverage on productivity. The waterwheel will be our metaphor for the interconnectedness of NPD's various components.

The New Product Creation Wheel

Figure 2.1 shows the New Product Creation Wheel. It depicts the principle of the vertical, "overshot" waterwheel—the most common of a family of waterwheel configurations. The wheel turns on a horizontal axis by the

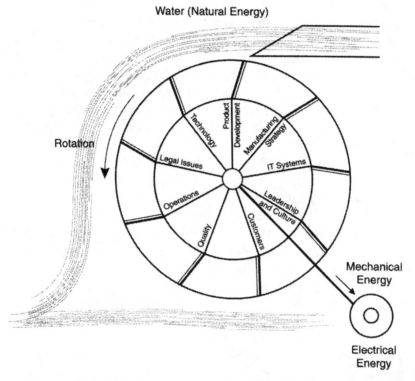

FIGURE 2.1   THE NEW PRODUCTION CREATION WHEEL—ANALOG OF THE NEW
PRODUCTION CREATION MACHINE

action of running water. As it turns, the wheel delivers useful work, such as mechanical action for milling and grinding or for driving an electric generator. Like its cousin the windmill, the waterwheel is one of human beings' first and simplest machines for creating "free" energy. More accurately, it transforms naturally existing energy into making agricultural and other products, by delivering power.[2,3]

The waterwheel symbolizes how new product creation is best practiced today. In earlier times (and even today) power was used in irrigation and to produce products ranging from smelted ores to beer mash. It's credited with broadening the commercial base beyond local townships by creating industrial and agrarian centers across the vast stretches of Europe and Asia.

I use the New Product Creation Wheel as a metaphor for new product development, for there are many analogies. The wheel draws resources from the energy of the marketplace in the form of creative ideas, market needs, and the supply chain. The organization focuses its energies through efficient processes to supply markets with the products it seeks. In the waterwheel it's the water velocity and the "hydraulic head"—the difference in water levels on either side of the wheel—that provide the energy needed to produce products. Entrepreneurs, a skilled workforce, technology, and an understanding of marketplace needs measure today's "business head." These are the factors that can lead to valuable product launches.

The New Product Creation Wheel offers still further insight into the ingredients needed for superior product creation. Notice that the wheel itself is a structure, organized with individual spokes that share the load. These spokes gird the wheel so that it may do its work without failing. In this metaphor the spokes are the key business functions that support new product creation. These nine spokes—each representing a chapter in this book—are bound together at the hub and provide the strength, cooperation, and discipline of the enterprise. These key business functions are:

- Product development
- Manufacturing
- Information Technology Systems
- Leadership and Culture
- Customers
- Quality
- Operations
- Legal Issues
- R&D and Emerging Technologies

The ancient waterwheel does indeed describe fairly well the dynamics of thoroughly modern companies—large and small—those that "do new product development right." Some top performers are known for superior strength in selected spokes. For example, they may excel at technological innovation or at production. Others are known for product quality and reliability. Still other companies are leaders in integrating and distributing information. Yet *total* perfection is a goal that seems always beyond our grasp. It requires mastery of *all* the spokes. No one seems to do it all, consistently. It's a company's weak spokes that make it vulnerable. But as you'll see in the ensuing chapters, the New Product Creation Wheel metaphor provides a useful conceptual model for continually strengthening your business's effectiveness.

2.2: Two Steps for Developing Valuable Products

Product development is at once simple and complex. It's simple because, as we'll see, developing new products only has two distinct steps. Yet it's complex because these two steps require thought, leadership, anticipation, patience, nurturing, and controlled speed. However, correctly implementing these two steps is worth every minute of your time and will give you a competitive edge like no other.

This chapter explains the significance of the first spoke on the New Product Creation Wheel—the new product development process. Successful new product development relies upon process, concurrent engineering, speed, and people. How a product is conceived, designed, distributed, priced, promoted, and supported is all-important. A new product delivery strategy involves carefully thinking through several vital strategic elements: product concept, product positioning, value offering, product art and design, market channels, and product promotion. My basic message here is that a *process* management approach for new product development should replace the traditional *project* management approach. We'll see in this chapter that the focus should be to manage the overall process of NPD; valuable products will then be the by-product of a genuinely good NPD process.

The two steps to excellence in product creation are (1) a steady stream of innovative ideas and (2) the process that allows you to turn these ideas into profitable products servicing markets with economy and delighting your customers. Let's have a look.

Step 1: New Ideas for New Products

Generally, new products are regarded as more tangible objects, which are ultimately bought by end customers. Products exist also as service components, as software, and as brand labels that command loyalty. Products, too, can be upgrades to internally developed business systems or processes that end consumers never see. Products can be advertising creations to promote products or to shape opinions. Generally, products are useful, intellectual creations, tangible or not, that are used inside or outside an enterprise.

Your road to successful product launches begins with continual market intelligence that identifies potential needs or opportunities. Once you understand what the market will welcome, your next task is the most fundamental of all: conceiving a valuable new product. Of course, having done your homework, you recognize that new product ideas often come from an outside opportunity and/or a need. But the job of translating those factors into an actual and effective product falls on you and your organization.

Therefore you should widely mobilize a continuing stream of new product development proposals from throughout the organization. Make it easy for people to float ideas, formalize, and submit them. All those who participate in these proposals deserve to be acknowledged and appreciated for their efforts. You should have a simple administrative procedure that encourages and facilitates new product proposals. This procedure ought to leverage the ideas across the entire company, not just those who run product-engineering functions. And those champions whose project proposals aren't accepted deserve a personalized explanation as to why. As important as these matters are, it's the easy part.

The hard part is how you can deal effectively with the blizzard of ideas and recommendations that (should) come from all corners of your organization. This leads us to "portfolio management." You can't—and *shouldn't*—take all of them on. You need a rational, objective process to evaluate project proposals so you end up selecting only the "best." Such an approach means not simply putting decision-making in the hands of one or two senior executives. There's no room here for the politics of pet projects. Everyone has biases. Everyone knows which are the "best" projects and yet can disagree strongly among themselves about particular choices. What you have here is the challenge of managing your portfolio of new product proposals. Investment bankers, fund managers, and others in the financial services learned long ago how to create and manage portfolios consisting of many disparate holdings. We can learn from them.

New products are the lifelines to your future. They are all different, and you soon find yourself choosing within a basket of fruit, not just picking out the best apples. Some projects are risky, others not; some are strategically vital, others not; some are costly, others not. Some projects simply must be given the go-ahead for regulatory compliance requirements. These particular decisions must be made "ex-portfolio." Otherwise, your goal is to select a collection of projects that, together, give you your best possible shot at a successful business future.

Keep in mind the four basic dimensions when managing a new product portfolio: strategic importance, financial return, likeliness of success, and urgency. All are more or less equally important. As "fruit" they're all different; you can't just add them up and pick those, say, with the highest revenue potential or the lowest risk. Rather, choosing requires a balancing act. You need a *process* for evaluating project proposals that, over the long run, will give you winners. These four dimensions of portfolio management provide the basis for such a process:

Strategic
- How, specifically, does the project align with your current and future product strategy?
- Does the project fill an important niche within the strategy?
- Is the project a new product or an extension of a current one?
- How likely is the project to spin off future new products or businesses?
- Will the project create or protect a competitive advantage?

Financial
- Do you fully understand the financial risks of *not* taking on this project?
- What are the expected costs, by project phase?
- What are the success factors for each phase of the project?
- What are the costs of bringing the project to market?
- What is the project's expected life-cycle return based on net present value, internal rate of return, or payback?
- Are you prepared to exploit this product fully and successfully?

The Risks Accompanying Project Acceptance
- Do you fully understand the technology and the development risks, and can you cover them?
- What are the business and economic risks?

- Do you have the resources to manage these risks?
- Do you understand the competitive downsides of *not* taking on this project?
- What market forces might arise to interfere with the project's success?
- Are there any other unexpected conditions (legal, regulatory, technological, etc.) that could arise to threaten the project's success?

Timing
- Is the proposed time frame realistic for launch?
- Do you understand the strategic and competitive losses of delaying this project?
- What is the economic penalty of delaying or killing this project?

Your objective is to maintain the overall portfolio so that it aligns with your business strategy and has a good balance with respect to risk, economic return, and competitive gain. It should have small and large projects; it should serve all market areas of your business. It should lead you to a successful future. In thinking through how to achieve these goals, *make sure* that each project accepted into your portfolio has at least one formal review, no exceptions. As we'll soon see when discussing the product development process, no project, once accepted, should automatically be entitled to continue through to product launch without critical justification along the way. Likewise, managing your new product portfolio should include a rigorous and comprehensive review of the *entire* portfolio, say semiannually. This twice-yearly lookover is your opportunity to step back and make adjustments that will ensure you are developing the best possible portfolio for the company at that moment. As a consequence, you may have to kill or postpone some specific projects in the higher interest of the overall portfolio. After all, your portfolio represents your company's future!

You have many ways to assess your portfolio; you need only to develop a methodology that can work effectively and uniformly across your entire organization. A good and simple starting point is to develop a scale for each of the four aspects listed above. For example, the "strategic" factor might have a scale running from zero ("is in clear conflict with our business strategy") all the way to ten ("is key to achieving our business strategy"), with specific steps between the extremes. Thus having constructed these four scales appropriate for your business, all projects in play and all those vying for acceptance can be ranked simply by adding up the four scores for each. Of course, those doing the scoring must have the wisdom and overall perspective of good, impartial judges. Once it gets political, all bets for process integrity are off!

But be aware that picking the winners by competitive scoring is deceptively simple, even if done with utmost fairness. You might find the resulting project portfolio somehow lacks the balance you seek. Yes, you need a balance of risk, economic return, and competitive gain, as mentioned earlier. But you also need balance across your business units, balance among large and small projects, and balance between incremental and truly new projects. Moreover, you might have removed from your list some projects that scored low because they carried high risk. But a truly balanced portfolio *should* include some risky projects—if they are associated with potentially high financial and/or strategic gain. The pharmaceutical industry has proved this over and over.

Another useful tool for selection within your portfolio is to create a list of "killer questions." Ask these questions of all candidate projects and answer them with a simple "yes" or "no." A single "no" answer is tantamount to killing the project, at least for that particular period. Here are a few such killer questions; add to them as appropriate.

- Is there a clear, competitive reason for making this investment?
- If successful, can we count on realizing the sales and margins as claimed?
- Will the project meet or exceed all legal and statutory regulations that apply?
- Do we have access to all the technology needed to make this project a clear success?

The message here is that the process is sovereign. Care and nurture your process of portfolio management, and it will take care of you.

You'll find that such a disciplined approach for project selection is vital to your future. You probably remember the most infamous product failure in the history of the computer industry: the Apple Lisa. It began with Steve Jobs's fresh vision to follow his company's popular Apple II product with one that would have a graphical user interface (GUI) and a mouse for easier human/machine communication. This idea was revolutionary stuff in early 1989 when Lisa had her debut. But the devil is in the details. Lisa was pricey ($10,000), heavy (48 pounds), and slow in performance owing to the GUI's large memory requirements. Despite mighty efforts to resuscitate the product with a newer, zippier model, Jobs pulled the plug on Lisa in the spring of 1995.

The lesson here is that vision, instincts, and courage are important, *absolutely* important! But so are the four aspects of portfolio management described above. They provide the discipline to balance visionary instincts. Had Jobs's team wrestled objectively with these portfolio aspects, Lisa may not have been born, and Apple itself may well have had a different future.

So don't pattern your portfolio management after the Lisa affair. Pattern it, instead, after the aluminum and packaging divisions of the French company Pechiney, S.A. Pechiney developed a rigorous process that ties together both the product development portfolio and the management of each new project. Conventional financial tools such as net present value and internal rate of return are used to rank each candidate project's expected sales volume and margins, and the cost reduction targets for improvements of existing products. The company also rates projects by such factors as urgency, alignment with their core competencies, level of risk, and profitability. Approved projects are required to have scheduled reviews during their journey through the process. No project is entitled to sail through the entire process unchallenged. Pechiney's goal is to maximize the value of its overall portfolio, year by year, by linking each project to its business strategy and to balance the portfolio in terms of exploratory projects, new products, and cost reductions. The result of this formalism is a portfolio of projects, each having passed rigorous business criteria and collectively in balance with regard to risk, competitive advantage, and profitability.

Another example of a disciplined portfolio management process comes from Medtronic, the $6 billion Minneapolis-based producer of devices to treat tremors and other neuromuscular diseases. Medtronics shapes its proposals through a process of cultivating groups of physicians who are likely to use their new products and who are willing to publish their work in professional journals. Medtronic's operating committee passes on all proposals that enter the portfolio pipeline. Proposals are judged competitively against both financial and affordability targets, with particular emphasis on choosing projects that will be able to sell in today's managed care environment. The process also has an appeal avenue for those projects that are initially rejected. In addition, Medtronic reserves a portion of the R&D budget to fund its "Quest" program for shaping exploratory, out-of-the-box ideas.[4]

As we've seen from managing the product portfolio, you may have several ideas incubating at once, some further along than others. Each product has to identify and compete for the right people and resources at various stages. Add to this milieu a dollop of risk that attends any new product development, and you can appreciate the difficult environment within which NPD occurs.

How best to navigate your way through these dangerous waters? The answer lies in rethinking old paradigms. The traditional approach is to regard each NPD project as just that—an isolated project to be managed. Someone is assigned to usher the project through each of the steps that have traditionally been used. He or she must compete for people and other resources and must simultaneously do battle with special interests while still meeting budget and quality requirements.

Clearly, the conventional *project-focused* approach for new product development is not the best way. It *suboptimizes* the NPD process. It forces a collision of special and competing interests among product engineers and managers. It can create needless discord. Most important, it can waste valuable time and resources.

By contrast, the *process-focused* approach of NPD borrows from the manufacturing arena. In earlier days manufacturing inspectors checked each widget as it snaked through the production line. The output was only as good as the inspectors' skill at finding and fixing defects. Now it's common knowledge that production excellence requires management of the *process*, not the widgets themselves. Process control uses tools, not inspectors. If the process is properly managed and continuously improved upon, then, absolutely, the widgets will meet all quality targets without the need for inspectors. The *process* is sovereign! And so it is with new product creation.

Suppose now that a product concept rises to the top of the portfolio heap and then gets formal approval—and a budget and resources—to establish itself as an initiative. Congratulations! But that doesn't mean it is entitled automatically to proceed all the way through to design and manufacture. Far from it. A new project should be required to "earn" that right at various stages along the path toward product launch. It can be killed at any stage in the face of negative new findings regarding risk, cost, technology, or market intelligence. The project can also be killed because of plain old discomfort from senior management. These people are ultimately responsible for defending the product to the outside community of investors, analysts, the trade press, distributors and dealers, and of course, customers. This "go–no go" decision gate tends to be subjective and sometimes can be very political.

Step 2: The Power of Process

OK, you now have a new product idea, one that has suffered through the Step 1 rigors of a portfolio management analysis: strategic thinking, financial and risk analyses, and timing considerations. You've asked the killer questions and didn't get a single "no" answer. Congratulations! You're now ready to move into the next step of new product development. Here's where you take your initiative from business case all the way to production. You must translate your excellent proposal into a product that can be manufactured with no wasted time, motion, or money—and that will be welcome in the marketplace. This is the hard part; this is where you enter the formal NPD process, which consists of four overlapping stages, listed below. We'll discuss them in greater detail shortly.

Business Case Justification—Develop the business plan around a specific product concept

- Emphasize market intelligence, product definition, and project planning
- Run a financial analysis: development timing and costs, staffing needs, financial paybacks
- Establish a firm product target cost—the absolute maximum cost of the product as agreed upon by all parties to the product launch
- Solidify channels, sales and marketing strategies

Concept Feasibility—Work toward rapid convergence on design and prototype evaluations; develop design criteria and plan for after-sales product support

- Evaluate and narrow the proposed technologies and design concepts; assess risk and competitive intelligence
- Make ready your technology: laboratory R&D to verify the concept or to develop the technologies that will enable the product
- Be thorough about design, testing, verification, and concurrent engineering
- Provide for design changes, customer feedback, product marketing, and after-market service calls and warranty costs
- Assure compliance with government and industry standards

Product Development—Complete product design and test; establish product and process quality targets; design process technology and qualification criteria

- Converge quickly on design
- Perform prototype testing and evaluation
- Comply with your process technology and design standards; quality targets, plans, and qualification

Pilot and Production Startup—Demonstrate production capability; launch product

- Design production processes; buy/build and install equipment
- Set up supplier and channel agreements
- Do pilot production testing; meet production process quality targets
- Hand off to manufacturing and begin production operations

The instrument for authorizing a project to enter the development process is your formally documented PDP. In general, all authorized projects should be required to pass through one or more decision gates provided for in this process document. Each authorized project should have to justify itself at various stages of the PDP to show why it should continue through the process—or else be shelved or killed. The principle here is that no project, once entering the process, should be automatically entitled to proceed all the way through the process unchallenged. No entitlements or pet projects. The process should require rigorous design reviews—as we'll discuss shortly—that form the basis for pass/fail decisions at the decision gates. This introduces discipline and integrity into the process.

What you need now is a robust, logical process that includes all these elements in the creation of valuable products. Such a process needs to be simple, yet complete. It also must be flexible enough so that it can accommodate the wide variety of new projects that will enter the process.

Sometimes a simple idea comes along that changes the very way you look at something. One such epiphany for me occurred years ago when I first *truly* understood that new product development should be treated as a process rather than a portfolio of managed projects. Ever since, this concept has been my guiding principle in the arena of new product development.

Figure 2.2 illustrates the general composition of a new production creation process. The heart of the process lies in the four overlapping ovals we've just mentioned above that make up the product development process (PDP): business case justification, concept feasibility, product development, and pilot and production startup. The PDP is not just some abstract concept—it's a living process. It must be tangible: thoroughly documented and used by people trained in its details. The PDP is there for *compliance*, not guidance. It *is* the company authority. It guides you through the process while allowing for some latitude and process simplicity in cases of small development projects, such as derivative products.

Schneider Electric–North America, formerly the Square D Company, stands as a good example of a company that has achieved excellence in new

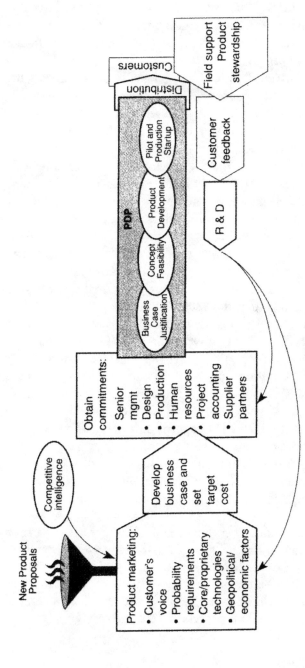

FIGURE 2.2   THE PRODUCT DEVELOPMENT PROCESS[3]

product development through superior process management. As a manufacturer of low- and medium-voltage protection products for residential and commercial buildings, Schneider Electric operates in a mature industry. Product differentiation and innovation are particularly difficult in mature industries. To ensure a continuing stream of innovation, in the early 1990s Schneider began to create what now is a truly world-class product development process, its PDP.

Schneider Electric's PDP contains all the basic features of the model described above. And theirs has been enormously valuable to their business. Their process has been imitated and used as a standard of excellence by other companies intent on upgrading their NPD processes. Lucent Technologies, Chemical Bank, Lexmark, and others have used it as a benchmark standard of excellence. The first full development under Schneider Electric's PDP was a product platform that included a new family of power-protection load centers. As part of this new platform, Schneider re-engineered its market channels, resulting in a significant pickup in market share. Its achievement was recognized in 1996 by the Management Roundtable's APEX Award for demonstrating product excellence, market share gains, best practices in product development, and effective teamwork.

Perhaps no industrial segment is more dependent upon efficient product creation process than the $300 billion/year pharmaceutical industry. This is a difficult business: heavily regulated, fiercely competitive, with long development cycles and huge investments and, of course, high risk. Yes, the odds for success are long: only one in about 10,000 entry products makes it through the FDA approval process, and only half of those make it to the pharmaceutical shelf. On average, it takes some 12 years to bring a new drug from R&D (80 percent of which is done internally) through clinical trials and then through the FDA approval process and on to market introduction. And the clock on patent protection (normally 20 years) starts early—when a chemical compound is first registered with the patent office. This narrow window of opportunity leaves little room for the developer to exploit the product commercially with exclusive rights and recoup R&D investments.[6]

If there is any industry crying out for efficiencies, it's pharmaceuticals. Future bets now are being placed on "combinatorial chemistry," using computers to create all possible combinations of organic molecules, then cataloging their potential for therapeutic applications. Also, clinical trials are being done on virtual rather than real patients via new computer technology. In this industry the process, indeed, is sovereign.

So far we've emphasized the need to manage NPD as a process, not just a collection of projects. In some respects it should be treated and managed much like a manufacturing process. To underscore this point, the table below summarizes the analogy between manufacturing processes and NPD processes. Each of the key features involved in production has its counterpart in the product development domain. This comparison makes clear the equivalence.

TABLE 2.1   ANALOGY BETWEEN PRODUCTION AND PRODUCT DEVELOPMENT PROCESSES[7]

Feature	Manufacturing	Product Development
Kind	High/low volume, repetitive, engineered products, assemble to order, job/project shop, cellular	Breakthrough, platform, derivative
Platform	Make or buy	Internal development or outsource
Capacity	Products produced per unit time	Performance to schedule
Speed	Product cycle times; processing and waiting times	Performance to schedule
Unit Operations	Unit processes and cells	Business departments (marketing, engineering, human resources, manufacturing)
Scheduling	MES, ERP	Product data management, new product releases, product scheduling, project schedules
In-Process	In-process work (= throughput x cycle time)	Actual/scheduled work effort
Quality	Process yields, rework rates	Iterations: change orders, revisions to complete work properly
Efficiency	Inventory turns; net downtime	Average development time/ critical path time; value-added effort/monthly available time; actual task time/minimum possible via CPM and other best practice methods

We've come to understand our production processes and make them very efficient. We know about process measurement, continuous improvement, scheduling for fast cycle times and minimum inventories, and so on. Now we're just beginning to understand the product development process in the same light. Manage the process, and the in-process work will take care of itself.

2.3: ORGANIZING AND IMPLEMENTING THE PROCESS

Now let's now dig deeper into the four sequential stages we outlined above—stages that are required of any robust product development process:

- Business Case Justification
- Concept Feasibility
- Product Development
- Pilot and Production Startup

Stage 1 of Your Process: Business Case Justification

Let's now have a look at the front end: after the filtering process for accepting new product proposals. Those that survive the Step 1 portfolio selection hurdle, new ideas for new products, now formally enter the product development process, or PDP. Each new project is now assigned to a team that plans and prepares the business plan for the project's entire life cycle. This is a crucial step, and experienced product and financial planners must lead it. They will forecast development costs and their timing, as well as overall project staffing needs. These projections are vital to determining the net present value and the internal rate of return on the investments required.

In this initial stage for managing your new product development process, you'll create and justify a business proposition. Here you must make a credible business management case and plan for the proposed new product. You've already done some of the analysis earlier, in the portfolio management process. But now your task is to develop a specific, overall formal business plan. Here's a structure—eight elements to help you begin:

PRODUCT CONCEPT

Just what is the product concept? Is it a new offering, or is it a derivative of an existing product? Most new products are extensions of current models. Truly "new" products are rare, and risky. However, the undeniable quickening pace of innovation pushes product groups in certain, almost predictable directions. *Forbes* magazine's editor-in-chief, Steve Forbes, captured a view of this future by observing, "Small jet-craft are starting to do to the airline industry what PCs did to mainframe computing, fractional horsepower machines did to turbines, mini-mills did to steel, cellular is doing to telephony, mutual funds are starting to do to centrally-managed corporate and government pension plans, and eventually will do to Social Security, and what the coming mini-generators will do to massive power plants.[8] They'll give customers more service, more flexibility, more control at less cost, as well as generate new products and services. It's all about power moving away from the machine-age center and toward individuals of the microchip era."

More likely your product is a derivative of an existing product, or a "line-extender" product. The business case justification stage of the process will be relatively straightforward because you have applicable history. But maybe it's a "platform" product—a new design built upon an existing chassis. An example of this comes from the late 1980s, when Kodak was losing market share in cameras to Fuji. They needed to move fast, so Kodak finished building the manufacturing facility for their new camera even *before* the design was completed—by practicing the principles of "concurrent engineering"—the practice of knitting together the activities of product design and process implementation needed to manufacture the product. Concurrent engineering enables design cycles to shrink, thereby delivering huge benefits by eliminating engineering changes in both design and process equipment. It cuts product costs, enabling products to be brought to market more quickly and competitively. Kodak used these ideas and mounted their offense by using a common platform strategy, enabling them to use a common production process for future generations of the product. It worked; they took back their market share.

Most product groups evolve incrementally; radical innovation is difficult and risky. Although incrementalism is most often the best strategy, there are times when a vision collides with new technology to create a whole new order of products and services. In the past two decades we've seen astonishing examples of this: think of the introduction of robotic assembly, flat panel displays, Web-based auctioning, customized products via rapid prototyping technology, and countless others.

Establishing your product concept deserves very careful analysis, initially with a broad canvas. Your design team should look at and consider alternative concepts that meet the requirements established in the original project proposal. They should sift through various options and converge upon the right one by a process of elimination. By doing this you will enjoy the confidence that your product development path is the right one for you.

PRODUCT POSITIONING

Next comes product positioning. Here's where you ask a few basic questions: Is the product truly an innovation? A close follower of an existing competitor? A commodity product? Example: In the 1980s Canon was looking for an approach to take market share from giant Xerox in the copier business. Xerox was betting on creating a strong service operation. Canon could not compete effectively in that arena and looked instead for a different business strategy. It settled on a simple but powerful approach: introduce copiers that simply would never need service! Canon accomplished this amazing feat by integrating all the components that were ever likely to fail into a single unit—the toner. This cartridge, after all, was the core component that customers were already conditioned to replace periodically. Canon took a fundamentally different product strategy; it redefined product quality as *seen by the customer.* No longer did offices have to suffer copier downtime, waiting for a service technician to make repairs. This strategy—a brilliant one—served Canon well. Today Canon enjoys a much healthier market share against Xerox. Their bold step of rethinking their product strategy may well have saved the company.[9]

VALUE OFFERING

Here's where you ask, why will the market respond eagerly to my product? What is its value to your customer? Is the product slotted to be low cost or high value, or to have prestige appeal? I recently bought a Sony portable recorder to make notes while away from my office. I quickly found that the 40-page operating manual, in awkward English, described endless and not-obvious combinations of buttons and screens that had to be mastered even to begin using it. The recorder may have been a technology marvel, but it didn't win the hearts and loyalties of its users. Customers seek distinctiveness and low cost; they look for differentiating attributes. How you deliver those values is a measure of your vision and genius.

TECHNOLOGY

Does the product embody new or established technology? My philosophy about product technology is that the best technology choice is usually proven technology. There's less risk in sticking to technology that is among your core competencies—not cutting-edge technology. ("Core competencies" is a term I'll use throughout this book; see Chapter 10 for a precise description of this term.)

But there are exceptions. We can learn a lesson here from Maytag Corporation, which for years had been a very respected but stodgy white-goods manufacturer until reinvigorated by the ascendancy of insider Leonard Hadley to the CEO position in 1993. For decades conservative Maytag had a policy not to be first to market with new technology. They preferred to be "right rather than first." All that changed when Hadley created a "skunk works" team to develop and test several innovative products, including a front-loading clothes washer. It was risky; the U.S. market has since the '50s offered almost exclusively top-loading machines. But Maytag's new Neptune product was such a hit that the company was able to increase its (already pricey) suggested retail price twice, yet still was pushed to increase production rates three times. Why the success? Back to basics. Neptune proved to use less water and was gentler on clothes, and Maytag took that message to the marketplace.[10]

INDUSTRY STANDARDS

It's fascinating to see how industry standards—or just plain convention—can "freeze" certain products and make improvements difficult, even impossible. Think of golf and tennis equipment, the placement of automobile control and accessory devices—even the VHS videocassette-recording format, which defeated its rival Beta format. Probably the premier example of the "frozen format" concept is the lowly typewriter. The keyboard was designed in the 19th century and configured in an apparent effort to slow typists down and thus reduce the tendency of those early mechanical contraptions to jam. Although later keyboard arrangements were offered that were faster and easier to learn, tradition prevailed. Today we're stuck with cultural inertia and a format we can't really change.

Industry standards have a lot to do with new product creation. Such institutions as Underwriters Laboratories, the FDA, NEMA, SAE, and ASTM place safety requirements on the design and testing of new products, in the interest of the general public. If your company falls under such controlling authorities, get involved in those standards-setting committees that influence your products. It takes time, but the rewards are worth the effort.

Also, pay attention to your product's end of life. We're entering an era in which recycling regulations more and more will dictate product disposition. This creates additional life-cycle costs, which must be factored into total product costs. In many cases the recycled material can re-enter the stream of commerce and find reincarnations in future products. In either event, end-of-life disposition must be an element in the product creation process.

PRODUCT SCOPE

Are there market opportunities for broadening or accessorizing your basic product lines? This often is an effective product strategy for increasing sales and capturing additional market share. One master of this strategy is Daimler Benz, which has successfully created an entire shadow line of products, including bicycles and picnic equipment, to market to their Mercedes Benz customers through their dealerships. A similar case is Harley-Davidson: their dealers' showrooms are crammed with motorcycle paraphernalia that both bikers and nonbikers covet. And then there are furriers that provide repair and alteration, along with storage service, to their customers. Manufacturers have cashed in on opportunities to offer product repair and maintenance services. Many businesses can expand their sales to existing customers through strategic accessorizing. A variation on this idea is to create a product pyramid—with a base that consists of high-volume, low-priced products and an apex that features just the reverse. Because of the higher margins at the top, profits can be made all the way up the pyramid while creating an entry barrier to competitors.

Here's a useful idea that connects directly with product strategy. Some businesses get stuck by seeing themselves as just a player in some well-defined market space. Within this space, gaining or losing market share is incremental. Growth opportunities are—or *seem to be*—rare. If you're a big fish constrained by market forces to swim in your own small pond, you'll always limit yourself. So, simply enlarge your pond! You'll then see yourself as a smaller player in a larger pond, with additional opportunities.

Roberto Goizueta, CEO of Coca-Cola until his death in 1997, was concerned about Coke's dominant position in the soft-drink market; there was little room to grow. Yet Coke had a minuscule share of the broader beverage market: water, tea, coffee, milk, and other soft-drink flavors. He reached out to these untapped *global* consumer segments with the Coke message, and the rest is marketing history. And similar stories come from Gillette (Sensor and Mach 3 razors, Oral-B dental products, and Duracell batteries), Disney (Disney Stores chain and theme parks), and others.

These leaders saw a larger vision and grew their companies splendidly with new product offerings.[11]

MARKET CHANNELS

There are a lot of channel choices out there, but the big one getting the most attention is e-business. Sure, it's risky—as any new business innovation is. But the risk is paying off for legions of startups and established companies. Among the high-profile converts are computer makers Dell Computer and Gateway—the number-one and -two direct marketers of PCs and related peripherals, network servers, Internet access, and software. These companies are enjoying tremendous inventory turns because they have their vendors carry their inventories. And they use their Web sites, television, and print media to inform the market how simple it is for customers—individuals, companies, and government entities—to "custom-build" their computers to meet individual needs and order directly off the Internet.

Success in such a "virtually integrated" environment requires a tightly coordinated supply chain management system. Top-notch suppliers are integrated as partners with the OEM's operations, and deliver quality and performance to their exacting standards. In this approach the Internet is more than just a sales channel. It provides the opportunity to transform traditional supplier relationships in a way to make the entire "virtual company" more efficient and responsive in addressing customer needs by sharing information and knowledge and getting immediate customer feedback. In the sincerest form of flattery, rival Compaq soon announced that it, too, will launch a direct sales initiative to smaller customers, using the Internet and telemarketing approaches.[12] Stay tuned for more!

PRODUCT PROMOTION

Is the product to be media-driven, promoted at the point of purchase, or traded on brand-name equity? Never discount the value of good will. Sears Craftsman tools for years have been promoted as high-quality, affordable products. Sears has consistently cultivated this reputation, in part through their famous guarantee that if the product *ever* breaks Sears will replace it free—no questions asked. A good product, together with a consistent message of quality and value, is a strong advantage that is tough for competitors to overturn.

These eight dimensions described above are your checklist for the strategic positioning of any new product. They should be used as an integral part of your decision-making process for authorizing new product development. Derivative products—those that are upgrades of existing products—normally stay the course with their existing product strategy. But even here, somewhat different strategies may be needed. For example, a product for the North American market almost certainly will require a different design and marketing strategy to be successful in, say, in Southeast Asia. It may call for new approaches as to value proposition, features, and distribution channels. Launching a new product that radically challenges one or more of the company's traditional product strategy elements is risky and requires a good deal of care and wisdom.

Having thought through your product checklist, you should place your product within the overall dynamics of your particular industry. This starts with developing a competitive analysis, a strategy, and an organizational plan for successfully launching and evolving your product. You may need additional market intelligence. And you'll surely need a crisp marketing strategy and operations plan. Prepare a thorough financial analysis for the product launch, including risk and uncertainty factors that carry through the product's full life cycle. Pay close attention to how you can best exploit the opportunities you see before you. And anticipate how you'll provide midcourse corrections for when, inevitably, plans don't play out exactly as written.

Your product plan drives the entire development process, through manufacturing, sales, and field support. It should be a life-cycle plan, not just a blueprint that ends with production. Opportunity and risk assessments should be evaluated, and product planners and marketing specialists should set firm target costs—*and* absolute maximum cost of the product. These target costs should be agreed upon by all parties to the product launch and should be held without compromise through the product development process. Mechanisms need to be in place for design changes, for customer feedback, for marketing the product, and for after-market service calls and warranty costs.

The technical side of new product creation may require laboratory R&D to verify the concept or to develop the technology that actually enables the product. Then there are the various steps involving design, testing and verification, and concurrent engineering to assure the manufacturing process is capable of producing the required quality targets. Attention also must be paid to compliance with government and industry standards. And never forget, the beginning point of every new product development proposal should be its link to customers. You must thoroughly understand the market dynamics and the opportunities that may lie within the market space for products or services that will attract your customers.

Your next step is to assign a process manager to the product. This person's job is to shepherd the product through the process. He or she is your ombudsman who "owns" the entire process. However, your PM does not have the authority to overturn the will of the interim process checks. Process management is a skill that is honed over experience gained by time. It requires strong leadership, good multitasking abilities, financial acumen, attention to details, and power enough to negotiate successfully for the people and other resources needed to make the project succeed. People with good process management skills are prime targets for advancement through management. I urge companies, as we do at Mascon, to elevate the position of project manager by requiring formal, certified training, as well as general project leadership experience.

Another decision that must be made during the business justification phase is autonomy. Will your company "go it alone," or should you work in partnership with others to launch this product? For example, in the mid-1990s Volvo AB, the Swedish auto maker, saw that keeping Volvo independent was vital in the climate of global competition and consolidation. By 1998, in an attempt to remain independent, Volvo announced a two-pronged product strategy. First, it planned to increase substantially its R&D investments in new products and to strengthen its joint venture with Japan's Mitsubishi Motors. Second, it launched its S80 sedan, a car designed to keep older and more affluent customers from defecting to rivals Mercedes Benz and BMW. This new auto was intended to provide the platform for a continuing series of future large "executive" Volvo models. It seemed a sound strategy, but it didn't work. Plagued by damaging competition in its truck unit, Volvo agreed in 1999 to be acquired by Ford—a move that would allow Volvo to focus and invest more in truck making. The message here is that autonomous strategies are not invincible and must be reconsidered periodically in light of changing market conditions.

Now comes the grand finale in the business justification stage—selling this new product idea internally to those having the power to authorize your project. Here's where politics enter. You've developed a clear and objective business plan for launching your new product. And now you must discuss the plan in candid one-on-one meetings with those who can authorize funding for new product proposals. Make sure they share the sense of importance you attach to this project. Go through with them the business proposition, the numbers, the risks, and the expected business payoffs. Tell them your staffing needs and whom you have lined up already. Get them personally involved somehow in the project so they have even more reason to see that it is successful.

Other features of a robust PDP include:

- The early, continuous involvement of customers and suppliers. Make them your partners, your confidants, and your advocates.
- A dedicated team. Guide it with a balance that reflects the project's main features as well as the experience and talents it needs.
- All information you can gather regarding customers' attitudes about the product, as well as service for the products.
- Attention to scale. Large companies commonly have more than one PDP process, especially when their business units differ significantly in size or in the nature of their product/service offerings.

This "front end" to the product development process is fraught with assumptions and vagaries. It is the most ambiguous stage of the entire process. It's also the most far-reaching, for poor intelligence and judgments at this point can get built into the product, with downstream consequences that may not be understood until much later. This front end is commonly referred to as the "fuzzy front end" precisely because of the vagueness of all the factors that go into building the business case for the product. And it is just because of this fuzziness that you must put your most experienced people on the task of building the business case. An error of a degree or two in the starting trajectory can lead to enormous errors when the project lands in the competitive marketplace.

New product creation requires vision—a good understanding of the marketspace in the years ahead. Vision is the basis for business strategy and can take you to better places than where you can end up just by incrementing yourself ahead. An excellent example of vision in new product development comes from Intel. In 1998 the personal computer market became ripe for a full-function computer that would sell for under $1,000. But early in his career at Intel, now-CEO Craig Barrett anticipated this strategic opportunity by leveraging not only Intel's design capabilities for low-cost microprocessors but also its superior capabilities in manufacturing operations. Although it didn't buy him anything at the time, he could see that excellence in manufacturing would sooner or later be requisite to remain a serious player in the personal computer industry. Starting back in the late 1980s, Barrett began to elevate Intel's manufacturing capabilities to true world-class status by improving technology, by making manufacturing more respected within the company, and by attracting the best people he could find. Result: their "sales per employee" ratio grew more than 50 percent per year from then on.[13]

The message here is the importance of attaching distinctive value to your new product—value in a form the customer can readily see and appreciate. And don't mistake true value with features that frustrate or annoy your customer!

Stage 2 of Your Process: Concept Feasibility

This phase brings the product down to earth. Up to this point, the product concept has been somewhat ethereal. It has lacked specific form and function; it's been abstract. But now that you have the business case firmly in mind, you can forge ahead to develop your specific product concept.

CUSTOMER INVOLVEMENT

Your customers are your ears to the marketplace. They'll tell you better than anyone in your company what new products will catch their attention. Your duty is to have an aggressive process for catching their ideas and bringing them back to your marketing and product development people. If you're in tune with your customers, you'll usually not be surprised at what they're telling you. They may be a bit ahead of you, but if you're in tune with a good listening process, you'll be on track. However, it's not unusual to find gold nuggets in your customers' voice—nuggets that can revolutionize your products and hand you new sales and market share.

MANUFACTURING INVOLVEMENT: CONCURRENCY MATTERS!

Just how feasible is your new product to manufacture? You won't have the answer until you get your manufacturing operation directly involved. It's got something crucial to tell you.

The single most important lesson manufacturers have learned from the past two decades of operational improvements is *concurrent* development. Introducing rapid and agile production depends upon coordinating product design with manufacturing process—"concurrent engineering." The difference between doing CE poorly rather than well is enormous! Many benefits are obvious: concurrency reduces or eliminates miscommunications and misunderstandings—problems that take time and resources to resolve. It also helps if R&D and design engineers have some direct experience in manufacturing engineering—and vice versa. Some companies wisely rotate their technical staffs so they can gain experience in both environments.

But there's another reason for practicing true concurrent engineering. In the early steps of product creation, the investment is small—large investments usually come later, when production equipment and operations are being made ready. However, the *decisions made* in the early stages weigh heavily on future investment requirements. A rule of thumb is that within the initial 20 percent of the product development's schedule, 80 percent of the total product costs are already locked in. That is huge—and potentially dangerous—leverage. It means things done poorly or just plain wrong in the beginning magnify downstream and will cost a whole lot more to fix later on. The message: Take extra time before locking in design and process features. Delay important decisions as long as possible and use that time to investigate alternative design scenarios and methods. Then, when you're sure you're right, proceed with your concurrent engineering and production planning efforts. Taking these steps is the essence of quick-response manufacturing, as you'll see in Chapter 3. Focus on rapid introduction of new products, cost containment, minimizing lead times, and eliminating non-value-added work. And intelligently work the gut issues of capacity planning, lot sizing, workforce management, and equipment qualification and selection.

CE is key to timely and cost-effective creation of new products. It knits together the activities of design and the process that will produce the product. Both functions—design and manufacturing—must work in concert for a smooth hand-off. From the design side, the practices of *design for manufacturing* and *design for assembly* ensure that the product design is appropriate for the production processes that will be used. Concurrent engineering also enables the design cycles to shrink, which delivers huge benefits by eliminating engineering changes in both design and process equipment. It cuts product cost, enabling your products to be brought to market more quickly, with competitive pricing.

As an example of the importance of concurrent engineering, consider the trend toward "late point product identification." LPPI, sometimes called "product postponement," is a fancy term for a simple concept. Across all industry segments, companies are more and more developing products that are in some sense "customized" to meet the specifications of the buyer. For example, a washing machine company may build a certain product but offer it with various features that can be tailor-ordered by the customer. The options might be in color, in the sensor and control units that manage the washing cycle, or in other features. Even a small number of feature options, when counted in the various possible combinations, can amount to a great many "different" products. Traditional product design doesn't account for this kind of "combinatorial" product complexity. Models having all the various sets of feature options used to be built in lots during the course of production. This practice resulted in a large finished-goods inventory just to be reasonably responsive to individual customer orders.

One of the cardinal rules of production is to minimize inventories, because they add cost but no direct value to the customer. The "build 'em all" practice was a just-in-case approach to production. "Let's make a dozen mauve washers to have on hand with automatic rinse sensing and with the two-temperature sensing module with three fabric choice settings. Sooner or later someone will want them."

A much better approach is to design the product with the forethought to add feature choices near the *very end* of the production line. All production units are to be exactly alike through the first 90+ percent of the process, and the customizing takes place as late as possible in the remaining 10 percent. GE and Whirlpool use this approach to produce variety in their washing machines. Motorola pioneered this approach with its "Bandit" line for manufacturing portable pagers. A customer could order a unit with up to 100 feature choices, and the unit would be built and shipped the same day. Zero finished goods inventories! LPPI is a growing trend among manufacturers, and it depends essentially upon concurrent engineering. It results in simpler and less costly production, as well as reduced inventories. It promotes the notion of "just in time" rather than "just in case."

SALES AND MARKETING INVOLVEMENT

Although you may have the best product idea on the planet and can manufacture it efficiently, it does you no good if you can't sell it. Therefore, get your sales and marketing folks involved during the concept feasibility phase of the process. Is the product to be media-driven, promoted at the point of purchase, or sold on the basis of your brand-name equity? As mentioned earlier, for example, for years Sears has promoted its Craftsman tools as high-quality, affordable products and has lived up to this promise, in part through its famous guarantee that if the product *ever* breaks, Sears will replace it free—no questions asked. A good product, together with a consistent message of quality and value, is a winning recipe that's tough for competitors to overturn.

R&D AND PRODUCT DESIGN INVOLVEMENT

The art of design, always important, is being elevated to ever higher levels. In earlier days products were designed primarily to be functional. Companies competed mainly on price. More recently a shift occurred—this time to quality. Now that all competitors know how to compete rather well on price and quality, the next epoch is emerging: *design*. Design—style and uniqueness—is becoming more and more important in the marketplace. Industrial design that emphasizes style is having a heyday, and trained designers are valuable members of product design teams. Undoubtedly, we'll see more and more use of stylistic design, which will create more markets for customers who'll make buying decisions based largely on eye appeal. We'll have much more to say about R&D operations throughout this book, including how to measure R&D effectiveness in Chapter 8.

Then, of course, there's technology. The saga of the Iridium project drives home the notion that technology should serve, not drive, new product development. Iridium was conceived at Motorola in the late '80s to be a worldwide telecommunications system not linked to conventional wireline or cellular transmission stations. Rather, it would have a network of low-altitude satellites encircling the globe to relay a call from anywhere to anywhere. But from the very beginning, when it left the Motorola labs to become Iridium LLC with dozens of international investment partners, it was troubled. It was troubled because it was marketed more as a technology than as a service. Both the unit and the airtime were too pricey even for upscale markets. The high cost was due in part to the satellites' low altitudes; they would re-enter earth's atmosphere in a matter of just a few years and burn up, requiring frequent launching of new satellites. Also, the handset was too bulky for convenient use. And it wouldn't work reliably within metropolitan building areas. And most egregiously, Iridium was locked into an advanced technology that was sure to change and mature in unknown ways, making it obsolete even before it went into production.

Iridium was a revolutionary concept but badly faltered early in execution. Motorola in this case was technologically driven and didn't pay enough attention early on as to how customers would use its new product. In March, 2000 Iridium LLC told a bankruptcy court it would liquidate its assets.

DERIVATIVE PRODUCTS

During the concept feasibility stage of the NPD process management, consider also the use of derivative products. This class of products includes those that are upgrades of existing products and those that evolve gradually from a relatively stable product strategy. For example, a product for the North American market may require a different design and marketing strategy in order to launch it in, say, Southeast Asia or Europe. Local taste or customs may weigh in heavily and influence its design. For example, the custom in Europe is to load a clothes washer from the front, not from the top, as in North America. Or industry standards may influence the design. Derivative products may also require new approaches for promoting their value and features and for mobilizing effective distribution channels. Launching a new product—even one that is merely an upgrade—can be risky and requires a good deal of care and wisdom. And, of course, even more so for derivative products that radically challenge one or more of the company's traditional product strategy elements.

PLATFORMS

Platforms offer another avenue to concept feasibility that can take some of the risk out of bringing new, valuable products to market. We're used to thinking about new products as being either incremental upgrades of existing products or truly new products. But there's another way to think about new products, and that's to think in terms of platforms—a new design built upon an existing chassis. Platforms are analogous to tables, in that they are built upon four legs: components, processes, knowledge and know-how, and people relationships (teams, supplier networks). Each new product version is based on a common chassis and uses new features to create the perception of a genuinely new product. It enables the manufacturer constantly to offer something new, yet not incur the cost of constantly re-engineering the platform itself. Platforms allow you to build successive product models or generations on a common design or technology. It cuts product development time and cost. It lets you use your existing production facilities for introducing successive new products, with substantial savings in process equipment.

The auto industry has been a champion of platforms, and has used this concept to great advantage. And the idea is rapidly spreading to applications in computers, entertainment products, and other areas where the market seeks a constant stream of "new" products. Platform design is becoming an imperative as the general pace of product obsolescence accelerates. Platforms can be used to create luxury models from commodity products. Companies having reputations for superior quality or high value can exploit the platform concept to introduce luxury models of commodity products. Here's how it works. You take a conventional product, like a toothbrush, TV, kitchen appliance, or shaving razor. Then you introduce a high-end line and advertise it heavily to market niches that appreciate quality and features. If all goes right, you can command premium margins that make even low-volume lines look good. That's the experience of Gillette's Mach 3 razor cartridges that shave closer. And of Maytag's Neptune washer that delivers on its promise to reduce energy costs—yet costs twice as much as some conventional models. Luxury products that spring from conventional platforms can soar—or they can crash. Requirements for success are a new idea, a novel twist, and superior performance—all backed by a solid brand name.

And platforms apply to more than autos, cameras, and razors. Computers are platform products; their operating systems are platforms on which various application software programs can run. In fact, a struggle exists within the industry to see whether a platform-free operating system, such as Java or Linux, can compete effectively against Microsoft or other platform products.

And yet the platform approach to product creation has its own obstacles. Creating the right platform architecture requires vision—vision of the future markets, competitiveness, and technology. Marketing a platform product requires balancing the vision of uniqueness with the confidence born of a tried-and-true product. It also requires a design team that can sustain its enthusiasm while making only marginal changes to the product.[14]

Product platforms apply as well to software development. Just as with hardware products, a succession of software products can be built upon a common architecture that consists of one or more core subsystems. The architecture itself may be open or closed (proprietary), fixed or scalable, and so on. It's supported by subsystems that draw from key technologies, such as object-oriented programming, relational databases, or the Internet. Products can evolve by building upon themselves without having to start from scratch each time.[15]

FIELD SERVICE AND ONGOING PRODUCT SUPPORT

The final stage in concept feasibility is to be able to structure methods to service the product in the field and continually support it throughout its life cycle. Here's your opportunity to shine; too many OEM manufacturers look at product support as a costly annoyance. You have two choices: do it yourself or outsource it. There are lots of arguments for outsourcing: it's not your core competence, it requires equipment and ongoing specialized training, and it may cost you less. If you regard product support as a maintenance issue, this may be the path for you.

On the other hand, product support can provide a strategic advantage if you look at it as a way to provide superior service and if you can use it as a conduit for customer attitudes about your service and about the product itself. If you take this path, decide now to make product support a profit center. You can do this by tying your costs to your product margin structure—costs built into the product to include warranties and guarantees. Train your service agents to be among the most customer-friendly people on the planet. Provide them with the tools they want and need to provide continuing customer feedback to your R&D, design, and manufacturing operations.

In summary, pay particular attention to this Concept Feasibility Phase. There's a tendency to get through this phase quickly so the team can get into the "real" work of product development. This can be a big mistake. Typically, although only about 10 percent of the project budget is spent in concept feasibility, the decisions made effectively lock in some 70 to 80 percent of the total life-cycle product costs. If the feasibility work is rushed, flawed, or incomplete, huge unbudgeted costs and delays are inevitable later on. Extra time up front in exploring various alternatives always pays back handsomely.

Stage 3 of Your Process: Product Development

Here's where reality meets the road. All that you've done in the first two stages now converges to focus on developing a specific product design, along with the process equipment and layout needed to meet production goals. It's a big task, not only in the engineering effort but also quite possibly in the commitments you must make in specifying and ordering process machines and related equipment.

Let's first talk about design. It ranges widely, from incremental changes to existing product lines, all the way to truly creative design that offers new technology, features, or appearance. The only common element across this span of designs is *function*. The starting point for any product design team is to understand the functions and standards that the product must meet. These may be safety-related features, size or weight targets, interconnectivity with other products or power sources, wear resistance, simplicity of use or service, or others. Be aware that in the case of derivative or platform products, there's a tendency to discount such functional considerations. It's easy to think of an incremental platform product as just carrying over an earlier design into a newer model of the same thing. But this can be a mistake. Perhaps simply by adding an additional functional constraint or requirement to the product, you can offer a product that is more interesting to the market. The first extreme is the simplest, so let's begin with it.

There's a universe of products that are candidates for creative incremental improvements—from razor blades to wireless paging phones. Most incremental or platform products are inspired by cost reduction programs. In these cases product design is less essential than the process technology that enables the cost reduction. The main issues here are process stability, product safety, and usability. Most frequently such a product is undetectable by users or consumers. It "feels" the same. The challenge to product developers is to make sure its performance is every bit as good as its nearest ancestor and that there are no added product liability issues. Thorough product testing must be an important part of any such new product design approach. The product may or may not have to meet industry requirements, but it must perform to the marketplace standards.

Then there's truly creative design—design that exploits styling or new technology to capture the heart of an existing market. A dramatic example of this was shown on a nightly news show.[16] The producers challenged the Palo Alto design firm Ideo to create and prototype a new and better shopping cart for supermarkets *within a week*. Ideo's self-described "eclectic" team interviewed shoppers, built storyboards and lists of creative ideas, and developed safety and other features to be improved upon. Their result—a working cart—featured a scanner technology that could eliminate the checkout line and included on-board modular hand baskets and plastic bag hangers, casters on all four wheels for added mobility, and various child safety features. The point of this program was to show the potential for improvement of even the most common products we use daily. It also demonstrated that at the heart of such "industrial invention" is a team of smart people with few inhibitions and the courage to challenge convention. Most important, the freewheeling approaches used by design teams like Ideo can be applied even to the most banal of products. Have you looked lately at the lowly corkscrew for opening wine bottles? If you haven't, you should; simple but clever design improvements have made masters of us all in the pulling of stubborn corks.

Look carefully for design—and process—patent opportunities, whether incremental or radical. We talk about this in some detail in Chapter 9, but its application starts with product and process design. Your product development process ought to include your internal procedure for recording notes and for patent filings. This is your opportunity to discourage competitors and to license your technology to noncompetitors. Keep in mind that process design, as intellectual property, is every bit as valuable to you as product design. And if you have reasons for not filing a patent application and you have a valuable product/process idea, consider making it a trade secret. Again, refer to Chapter 9 for guidance on how to pursue this avenue.

Let me quickly take you back to the early 1980s, when the subject of product design began to change rapidly. It began with the development of "design for assembly." DFA was motivated by the introduction of more sophisticated process technology—such as robotics, materials handling systems, and other forms of automation. Engineers soon saw that if they were to design their products just a bit differently than before, they could capitalize upon the speed and labor-saving potential of automation for less costly assembly. The now well-established design practice of DFA began with a simple concept: design so that assembly can be accomplished from one direction only, which allows automated assembly to be used. DFA then quickly generalized to design for manufacture, for serviceability, for cost, repairability, usability, maintainability, disposability, and so on. The principles of design for "X," DFX, are now part of the formal training of design engineers around the world.

If you're like most industrial product or service providers, product development is a core value of your company. Product development, and maybe even R&D, is vital to your competitiveness. However, free your thinking to consider partnering with someone outside your company to help you improve your new product creation projects. There are many sources—universities, not-for-profits, government organizations, and specialized design organizations that can provide cost-effective technology and integration functions. This approach is becoming especially interesting to companies whose products are becoming ever more complex—with embedded software and firmware. If your core competency is, for example, mechanical design, it might benefit you to partner with someone that can help carry you into a new domain of opportunity. You may be surprised at the ideas and value you can find within easy reach.

Another important component of product development is the technology for developing, sharing, storing, and accessing product designs. Computer-aided design (CAD) tools are essential today, even with the most ordinary product lines. They can do the styling as well as the engineering—stress, thermal, dynamic, and fracture analyses—and provide design guidance for the environment in which the product will actually be used. CAD's twin, computer-aided manufacturing (CAM), provides similar analyses from the production arena. This is truly marvelous stuff. But frequently there's a hiccup because of the inability to integrate these data files with other information systems serving production and distribution.

The choke point for many product development organizations is quick access and sharing of current design information. This problem may be less acute in small organizations in which people can interact daily and there's provision for central storage and retrieval. But for most, a product data management system is now essential. I'll touch on the importance of PDM systems technology again in Chapter 4. But it's important to mention here the necessity of cutting time in your design phase by sharing configuration status internally, as well as with vendors and other partners to your development projects. Having a secure system that can trade design data within your collaborative network can do wonders for your development operations. PDM can take design information from CAD systems and produce drawings and develop part numbers and bills of materials.

Having the ability to create a 3-D product in software, to look at it from any angle, to section it and produce it to any scale has created a vibrant new industry: rapid prototyping, RP. As we'll see in "Tool Power!" (page 53), RP is a growing collection of technologies that enable designers to hold in their hand this afternoon a physical model that the design team worked on this morning. RP is driven by 3-D CAD files—or by PDM systems—and produces the physical model in plastic, metal, layered paper, or other media. RP is also being used for production tooling for plastic parts and for rapid tool making. Its impact on new product development is enormous. If you don't already have such a system, I suggest you to look into this technology.

As a final suggestion I urge that your team become proficient in some of the various tools that are invaluable in the product development arena.

There are many great tools out there that help product developers do their daily work more effectively. We'll have a look later in this chapter at finite element analysis, rapid prototyping, and process simulation. And in Chapter 7 we'll discuss some key quality tools, including process mapping, benchmarking, Six Sigma, and quality function deployment ("house of quality").

All design, engineering, materials, and production planning are to be completed in this stage of the NPD process. The "deliverables" include the final product design and specifications. The quality plan, including production and shipping quality control and field support, is agreed to. This plan also includes suppliers and the training and other support they'll need to synchronize with your product launch. Manufacturing, tooling, and supplier selections are finalized. The go-to-market plan is finalized, covering the appropriate bases, including promotional and advertising, trade shows, direct marketing, and customer alliances. And in this phase of the NPD process, your after-market product support plans are developed and ready to go.

DESIGN REVIEWS

It's hard to overstate the importance of a rigorous design review in the process of creating new products. It's really a simple idea, and most design teams use it routinely. However, it is so often misused that it's worth our taking another look at it.

The intent of a design review is to step back and look critically and objectively at a design project. The review sets aside time for the design team and other stakeholders to ask the gut questions about being on track and about new concerns that might compromise cost, schedule, or performance. The purpose, of course, is to assess the state of the project. But it's easy for objectivity to go out the window when the team summons itself to be critical of itself. I've seen design reviews conducted over lunch at the plant cafeteria, with all the rigor of a weekend dress code. This is not a design review; it's merely an exercise in ticket punching.

The mark of a good design review is how many problems the team can identify and frame for correction. It's not about pointing fingers or assigning blame; rather, it's about doing everything possible for the team to make the project succeed—or if need be, to redirect or kill it. A real design review is rigorous. Participants include not only the key project team members but also one or more senior executives from engineering, manufacturing, and/or marketing. Some of the best design reviews I've seen have included one or more people from outside the company: a user, customer, or technical expert who can provide insightful, objective opinions about the project. After all, you should be seeking out real or potential problems—and the thoughtful, unbiased people who can provide just that.

When should a design review be scheduled? Generally, when the project is far enough along that much is known about it, but not so far along that it would be very difficult to step back and take another direction or develop alternative concepts. And don't limit yourself to a single review. Except for small, narrowly drawn projects, it's good practice to schedule design reviews at significant markers, such as completion of feasibility, when the design approaches completion, and just before hand-off to manufacturing.

Good design review practice sees to it that the review is treated as a formal event. It's just more effective when embedded in an atmosphere of rigor and process. This means providing advance notice with a complete agenda and a list of all invitees. It's often useful to schedule it off-site to avoid routine distractions. Someone should be tasked to make and distribute a thorough record of the proceedings. And most important, give it time! Depending on the scope and complexity of the project, a design review of a narrow or "routine" project may run a half day. Review of a larger or more complex project may easily go for a day or more. And at the conclusion, specific actions and follow-ups should be assigned so that the project itself is the beneficiary of the review process.

Stage 4 of Your Process: Pilot and Production Startup

This final phase demonstrates manufacturing's capability to achieve your product line's quality goals, and then launches production. This phase may be little more than a formality if the product is a simple line extender or a minor enhancement of a current product. Otherwise, pilot production is a key element in your product's launch.

It involves designing and developing the production architecture that best meets your requirements. As we'll discuss in the next chapter, there are choices to be made based on production volumes, level of automation that can be exploited, and how much customization production units or lots require. You may launch the product on an existing production platform, in which case the needed process engineering will likely be straightforward. If not, you will require a significant rework or a newly engineered production process.

Then you'll need to identify the process equipment you'll require and work with manufacturers and system integrators to find the equipment you'll need to meet your process specifications. Typically, this involves quality monitoring and control systems, buffers, inventory stations, kanbans, materials handling equipment safety devices, and all the rest. This can be one of the most difficult and stressful phases of a new product launch—because of the many options and trade-offs available and because of the many party negotiations you'll get dragged into. But it's the heartbeat of your new product, so commit considerable energy to it.

This preproduction environment should definitely be developed as the actual and final production process. Preproduction is your stage rehearsal—it's there to search out the bugs and to demonstrate compliance with the quality yields and defect targets you've planned for. It's also the training arena for your production operators. When you've trained those needing to be trained and you've demonstrated the quality capability of the pilot production process, you merely flip the switch and it becomes your real production process.

Now you are ready for smooth production startup. Congratulations: if you've done your homework right to this point, this should be the most rewarding stage of your new product launch. The process is critiqued, and the quality plan and measures are reviewed. Production people are trained and qualified. All project records are archived in keeping with company policy. You're on your way!

Now let's step back again for a moment. Pay particular attention to the product development stage—the second of the four stages we've just discussed. There can be a tendency here to get through the concept feasibility step quickly so that the team can get into the "real" work of product creation. But haste at this point is a grave mistake. To repeat, although only about 10 percent of the project budget is spent in concept feasibility, the decisions made effectively lock in some 70 to 80 percent of the costs. If the feasibility work is rushed, flawed, or incomplete, huge unbudgeted costs and time delays are inevitable later on. Extra time up front to explore many alternatives always pays back handsomely. So give it the time and attention it deserves. Move ahead with the best product concept only after it's been tested against other concepts and has emerged as the best. And at the end of this stage make sure you have a rigorous, formal design review.

Throughout this overall process of moving from stage to stage there will be degrees of overlap. Expect this; there is time and coordination involved in "handing off" from one stage to the next. But the important point is that a "go-ahead" or "kill" decision at the end of each stage should be made at some level above the process manager. This decision normally follows each design review. Another important point is that all product records should be archived—preferably electronically—at the conclusion of a development project. This discipline is a small but important step along the path toward creating a learning environment within the company.

My advice is that if you haven't done it already, put in place this formal process for new product development—or one of your own choosing, just as long as it's a process that accommodates all the elements involved in product creation. Then manage your process, as well as the new product portfolio. Put discipline into this process by having documented procedures that set out the requirements for authorizing a new product launch. This process requires all the front-end elements we've described in the four stages, with special attention to the concept feasibility stage: market analysis, financial development costs and projected sales streams, risk analysis, and plans for market launch. And make it a point that *everyone* involved is trained in and understands the procedures and approval processes of your product development process.

The beauty of a documented, disciplined process is that it can be *measured*. Which brings me to include in your PDP some realistic metrics that you can apply periodically to evaluate how efficient your PDP really is. This will give you added control and confidence in your process and will lead to continuing improvement. I'll stress throughout this book the need for identifying appropriated performance measures for R&D and NPD processes. Well get to R&D later in this chapter; measuring product development processes will be addressed in Chapter 8.

2.4: SPEED IS *EVERYTHING*!

More and more, product creation depends not just on processes but on *fast* processes—to outsprint your competition. Companies in every sector are seeing the value in accelerating their efforts to bring new products to market. Why? For two basic and compelling reasons. First, getting a jump on your competition is both critical and rewarding. It can bring direct and handsome dividends. When you set the new standard, competitors have to play catch-up, an expensive and often risky effort response. In short, it hands you a strategic advantage.

Second, sprinting through your development process brings you additional, indirect dividends. Doing the right things even faster forces you to rationalize and streamline your process and to strengthen collaborations among team members. Enormous hidden costs are associated with leisurely processes. One of these unseen costs is the tendency toward "feature creep." Feature creep occurs when your engineers add little extras to the product because it's easy to do in the design phase. Their argument is "I can easily incorporate this added feature in the product now, so I will because it will be very expensive to do it later. Besides, the customer will appreciate it." I'm convinced that's what ran through the mind of the person who designed the voice recorder I mentioned earlier—the one with so many cute features it was, for me, worthless.

This insidious tendency is costly and must be stopped. The best way to stop it is to enforce strict adherence to approved design criteria and target costs, as discussed earlier in the concept feasibility stage of new product development. All product features must stand the test of meeting market needs and being competitive with product costs.

How much cost can be avoided by collapsing development cycle times? It depends on the specifics, but in most cases you can expect a 30 to 50 percent reduction in development times. Yes, it takes work. You must rethink your process from beginning to end and create a new model based on the process of product development laid out above. As a result, you can collapse your product's development cycle by as much as a third or more. These stakes are well worth your concern and commitment. They were worthwhile to Deere & Company, which set a goal to cut development time by up to 50 percent by making more use of rapid prototyping, iterative computer-aided design, and virtual reality tools.[17] Chrysler achieved similar cycle time savings when launching their 1998 Dodge Durango vehicle.[18] Such companies that have had speed as a target for improvement have benefited enormously. These stakes are worthy of your concern and commitment.[19, 20]

In their classic book, *Product Development Performance*, Clark and Fujimoto[21] concluded that there are three key measures of product development performance:

> *Leadtime:* how fast a company can move from concept to manufacturing or to market
>
> *Productivity:* the level of resources needed to take the project from concept to a commercialized product
>
> *Total product quality:* the extent to which the product satisfies customer requirements and expectations

Improvements in integrated product and process design—which we know as "concurrent engineering"—must include advances in all three simultaneously. Furthermore, achieving gains in development cycle times depends upon a company's consistency of leadership, technical skills, and attention to strategy and culture. Efficiency in new product creation generally equates with fast-paced, effective work processes. Speed is a result of good organizational and systems integration. Moreover, as Clark and Fujimoto found, there is a consistent linkage between good product creation and good production processes. Each shares with the other a focus on production throughput, reduced inventories, continuous information feedback up and down the process, increasingly higher levels of product quality, and success at doing the right things right despite unexpected events.

Toyota is an auto maker that, perhaps more than any other, has pioneered improved design and production processes. It is regarded as the standard for excellence in total quality, concurrent engineering, lean manufacturing, and reduced cycle time in both NPD and the manufacture of better cars. Toyota's development process is constantly being tuned, improved, and re-created. It's been studied by managers and MBA students and emulated to some extent by nearly every other auto maker. One innovation Toyota found useful in reducing the time to bring a new product to market seems paradoxical but has proven very effective. Let's have a look.

The usual approach to managing a complex product, such as a new auto, is to sequence steps in series and in parallel. The purpose is to make firm decisions as early as prudent. Early decisions have the advantage of building the project upon a rock-solid base of fixed markers and eliminates second-guessing and revisions. However, Toyota has experimented by questioning this conventional wisdom. Rather than making firm design decisions along the way, Toyota allows these decisions to float along while alternative approaches are investigated. Over time, and as the project proceeds toward completion, these "fuzzy" decision points are revisited and the various alternatives evaluated in more recent light. Of course, some basic decisions must be nailed down early on, like the choice of engine or the chassis platform, because so many other decisions depend upon them. But delayed decisions on secondary features and issues of styling, subsystems design, and such can lead to better decisions. Toyota's experience is that this approach often leads to wiser choices and, paradoxically, to overall shorter development cycles. There's no reason why this approach can't work for other kinds of new product launch.[22]

2.5: THE SUN NEVER SETS ON NEW PRODUCT DEVELOPMENT

Another factor in the speedy delivery of new products is the development of virtual teams. One of the biggest challenges facing new product creation today is how best to manage it in a multinational environment. Global companies find using global teams for product creation somewhat easier because they have international presence. A regional company, by contrast, may not have established international connections to enter directly into partnerships to get close to broader markets. But in either case here's a simple truth: both markets and technology are now global. Today markets and market access vary widely around the globe, but technology is technology everywhere. In recognition of this fact there now is a trend for many companies, large and smaller, to choose to centralize their R&D capabilities in one place. There's no particular advantage for multi-site R&D labs. Rather, companies can concentrate their resources and talent in one area—usually where they have historical roots or where they have access to the intellectual capital they require.

New product development must, of course, still serve the particular requirements—tastes, standards and regulations, and the like—of regional markets. And companies can develop product concepts simultaneously, even across the globe, with enough telecom bandwidth to share large files from computer-aided design and other teams. Indeed, the sun need never set on NPD. Teams can collaborate virtually and quickly to develop product concepts and launch new products with rapid efficiency.

This is a fascinating era for new product creators. Multinational companies routinely develop products tailored for local markets around the world. And it's not just the multinationals; companies much smaller in scale are partnering with each other all across the global village to create valuable products. Consider Novosoft, a small software company with technical operations located in Novosibirsk—in Siberian Russia. Novosoft was started in 1992 and is run by the president, Philip Brenan, from his office in Houston. Most of his customers are small U.S. companies. Brenan uses the Internet for everything from setting contractual terms with his U.S. customers to monitoring the progress of projects. Distance no longer is an impediment to doing business!

Transcontinental product development makes good business sense. Technology has freed companies from the constraints of distance and time like never before, allowing them to tap productive talent wherever it's found. India, Russia, Israel, and other nations often can outcompete others in the business of software development. Southeast Asia has a similar edge in electronic manufacturing and assembly. Choosing partners now is a matter of capabilities and cost, not distance. Companies are wired for high-bandwidth voice, video, and data transmission, and all can be, virtually, together at any time, any place.

My own company, Mascon, is a full-service information technology (IT) provider with major operations at Chennai, India. We have clients throughout the world and routinely work around the clock, seven days a week. At the end of their day, software experts in Chennai download their work to our Schaumburg, Illinois, office for further work and testing while they sleep. Twelve hours later Chennai picks up the ball again from Schaumburg, and the cycle continues. Both teams are in voice and data communication at the beginning and the end of each team's day, so there is person-to-person contact twice a day. The work gets done faster and better, and everyone wins. The project itself never needs to sleep.

Such also is the experience of companies as different as Motorola and Ford. Information technology takes its own kind of project planning, and language can be a challenge. Yet many companies are developing a history of successes with global development teams.

However, as in all things, there is risk in virtualdom. Challenges can attend this global development proposition. SAP, the German enterprise resources planning (ERP) systems builder, has generally enjoyed phenomenal success. Its R/3 product line has been the envy of the industry and the choice of thousands of companies worldwide. These systems, described in Chapter 4, are costly to install and to maintain, but SAP has set the benchmark for automating internal operations such as financials, manufacturing, and human resources.

In the mid-1990s, SAP developed plans for a new generation of packaged software products, its New Dimension line. This product was to provide more functionality in supporting sales forces, supply chains, and customer needs. SAP brought together, virtually, a team of some 5,000 software developers residing in Germany, India, California, and Russia to develop New Dimensions. But it stumbled, not because of time zones, but because SAP failed to create a tight specification for the product. Consequently, internal differences and disputes sprang up about product features and architecture. Time was lost; some customers defected to such rivals as Oracle, Baan, and PeopleSoft. The leakage in customer loyalty wasn't a knockout blow, but it left SAP somewhat bruised.

The lesson here is that global concurrent development can work to your advantage. It can save you time and investment, and it can help you expand your markets. But it clearly requires coordination of systems, tools, and ideas. It calls for organization: clearly drawn roles and responsibilities, authorities, and timetables. Without this discipline, you run the risk of managing some level of chaos—and that can set you back.[23]

2.6: Tool Power!

Successful new product development relies upon people, product ideas, process, concurrent engineering, and speed. To this point I've emphasized the process. The process *is* sovereign—it takes you where you need to be. The leadership and teamwork needed to implement this process are also vitally important and are addressed in Chapter 4.

But execution requires tools, and there are many that are revolutionizing the practice of product creation. There are hundreds, if not thousands, of tools used in new product creation. Most are in the public domain; some are proprietary. It's not my intention to survey them; rather, I'll draw your attention to three that are revolutionizing the process of product creation:

Finite Element Analysis
Rapid Prototyping
Process Simulation

Finite Element Analysis

The most powerful technical development affecting the efficient creation of valuable products is 3-D solid modeling using finite element analysis (FEA). This 40-year-old technology has only recently achieved incredible utility to do high-speed computing. FEA allows designers to create, in software, detailed structural designs at the component or at the product level. The designer can quickly analyze structural and thermal integrity, vibration characteristics, fatigue and fracture resistance, and other design characteristics. FEA reveals the industrial design image aspects of shape and texture and shows how the design looks in various colors and lighting. It allows rapid revision of designs and the creation of "virtual products" that can be seen and "used" in three dimensions from any aspect and at any level of detail.

One application that dramatizes the power of FEA is Boeing's 777-airplane program. Boeing engineers significantly reduced the traditional costly rework caused by part interference and fit problems by preassembling the entire aircraft on the computer. They used three-dimensional structure and literally "assembled" the entire structure and visualized it just as it would be seen on the production floor. They "saw" how large cargo packages could (or couldn't) be maneuvered into the cargo hold. They were thus able to short-circuit the traditional parts and structural rework by designing the right components for assembly in the first place.

Boeing launched the 777 twinjet in 1990 and in the process saved 50 percent in time and cost by eliminating change orders, errors, and rework.

A similar story of the power of virtual product design comes from Chrysler's Jeep Grand Cherokee creation. Chrysler eliminated two build-and-test cycles that had traditionally required physical models. The new technology cut its overall design cycle by a full year and handed Chrysler a staggering payback.[24]

Rapid Prototyping

RP technology was born in the 1980s to accelerate the cycle time for creation and evaluation of various product concepts and design. Having the ability to create a physical 3-D product from software, to any scale, can be enormously valuable for designers and manufacturers. Today RP includes a growing collection of technologies that enable you to hold in your hand—this afternoon—a physical model that your design team worked on this morning. Such models aid designers by letting them get the actual "feel" of the product before locking in the final design specifications. RP takes 3-D CAD files and uses a variety of technologies to create the physical model.

Rapid prototyping began with stereolithography machines designed to build prototypes "additively," layer by layer, using liquid polymers or metals. Soon after, a similar technology was developed using layered paper mockups, sintered sand, investment casting, and other materials. RP has also been used for production tooling, for quickly making plastic parts and production tools. Its impact on rapid product development has been huge.

From these beginnings RP has now graduated to produce "one-off" or limited runs of production products in metal or other materials, using both additive and subtractive (material removing) techniques. Scientists at Stanford, UC Berkeley, MIT, and other research centers are advancing this technology, which soon will enable the production of products having directional properties and imbedded devices—products that until now have been impossible to produce. Eventually this technology will have a vital application in the production of mass-customized products such as medical implants.

Process Simulation

Still another valuable product of the computer era has the extraordinary power of simulation technology. And you should be aware of the advantages that process simulation can bring to your product development and production operations. One of the most widely used applications is for simulating manufacturing processes such as unit operations: cutting, drilling, grinding, finishing, and so on.

But from a concurrent engineering standpoint, the real action for process simulation lies in its ability for virtual run-throughs of any kind of manufacturing process. You simply model your line or lines—with all their complexities of unit process equipment, inventory stores, manual operations, and the like. Each such unit or station is characterized by its cycle and transit time to the next operation. You can model line, cellular, or functional processes in deep detail, with parallelism, feedback, and feed forward routing of in-process work and with statistical characteristics. Once completed, the entire process can be "started" and run until it stabilizes. At that point the process reveals its steady-state condition in terms of queues and bottlenecks, inventory gluts and depletions. You can then modify or reconfigure the process to speed it up and easily examine the "what ifs"—what if this equipment goes down or what if another machine or operator is added to the production process or what if the throughput is to be increased.

Process simulation is also very enlightening for designing job shop and short-run production environments. And the applications of simulation don't stop there. Simulation is being used for entire business and university environments—modeling business transactions, risks, and competitive factors to evaluate how changes will affect business results. It just makes good business sense to have, or have access to, good modeling and simulation capabilities to help you make better decisions.

In fact, computer-based design and simulation tools are becoming essential for reducing cycle times for new product development. These tools enable improved decision-making for new product concepts, for marketing, for modular and platform design concepts, for prototyping, and for virtual testing new product concepts. These same tools also offer predictive abilities that can help in making good product and life-cycle decisions. An example is Motorola's approach to product prototyping. Instead of linking prototypes to various project phases, Motorola found more value in "periodic prototyping"—creating prototypes on a given date each month. The periodic prototyping gives its engineers and managers a better evolutionary understanding of product development and its connection—literally—to today's product and process design information.[25]

2.7: CREATING SOFTWARE PRODUCTS

Developing valuable products is certainly not limited to tangible products and related services. Software algorithms and systems are becoming inextricably bound with the hardware and networks they serve. In fact, software development is best done with a process model that has all the features we've just discussed. Software development ought to be subject to an established process that includes:

- Requirements analysis
- Functional specifications
- Systems analysis and design
- Development and testing
- Implementation and field support

The process should be repeatable, measurable, and continuously improved. It refines itself by learning from its experience, and translates that learning into shorter cycle times and better customer service.

Just as manufacturing and service companies often seek quality registration with the International Standards Organization ISO 9000 or the closely related QS 9000 standard for the auto industry as evidence of their quality achievements, these same avenues are available for software development products. Perhaps the leading model for advice and qualification of software development processes is Carnegie Mellon University's Software Engineering Institute. SEI has developed a description of the various stages through which any software organization committed to continuing improvement must pass. These stages include defining, implementing, measuring, controlling, and improving their software process. The model provides useful guidelines for improvement strategies by identifying the most critical issues the organization will face in the future.

SEI's Capability Maturity Model (CMM) is a recognized standard for measuring excellence levels among industrial companies' software development processes. This model uses a scale to indicate just how well disciplined and documented an organization's software process really is. This model consists of five distinct maturity levels that characterize software organizations. It provides specific guidelines for companies wishing to improve their software processes over time. Each level requires a strong focus on the organizational aspects of development and generally less on the technical aspects. Figure 2.3 illustrates these five levels of the CMM model.

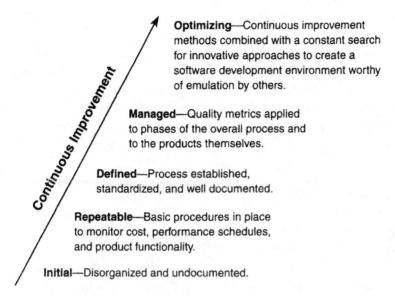

Optimizing—Continuous improvement methods combined with a constant search for innovative approaches to create a software development environment worthy of emulation by others.

Managed—Quality metrics applied to phases of the overall process and to the products themselves.

Defined—Process established, standardized, and well documented.

Repeatable—Basic procedures in place to monitor cost, performance schedules, and product functionality.

Initial—Disorganized and undocumented.

FIGURE 2.3   THE CAPABILITY MATURITY MODEL

Only a few companies—less than 1 percent—qualify for the optimizing level. Those that have include Boeing's Defense & Space Group, IBM's Federal Systems Company, Lockheed Martin Federal Systems, Motorola India Electronics Ltd., and the Software Engineering Division of Odgen Air Logistics Center at Hill Air Force Base, Utah.

Software development finds itself becoming more complex with time because of its need to be integrated with various companion systems, such as factory automation, enterprise resources planning (ERP), groupware, and telecom systems. The need for access by various users and integration with information technology systems has driven the focus on process, just as it did with the evolution of product development processes.[26] Companies that generate software internally now have formal protocols for developing that software. And as with production and other internal processes, making abrupt improvements requires internal training and close coordination if they are to stick. Instructional "face time" is important, even if that face time is on a Web site, which is becoming more useful as supplementing or even substituting for conventional training.

Generally, there are two different approaches used in new software creation: waterfall and prototype. In the waterfall process, as one phase is completed and the next begun, further experience and new requirements may create a need for corrections or modifications to earlier phases. It allows for an iterative process; one can go back and make adjustments based on more recent information. The waterfall process is commonly used in development application environments. By contrast, the prototype approach requires each phase to be completed, tested, and approved before the next phase is begun. It is a serial approach, used in contractual agreements in which the acceptance procedure doesn't allow for iterations.

2.8: Wrapping It Up—Measuring Your Processes

The real power of our process model for new product development—hardware or software—lies in the ability to measure the process. It's just like production operations in which quality products are assured as a result of statistical process, quality control, and related tools. However, measuring the NPD process is a bit more complicated because here the "widgets" are all different, in contrast to the sameness of high-volume production operations.

Many metrics are available for measuring the efficiency of a new product development process. What matters is that you select a few that make sense for your business environment, then use them consistently to watch for year-to-year changes. Think of this as an annual physical. Your physician takes various measures of your body's efficiency: weight, pulse, lung capacity, audio and vision tests. No single test can be a reliable indicator of your body's overall condition. But taking them together, an experienced practitioner can make an evaluation, then determine whether you are more or less healthy than a year ago and what you can expect in the future if you continue your lifestyle.

Table 2.2 provides some useful process metrics for new product development, as developed and used by Hewlett-Packard and other leading product developers. Begin by using some or all of these, and be on the hunt for other process indicators that may apply to your specific business.

As much as I advocate the process view for developing valuable products, there is a cautionary note. We think of processes—especially production processes—as being "in control," with only acceptably small variations. The process shepherds the products throughout the production process. But NPD *is* different. No two projects are exactly alike. Different project leaders and team members manage them. And all new products are vulnerable to the whims of the marketplace and the economy. "In control" here really

TABLE 2.2   METRICS FOR NEW PRODUCT DEVELOPMENT PROCESSES

- **Impact of Process**
  Throughput: Number of new/improved products commercialized per year.
  Capacity: Number of new/improved product development projects in the pipeline, as a percent of last year's figures. Also as a percent of comparable figures five years ago.

- **Impact of Technology**
  Technology Share: Ratio of the number of company-owned patents to that for all comparable patents from all competitors.
  Patent Utilization: Percentage of your company's active patents that are actually incorporated into or used to defend commercial products and processes.

- **Impact of Speed**
  Cycle Time: Time improvement in launching new or derivative products.

- **Impact of Sales**
  New Sales: Sales (in $ and %) from new/improved products released in the prior year. From new/improved products released in the prior three years.
  New Sales Ratio: Ratio of current year sales revenue from product developments commercialized in the five prior years, to the total current year sales.

- **Impact of Costs**
  Return from Product Development: Percent of net income from products developed in the past five years.
  Cost Savings Ratio: Ratio of current year savings in cost of goods sold from product changes or process developments adopted in the five prior years, to current year gross profits.

- **Impact of Project Management**
  Break-Even Time: Time in months from project go-ahead to when project's new profits equal the development investment.
  Break-Even After Release: Time in months from manufacturing release to when the project investments are recovered in product profits.

---

means "control of risk." A good product development process is highly effective but of course doesn't automatically ensure a winning product.

Take, for example, Casio Computer's experience when, in 1995, it launched a small digital camera, the QV10. Forecasts were for modest sales of about 3,000 units per month based on a recommended point-of-purchase price of $550. Casio knew that their sales of conventional film cameras had been in decline for several years and that customers were switching to inexpensive "throwaway" cameras. But Casio failed to anticipate the huge potential market for the particular features unique to digital cameras. These features included the ability to see instantly what the picture would look like if taken as aimed. Moreover, the QV10 provided the user the ability to load easily the picture into a computer so that it could be viewed on a home TV, used in marketing materials or on a Web site, transmitted via e-mail, or used in similar ways. Shortly after the QV10 launched, demand was so strong that Casio had to add more capacity so as to produce some 80,000 units per month—more than 25 times the original market forecast! The market found a new way of using what was considered a conventional product. As a result, the new capability of "temporary imaging" found a thirsty market in home and commercial use, and the product simply took off at a rate that was not anticipated. For Casio this was a "good" problem because they were able to mobilize extra production capacity.[27]

Yet there are many ways for an attractive new product to fail. Falling victim to bad first impressions is one. Take the case of the Apple Newton communicator products, designed as portable personal communicators for workers in hospitals, trucking, and other industries that rely on interteam communications. These products, dubbed MessagePads, first came under development in 1987 and hit the market in 1993. From the beginning, though, they were plagued by their inability to recognize the user's handwriting—a much-heralded and key feature of the product. So flawed were the first products that the Newton became the butt of jokes on late-night talk shows. Moreover, at a retail price of about $1,000, they were simply too pricey for the mass market. Subsequent versions performed much better, and wireless paging and other features were added. But the products were doomed early and were just too far ahead of themselves. Interim CEO Steve Jobs finally killed them in 1998.

2.9: IDEAS FOR ACTION

1. If you haven't already, get your senior people responsible for R&D and new product creation professionally involved in such organizations as the National Association of Manufacturers, the Industrial Research Institute, the Management Roundtable, or others as appropriate. There's much to be learned outside your walls.

2. Create standing benchmarking councils for product creation and manufacturing. Have them work with companies that have best-in-class design and production capabilities. Share information; you'll get back more than you think!

3. Commission a thorough review of your product strategy in terms of the eight elements described earlier in this chapter, and look for opportunities and threats. Pay special attention to unnoticed competitors, existing and potential, that may share the same technologies or supply chains as you.

4. Revisit the ways your product/process projects are conceived, reviewed, and selected for funding. You have much to gain by having a disciplined approach to managing your product development portfolio.

5. Examine your product creation process. It should be in step with the ideas of this chapter, disciplined and well documented. And it should be used faithfully! Your managers need to be knowledgeable of its details and the issues involved to make it work. Have a review and evaluation of your process annually and continuously improve it.

6. Put in place a process to train your people periodically in your methods of new product creation, focusing on your own PDP, on new design tools and methodologies, and on improving project management skills.

7. Use formal design reviews at critical points in your product creation process. Involve the right people, including outside experts when appropriate, to challenge approaches and to contribute ideas early on in the process.

8. Consider whether your future may include virtual product teams. If so, prepare for it by appointing appropriate leadership and planning for the technologies to enable it.

9. Put in place measures for evaluating your PDP, using as a guide those outlined in Table 2.2.

Chapter 3

Manufacturing Strategy
The Other Half of Concurrent Engineering

Let's begin this chapter by looking at the manufacturing spoke of our New Product Creation Wheel. The waterwheel, developed before the modern era, evolved such that two thousand years later it would initiate the giant advances that would lead European and Asian feudalism into the age of industrialization. During that later period the waterwheel became the engine that enabled milling grain, forging iron, sharpening tools and weapons, sawing logs, pressing olives, and making wool cloth and countless other products. Indeed, it was the first general-purpose mechanical workhorse. The manufacturing spoke's role was to produce a particular mix of products for villagers who depended upon the wheel, directly or indirectly, for their livelihood. For the most part that role was simply to avert flooding of farmlands and, later, to provide an engine for milled grain. But by the 17th century the waterwheel had evolved to the point that it could produce a variety of products. The workhorse had become a production engine.

Just as waterwheels became capable of manufacturing particular products, modern industrialization provided the products and services that people need and that enable people to have jobs and that draw investors to businesses. Just as the waterwheel's manufacturing spoke needed to be sturdy, so too must modern manufacturing processes be robust and reliable.

Today's manufacturing environment descended directly from the medieval waterwheel. In this chapter we'll see that production systems come in many forms. There have been enormous improvements, especially since the early 1980s. We've learned about robotics and sophisticated scheduling and control methods. Total quality, kanban, just-in-time, and a host of other concepts are topics of discussion over lunch. Yet a wide gap still exists between understanding the elements of good manufacturing practices and harnessing them to best advantage. Everyone knows the concepts, the buzzwords of manufacturing. But it takes wisdom, courage, and effort to put them to work for you. In this chapter we'll focus on three key factors that are vital to superior production operations performance: manufacturing strategy, the supply chain, and manufacturing systems design.

One key to effective strategy is the supply chain that connects the supplier to the manufacturer, and then the distribution chain from the manufacturer to end customers. This notion of manufacturing is central to the "value chain" that reaches all the way from the raw materials producers to the ultimate product consumers. The customer may not realize the many contributing links in this chain, but unless it's efficiently managed it can ruin a business. Fewer middlemen and faster cycle times are good starts. The supply chain element of manufacturing focuses on the industry rather than the enterprise.

Another critical factor of manufacturing is the production systems that produce products. Of course, a basic distinction exists among continuous, batch, and discrete products. And even beyond those differences some products are made by additive processes, such as assembly and coatings; others are made by subtractive processes—such as products made with machine tools that cut or thread. Each approach has its merits and disadvantages. Moreover, some items are products made in high volume, while others are individually designed and produced, as in a job shop. Manufacturing systems design must match the level of production complexity to the product complexity.

Supply chain management and production systems are simply different aspects of production—features that can be designed and managed to accommodate the requirements of the products of manufacturing. As a manager, it's your responsibility to see that these processes evolve over time to become ever more reliable and efficient. In this way you can deliver more and more value to your customer.

To begin, here's what drives the production function: manufacturing strategy.

3.1: YOUR MANUFACTURING STRATEGY

New product creation—and all that supports it—demands a sound manufacturing strategy. It's much more than just a vision or mission statement. The strategy is your blueprint for fighting the good competitive fight. It's your intended destiny. It should lay out your principles of what and where you produce: the nature of your design and production processes, your goals for competitive advantage, your key technologies, your supply and distribution tactics, and of course, how you intend to delight your customers. Most important, your manufacturing strategy must support your company's business strategy and be a living, valuable presence.

So what exactly *is* a manufacturing strategy? Think of it as a key pillar of your company's overall business strategy. It spells out just how production processes are to be designed and managed so as to secure your desired future. It specifies what production is done where and how. It ties your raw materials and parts suppliers to your production sites. And it provides perspective and a blueprint to gain competitive advantage through manufacturing. Table 3.1 outlines a manufacturing strategy. Use it as a template, tailoring it, of course, to the particular needs and requirements of your company and your industry.

Most of the strategic plan elements in the table are straightforward and can be controlled internally. The team that drafts a formal manufacturing strategy can fill in the blanks after it gets and filters information from key managers. Let's begin with your supply chain.

3.2: CARING FOR YOUR SUPPLY CHAIN

Your supply chain is your lifeline. Those companies that provide the materials and components you need for production are partners that share in your quality-improvement initiatives. These partnerships work best within cooperative, noncontentious arrangements. They may carry your inventories. And increasingly they may be taking on responsibilities that used to be yours but that they can often do more cost-effectively. Gone are the days of adversarial relationships. Your suppliers are now your extended family.

Your suppliers should be:

- Enabled by technology to communicate and share information readily
- Evaluated on total cost, not on unit price

TABLE 3.1   ELEMENTS OF A MANUFACTURING STRATEGY

Executive Control
  Who (person or council) is responsible for implementing and managing the manufacturing strategy? Issues:
  • Organizational structure for manufacturing operations and support functions
  • Rationalizing facilities and factories
  • Make/buy strategies for components, products, and automation
  • Method of cost allocation

Maintaining and Leveraging Core Competencies
  Continual improvement of internal processes that impact core technologies and practices. Issues:
  • Materials engineering
  • Design tools, practices, and concurrent engineering
  • Process technologies and methods
  • Project management

Operations
  Effective use of production methods and technologies for competitive advantage. Issues:
  • Capacity and facilities
  • Production equipment, systems, and classifications
  • Inventory reduction and management
  • Reduction in product cost
  • Competitive products and process analysis
  • Production planning, scheduling, just-in-time, bills of material, and materials control
  • Purchase methods: volumes, flexibility, and engineered products
  • Tools and best practices
  • Concurrent engineering environment
  • Equipment maintenance: preventive and total productive maintenance

Quality
  Implementation of an effective policy for total quality management. Issues:
  • Baselining, benchmarking, and goal setting
  • Defect measurement, prevention, monitoring, and intervention
  • Cycle time measurement and improvement
  • Continuous improvement: process innovation and re-engineering
  • Measurement of process capability
  • Certifications and registrations

Intellectual Property
  Policy for creating new patents, licenses, and trade secrets. Issues:
  • Establishing goals, strategies, and measurements
  • Processes for competitive intelligence-gathering
  • Rewards and recognition

Continued

Supply Chain
The philosophy, implementation, and maintenance of suppliers: selection, mutual commitments, and cooperation. Issues:
- Linking your materials management strategy with your supply partners
- Supply chain management
- Teaming with and training suppliers
- Integrated logistics
- Hedging and future strategies for purchasing commodities
- Stock and stockless strategies

Distribution
Development of effective go-to-market ideas by harnessing the power of your sales force, distributors, factory reps, and other partners. Issues:
- Developing and keeping your star distributors
- Managing channel conflicts
- Training your distribution partners
- Keeping your distribution partners current with new products/services

Transcending Geography
Harmonizing your new product development methods among business units and affiliate companies and across distance and time. Issues:
- Coordinating decision-making protocols
- Providing groupware and other technologies for virtual meetings, transfer of drawing and information, making use of Web and Internet tools, etc.

Competitive Intelligence
Effective processes for intelligence gathering to keep abreast of your competitors' new product development and production practices. Issues:
- Organizing for intelligence-gathering
- Charting and educating the principal participants
- Educating everyone about the purposes and methodologies
- Keeping track of results and measuring the process

Employee Loyalty
Policies specific to ongoing training and education of people who are part of your worldwide manufacturing organization. Also, any special goals and strategies necessary for recruiting and retaining high-caliber people within your organization. Issues:
- Skill-level assessment and improvement
- Reward systems
- Leadership and training
- Culture and empowerment

- Capable of delivering on a just-in-time basis
- Committed to replenish inventories on a continual basis
- Brought in very early as partners in new product development
- Contractually committed to continual cost reductions

Paying close attention to your supply chain pays real dividends. Experience has shown that cost reductions of 20 percent or more are achievable in purchased materials; maintenance, repair, and operations (MRO); development time; and manufacturing costs. But such success can be achieved only if a consistent set of performance measurements is used to track improvement. These measurements provide a road map for achieving superior performance. Here's a useful starting point for thinking about the all-important issue of measurement:

- Performance Quality

  On-time delivery
  Product and purchased material quality
  Order fulfillment
  Damage frequency
  Percent returns

- Cycle Time Reduction

  Development time
  Quote-to-cash time
  Response time to customer inquiry
  Lead time for order fulfillment

- Inventory Management

  Inventory turns
  Inventory obsolescence
  Days supply of inventory

- Production Operations

  Production plan achievement
  Forecast accuracy
  Capacity utilization
  Stock-outs and back orders

- Business Costs

  Development costs
  Product manufacturing costs

Supplier selection and training costs
Total supply chain costs

Let's now look at the payback potential from enlightened outsourcing practices. In the mid-1990s Procter & Gamble committed to a fundamental review and improvement of its supply chain management practices. They had thousands of customers, hundreds of suppliers, dozens of plants, and ten distribution centers. To get their arms around this complexity, P&G installed a geographical information system (GIS), linking it with operations management algorithms for planning and coordinating regional supplier and plant partnerships. As a result, they were able to improve their information systems so that orders, payments, suppliers, production, and shipment could be much better coordinated. GIS leveled out their inventory surges and brought kudos from their customers.

Inspired by these early successes, P&G management then sought to improve their distribution logistics and locations. While doing this, they uncovered a major nugget: a key to improving a product proliferation problem. Like many manufacturers, P&G faced increasing frequency of new products and derivatives thereof. They found they could better manage this proliferation by keeping inventories of their base, or generic, products separate from their inventories of custom or differentiated products made therefrom. They learned that customization should be completed as late as possible in the process—a concept discussed in Chapter 2 as late point identification or product postponement. The product is kept as generic as possible through production, and the product differentiation is added as the last step—when there is a customer order in hand.[1]

Another vital link in the supply chain is the management of MRO functions, mentioned earlier. Everything I've discussed earlier about supply chain management applies here as well. Companies now are forging more intimate relationships with their MRO suppliers as key partners in their business. Trends include strategically reducing the MRO supply base, reducing variation among MRO products and services across a company's business units, providing better MRO services, and improving up-time of unit process equipment. And here again, e-business is bringing transaction efficiencies, from searching and selecting among online catalogs to paying by electronics funds transfer.

All these approaches to improving supply chain management would be mere platitudes without appropriate use of information technology. Electronic data interchange (EDI) is a key part of this technology because it allows field engineers and salespeople to do their work on the spot, eliminating precious time and transaction disputes. EDI has become a cornerstone of the automobile industry's competitive renewal. Honda, for example, has converted 40 percent of its U.S. suppliers—companies that were still using paper-based transactions—to EDI, saving both parties time and cost. And derivative benefits usually follow: rewards such as faster communications with supply partners and better control and reduction of inventories.[2]

Yet EDI sometimes has difficulty navigating across multiple enterprise resources planning (ERP) platforms that are used by supply chain partners. In some industries it is even more challenging to look at an *integrated* chain, with each link being run by its own stand-alone ERP. We can therefore expect to see alternative technologies to supply chain management that will overcome such constraints. It might be a single, standardized network capable of orchestrating all partners within a given supply chain. Or it might be the recently developed extensible markup language (XML), a Web-enabled, natural language that users can more easily work with. Whatever unfolds, you can be sure that new tools will emerge to offer even better chain supply efficiencies.

Outsourcing—especially contract manufacturing—is becoming an important dimension of cooperation. Contract manufacturers in the electronics sector, for example, have done very well, outperforming the overall market growth as measured by the Dow, S&P, and NASDAQ indices. A good example is Solectron, a contract manufacturer and an early (1991) winner of the Malcolm Baldrige National Quality Award. In 1998 Solectron announced that it was taking responsibility for Mitsubishi Electric's cellular telephone manufacturing operations—a tight fit with Solectron's basic business. It was the first time a major Japanese company had entered into such an outsourcing arrangement with a U.S. manufacturer. And in April, 2000 it purchased Nortel's worldwide inventories of printed wiring boards, components and subsystems, further strengthening its capacity to serve. No doubt it's a harbinger of similar international outsourcing arrangements.[3]

Supplier certification is an important aspect of supply chains. You want your chain partners to perform to certain standards. In some industries such certification is mandated. The automotive industry has been the most aggressive. The growing importance of having been certified under the QS-9000 standard (an enlargement of the ISO-9000 standard) is just one indication of the commitment required for being a player.

In 1998 farm equipment manufacturer John Deere announced its new company-wide supplier-rating process. Under this system Deere trains, monitors, and measures some 500 suppliers monthly—by tracking their progress on quality, on-time deliveries, and cost improvements and evaluating their working relationship with Deere. Like many other companies that have increased the proportion of parts purchased from outside vendors, Deere has found this rating process strategically vital. Those suppliers that "make it" are no longer subject to the game of trying to win a competition on price alone. This program is critical to Deere's future because the company has increased the percentage of parts purchased from outside suppliers from about 50 to 70 percent. And it keeps relationships more honest. For example, it doesn't penalize small companies that produce quality parts but may be short on product engineering capabilities.[1]

Packaged supply chain management software can be essential to making your supply stream responsive and predictable. This technology, in combination with close "win-win" agreements with your suppliers, provides a huge strategic advantage. It enables you to establish your requirements for parts and materials with suppliers a week or so ahead rather than monthly or quarterly. You can reduce inventories and safety stocks. You can more effectively harness the power of flexible and agile production methods.

And there are other approaches aimed to improve supply chain effectiveness. Much hoopla is being made over the notion of supply chain "disintermediation." Disintermediation is a fancy word for eliminating links in the chain and for finding faster, more effective ways to use the remaining links. Channel disintermediation is a new way for making your supply chain more efficient.

Here's another: focus on improving value for your distributors and resellers. Such companies as Ingram Micro, the computer reseller of Microsoft, Compaq, Hewlett-Packard, and other products, succeed by offering unbeatable service, such as carrying and managing inventories and offering same-day custom assembly ("channel assembly") and shipment of orders to its 1,500 vendors. Their "product-pull" strategy is reducing inventories from some six months to less than two. And their process discourages the traditional practice of "channel stuffing," in which manufacturers dump extra product into the channel just before the end of the month to make their numbers look better than they really are.[5]

A growing number of companies are embracing vendor-managed inventory (VMI) agreements with their supply chain partners. Wal-Mart pioneered this practice in the late 1980s. They held their suppliers responsible for stocking shelves and for promotional information—in exchange for providing prime shelf space. Today manufacturers as well as retailers and distributors are finding they can increase their capacity utilization by using VMI to smooth out production flows and decrease cycle times. Excess inventory is a buffer against demand uncertainty, and increasing capacity utilization encourages yet more inventories—leading to a spiral of excess. However, Vanderbilt University's Eric Johnson has found that VMI enables manufacturers to lower their excess capacity needs, therefore increasing their production efficiencies. Of course, any change in production strategy must be carefully planned and implemented so as not to degrade current production operations in the process.

You'll also benefit from helping your channel partners reduce their inventories. 3M's Dental Division, a 1997 Malcolm Baldrige Award winner, has done just that. They've used supply chain optimization software (Texas-based i2 Corporation) together with committed partnership teams to achieve inventory turns of 12 or better. As a result, 3M Dental was able to guarantee product delivery within four days of order to anywhere in the United States. This is truly an agile company: 300 employees responsible for a product line numbering some 1,300.[6]

Here's another success story. Weyerhaeuser's door-making division was stuck with a clumsy, inefficient, and error-prone process for taking orders, and for parts and materials purchasing, assembly, and delivery. They suffered with a near infinity of design and pricing options. As they looked ahead toward a murky future, Weyerhaeuser decided instead to take a bold gamble. They installed an intranet to link their customers and suppliers and acquired software to manage inventory and locate best pricing. They extended their intranet to the outside, creating a secure extranet to allow customers to see product information and place orders—which then go immediately to the shop floor. This new process reduced order cycles from weeks to minutes. Moreover, it enabled Weyerhaeuser to change their business. They moved from serving small orders to serving major customers such as hotel and offline builders—and more efficiently and profitably. It enabled them also to disintermediate. By eliminating distribution, they could serve their customers better, faster, and more profitably. Weyerhaeuser remade itself from a struggling, moribund business to a growing, agile, and profitable operation.[7]

A classic example of disintermediation is Flowers by Wire. In the old paradigm the customer would pick up the phone and call a local florist, who would be responsible for taking the order (and the money) and making sure the local florist in Mom's town would fill and deliver the goods. Sounds simple, until you consider the intermediate steps: the flower growers ship flowers to a wholesaler, who ships them to a distributor, who ships them to Mom's florist, who in turn creates the artistic arrangement and drives it to Mom's house. Lots of expensive and time-consuming steps.

Think of the potential for greater efficiency. Imagine, instead, that you go to the Internet, connect with a florist network, describe your needs, and enter your order. Your transaction instantly makes an electronic transaction directly with a group of full-service flower growers. The florist network then uses delivery channels to take flowers from their growers' grounds to the recipient's door within 24 hours. In this particular case, the growers "bid" electronically for your order, and the winner accepts responsibility for getting the flowers to Mom's local florist, who assembles the presentation and delivers your order, personally and directly, to Mom.[8]

In fact, that future is happening today with the advent of e-business. Expect to see a huge growth of streamlined businesses thanks to this new business medium. The explosive growth of e-commerce ("e-tail") is redefining purchasing transactions up and down the supply chain. Today some 10 percent of the industrial U.S. market uses it, and that figure is increasing rapidly. Why, Intel's online orders had reached $1 billion per month by the end of 1998, up from zero just a couple of years earlier. And think about the worldwide opportunity, considering that only 1.6 percent of our planet's inhabitants are now trading on the Internet.[9]

One of the most important applications of e-commerce is putting catalog information directly online for your customers to access. In a move reported in *Manufacturing News*, in 1996 General Electric mandated the use of its e-commerce system to rid itself of paper-based transactions.[10] Partner companies now search GE's catalogs for product offerings. Electronic funds transfer—as well as exchange of proprietary information—is then executed over the Internet. And GE divisions can interrogate the database to find and bid on products offered by its suppliers. This "trading process network" is beginning to revolutionize how GE—and other companies—works with its supply chain partners and with direct customers.

Dell Computer has gone after excess inventory as if it were a thief that steals its cash and numbs its productivity. Dell presently counts its finished-goods inventory in about a week. Its goal? To measure it in minutes! By establishing individualized Web pages for each of its top suppliers, Dell enables suppliers to enter their (secure) site and find out in real time Dell's demand forecasts, immediate customers, and other details important to its markets. This technology is not just a technique; it's a *business process* chock-full of intellectual property that provides Dell with a market advantage.[11]

And Dell is not at all unusual in its zeal to improve supply chain management. The difference is that Dell and the many other companies that put such priority on supply chain management make it a high *strategic* initiative. It's not an effort or a program; it's not measured by incremental improvement. Rather, it's a search to revolutionize the supply chain process as a way to grow and strengthen the business. It challenges you to think fresh thoughts about your go-to-market business processes. In many cases the best solution is the simplest. Home Depot found itself saddled with the costs and delays of moving goods from supplier to warehouse to retail site. The solution was obvious: eliminate the warehouse! Now nearly all merchandise moves directly from the manufacturer to Home Depot's retail outlets.

There's a variety of levers you can pull to retune your supply chain management. Here's a checklist to start with:

Cooperative agreements
    Pricing
    Backlogs and reservations
    Advertising and promotion

Supplier ratings
    Quality, delivery, cost

Financial agreements
    Financial institutions: credit lines and cash transfers

Purchasing approaches
    Blanket orders
    Stockless purchasing and purchases without invoices
    EDI; e-commerce

Workforce
    Flexible hours and part-time employees
    Surge protection: agreements with temporary agencies

Inventory strategy
    High turns replacing buffer stocks and finished-goods inventories

Logistics
    Warehousing
    Demand predictability

Order fulfillment
Controlled exchanges of forecasting, production, and inventory
  control information

Transportation
  Modes: air, rail, truck, sea

Tying it together
  Vertical integration
  Close partner ("keiretsu-like") networks
  Information, knowledge, and learning technologies
  Other technologies: point-of-sale scanning, etc.

3.3: PRODUCTION METHODS: MATCHING YOUR APPROACH WITH YOUR BUSINESS

Beginning in the 1980s, we were inundated with manufacturing buzz. We heard of the triumphs of CIM (computer-integrated manufacturing), CAD (computer-aided design), CAE (computer-aided engineering), CASE (computer-aided software engineering), CALS (computer-aided acquisition and logistics support), JIT (just-in-time), and on and on. Each creed vied for the role of America's savior to improve America's production shortcomings. By now these and many other approaches have sorted themselves out. Experienced people usually can identify the hype from the truth. They know which approaches are best for a given business or production environment. Still, there's more than enough mysticism about manufacturing to go around.

I'm reminded of the late Carlton Braun, fellow Motorolan and good friend. He'd talk about manufacturing at the drop of a hat, arguing that manufacturing is simply a process of material conversion. To those who focused only on the technological aspects of production, he'd say, No, it's not about manufacturing systems—just material conversion. It starts with a product plan, then managing the inventories, throughputs, and cycle times. Add a pinch of total quality and *voilà*, you have a robust recipe for manufacturing anything: widgets, home construction, software—whatever. And don't you know, he was right?

CIM is a field that addresses all automation processes that directly affect production. It stresses shared information both within and outside the production facility. Its uses the tools of computer-aided design/engineering (CAD/CAE) for design, decision support systems (DSS) for information, and manufacturing execution systems (MES) for automation control. CIM plays the role of maestro—it orchestrates all the manufacturing elements:

Product creation
Production planning
Production control
Production equipment
Production processes

As broad as it is, CIM is but a part of something larger. It can be thought of as the manufacturing component of enterprise resources planning, or ERP. We'll have much more to say about ERP in Chapter 4. But for now let's just say that it is a tool for coordinating *all* the elements of production—inside and outside the production floor. In particular it consists of sales forecasting, resource requirements planning, purchasing, order entry, materials management, master production planning, capacity requirements planning, production scheduling and control, total quality management, and finance and cost control. It is indeed a very comprehensive tool. Computer-integrated manufacturing goes much deeper into the production processes than does ERP but is much narrower in scope. In contrast to CIM, which "runs the production processes," ERP is a management tool that "runs the company."

High performance in manufacturing requires matching the manufacturing approach to the particular production environment. For example, discrete-parts manufacturing has different requirements than continuous-flow, or process, manufacturing. Process manufacturing is designed around a collection of units through which material is transformed into the final product. It consists of a series of highly controlled steps. Such products as metals, chemicals, and foodstuffs are familiar examples of process manufacturing. By contrast, discrete manufacturing deals with unit processes, in serial or in parallel, of course, and results in the production of individual units or assemblies.

Production Approaches

Discrete manufacturing, like process manufacturing, is best accomplished by "pull-through" rather than "push-through" processes. To avoid excessive in-process inventories, work is paced to advance only at the level of the next workstation's capacity. Discrete production environments are many, and each has its own characteristics as to setups, scheduling, statistical process/quality control, inventory stores, process control, skills of production workers, and equipment maintenance procedures. A summary of the various kinds of discrete production is shown in Table 3.2.

Manufacturing is a crucial element of a company's competitive strategy. Moreover, the accelerating pace of new product introductions and the demand for distinctive and custom products has forced production environments to become even more efficient and flexible. These requirements have given rise to two complementary visions of production strategy: *lean* and *agile* manufacturing. Elements of leanness and agility—measures of speed—apply to the six production approaches described below. These ideas will be part of manufacturing's future, so here's what they are and what they can do for you.

Lean manufacturing stormed upon the manufacturing stage in 1990 with James Womack's book *The Machine That Changed the World.*[12] It showed Western managers how better autos can be built by eliminating waste and by using ever fewer of all the inputs to the production process: space, inventory, human effort, engineering time, and capital investment.

TABLE 3.2   CHARACTERISTICS OF DISCRETE MANUFACTURING ENVIRONMENTS

Dedicated—High-volume line-flow production of identical or highly similar products, with few or no changeovers

Cellular—A dedicated grouping of two or more clusters of production cells, wherein each cell produces products in identical groups or lots. In-process work moves within a cell where value-added operations (machinery, molding, component placement, assembly, etc.) are performed until final completion. Used in batch flow operations, with low to mid-volumes.

Flexible—Low- to mid-volume production of different products without retooling or other changeovers. Enabled by robotics and other flexible automation devices.

Job Shop—Production of unique or small lots, each requiring different routings and operations. Includes rapid prototyping processes. Functional layout; irregular flows.

Flow—A production process in which in-process work proceeds from beginning to end without interruptions or delays.

Quick Response—A combination of production strategies used in custom-engineered products or products having a large number of options.

In-process work is pulled along, and value is added at each successive step. Quality is monitored throughout the process. If a problem arises, it is corrected right at the source. Leanness makes fastidious use of visual order. The only tools in the workspace are those required for the job—each in its own place and regularly cleaned and calibrated.

Leanness or "quick response" manufacturing means producing an existing portfolio of products quickly, effectively, and to very high standards. Leanness relies on the tools of TQM, especially continuous improvement, to reduce defects and cycle times—and, of course, to please customers. Pure leanness is best suited to dedicated-flow and some cellular production environments that change only a little, if at all, over long periods of time.

Agility has a different objective: your ability to thrive in an environment of continuous change. Particularly suited to companies that must respond to rapid changes in market opportunities, agility enables you to adapt very quickly to variations in products and product requirements. Exploiting opportunities in such an environment demands the continual introduction of new and modified products and services, often in highly fragmented and constantly evolving markets. Agility draws from the principles of lean manufacturing, but its emphasis is more on rapid adaptability. Agility is best suited to discrete operations, as in flexible, batch, and job shop environments.

Leanness and agility are key determinants of production speed. In their classic book, *Product Development Performance*,[13] Kim Clark and Takahiro Fujimoto discuss the benefits of speed. Their research has shown that speed is associated with:

- A company's pattern of consistency in their total development system, including organizational structure, technical skills, problem solving, processes, culture, and strategy.
- Firms that work fast and effectively and therefore tend to be highly efficient. Firms that are slow, on the other hand, often have low productivity.
- Good product development processes, which in turn are a result of good organizational and system integration.
- Good product development performance, including lead time, productivity, and total product quality. Improvements in integrated product and process design should include improvement in all three simultaneously.

- The linkages between product creation and manufacturing. Each shares with the other a focus on high-speed throughput; reduced inventories; continuous feedback from downstream to upstream; rapid and effective problem-solving; ever higher quality, speed, and efficiency; and success at doing the right things right despite unexpected changes.

But here's a word of caution. Leanness, like other manufacturing approaches imported to the United States from Japan, often presents cultural roadblocks when implemented here. In particular, the concept of total trust within the supply chain is not so easily accepted. Lean manufacturing often requires considerable reskilling and cultural reorientation throughout the chain for it to work to expectations.

A particular industry—residential furniture—makes a compelling case for agile production methods. A diffused industry consisting of thousands of manufacturers and retailers, this largely cottage industry in its eagerness to attract and please customers has had a history of offering virtually any combination of style, color, and material the customer selects. Of course, all these choices lead to a great deal of handwork, long delivery cycles, and high embedded costs. Century Furniture, for example, theoretically can offer some 1.7 *billion* unique combinations across its 3,500 sofa and chair product lines. Moreover, much of the furniture industry's marketing messages have bordered on hucksterism—commercials offering teaser interest rates and long delayed payment schedules—which shouts to potential customers that pricing is inflated. Indeed, here's an industry that is ripe for consolidation, for narrowing product choices, and for adopting the tools of agile manufacturing.[14]

A comparison of lean and agile production approaches is shown in Table 3.3.

Considerable skill and experience are needed to design a production layout for a particular kind of manufacturing—such as for batch, job shop, or high-volume production. The capacity, the cycle times, and the sequencing of process equipment all must work together as a synchronous process.

Process modeling and simulation tools are among the most essential in the plant manager's arsenal. They make possible the efficient design of process systems, cellular production environments, and so on. And this technology, like most others, is advancing rapidly. It's now gone beyond the graphical simulations of production processes—where it won acceptance as a major advance in designing production processes. Researchers at

TABLE 3.3   FEATURES OF LEAN AND AGILE PRODUCTION ENVIRONMENTS

	Lean Production	Agile Production
New Product Development	Use of design for assembly/manufacturability and concurrent engineering. Design engineers experienced in production. Rapid product changes as needed.	Same, but with emphasis on product platforms for rapid introduction of new product families.
Customers	Close, long-term relations with key customers, emphasizing quality.	Same, but with a constant mix of new services and information. Provides custom products—produced on demand.
Suppliers	Long-term relations built on trust, mutual commitment, and total quality management	Same, but with emphasis on full integration of supply chain.
Management	Flat organizations; empowered workforce; regional focus	Same, but with less regional focus and more attention to changing environmental and related issues.
Workforce	Stable, well-trained workforce as a fixed, not variable, cost. Stable employment; few job classifications. Decision authority at lowest effective levels. Bonuses tied to team and to company performance.	Same.
Facilities	Smaller factories, close community ties. Efficient use of space, inventories. Flexibility more important than utilization. Inventories and equipment openly visible.	Use of space that stresses speed and adaptability; more emphasis on shared resources among facilities.
Processes	Flexible automation and late-point identification. Processes fully defined, fully characterized quality measurements.	Flexible production centers that are reconfigurable, scalable, and modular. Real-time, closed-loop process control. Flexibility even more important than in lean production.

Continued

| Inventories | Reduction of parts and in-process work. | Same, with more emphasis on finished goods inventories and JIT and kanban for managing inventories. |
| Quality | Defect reductions and root cause analysis. Wide use of statistical quality process and quality control. | Same, but with emphasis on customer delight over full life of product. |

Georgia Tech and elsewhere are now using it "off-line" to drive and assess the performance of *actual,* not simulated, processes—thereby finding even better ways for improving these processes.

In the final analysis, the keys to high-performance manufacturing are continual process improvement and total quality control. Process improvements depend upon higher speeds and lower costs. Quality improvements, which I'll cover in Chapter 7, depend upon reducing errors and cycle times.

Here's a success story. Consider the renaissance that awakened New Jersey–based Electronic Measurements Inc.—EMI, now a part of Lambda EMI, Inc.—which has manufactured AC-DC power supplies, converters, and accessories for half a century. Finding itself in a competitive stall, it embarked in 1991 upon an ambitious campaign to adopt true world-class manufacturing practices by benchmarking the best companies it could find: Harley Davidson, Pitney Bowes, Varian, and others—companies in noncompetitive markets but with reputations for excellence. EMI learned from them and then set out to realign and streamline its production processes, focusing on five areas:

Management:
- *Master Scheduling:* Scheduling to approach "real time" and to maximize the utilization of all processes.
- *Supplier Networks:* Building and improving cooperative, responsive relationships with all direct suppliers.
- *Lot Size of One:* Rejecting the old notion of "economic order quantity" and replacing it with the principle of "lot size of one"—thereby creating an environment that thrives on flexibility and responsiveness.

People:
- *Process Orientation:* Training and engaging everyone in process ownership: meeting or exceeding all internal and external customer expectations.

- *Skill Diversity:* Creating a "knowledge-worker" ethic throughout operations.
- *Housekeeping:* Instilling the discipline to keep the entire production area neat, orderly, and ready to serve internal customers.

Quality:
- *Process Ownership:* Emphasizing self-inspection at each process step and continually reducing non-value-added handling and staging.
- *Defect Reduction:* Understanding that quality is the result of process control.

Processes:
- *Cellular Manufacturing:* Providing cross training to reduce overall cycle times.
- *Balanced Line Flow:* Balancing operations for maximizing throughput, resulting in less inventory and less unused capacity.
- *Pull Systems:* Adding value to in-process work as late as possible, at the internal customer's request, thus reducing in-process inventories.
- *Visual Control:* Using kanban (visible cards) methods for seeing work status instantaneously.

Environment:
- *Process Changeovers:* Minimizing cycle times associated with tooling and other process adjustments.
- *Compact Plant Layout:* Using "focused factory" principles to streamline processes and eliminate non-value-added activities. Basing measurement on asset utilization, economic value added per unit of space.
- *Preventive Maintenance:* Giving operators the responsibility and authority to keep their equipment at peak performance.

Was it worth the effort? You bet it was! Within the decade EMI achieved ISO 9001 registration, increased productivity by 200 percent, reduced work orders by 70 percent, doubled production rates while reducing floor space by 80 percent, achieved an 80 percent improvement in quality yields, and significantly reduced the number of job titles. Sales and profitability also soared. It was a bold commitment to transform the very way the company did business, and it paid off handsomely.[15]

Mass Customization

As industries have learned to master agility, a fascinating and potent application has emerged—*mass customization.* The idea here is that certain kinds of products—clothing and footware, bicycles, pagers, eyewear, even the particular amenities in a luxury hotel—can be tailored to the individual customer. These examples are just a few of a growing market for custom products that can be provided "immediately," or nearly so.

There are degrees of customization. At one end there is the relatively simple level that we associate with having a hamburger "your way" or configuring a PC to your choice of available options. At the other extreme is the full customization we see in fitted clothing and in sporting equipment such as custom golf clubs and bicycles. Managing mass customization well—at any level—is not easy. It requires a tight information exchange with customers, as well as the advanced production systems required to create "unique" products economically.

The key, of course, is gathering the right information on the spot. Panasonic National Bicycle Company, part of Japan's National Bicycle Industrial Company, is a pioneer in the art of mass customization. A customer walks into one of their shops and gets fitted for height, weight, and size dimensions on an adjustable bicycle frame. This information is sent electronically to the factory, which then fabricates and ships the bike to the customer *the same day.* These products command a higher price, some 20 to 30 percent over comparable mass-produced Panasonic bicycles. And the market is "incremental"—it doesn't take away from traditional market. It is, in fact, setting a trend.[16]

A similar case is eyewear retailer Paris Miki. Customers go to the nearest optician, where their faces are digitally photographed and measured in several ways. They identify the kind of "look" they want, and pictures instantly appear showing various frames on their face. By viewing various eyewear and facial combinations until they find "right" look, customers in an hour can leave the shop wearing unique, custom-crafted glasses.

In the 1980s Motorola's pager division pioneered mass customization of electronic products, scrapping their conventional pager-making process, which took some three weeks from order to product shipment. As I described in Chapter 2, replacing it was an entirely new process whereby a pager could be customized to the customer's specific set of options in two hours from order receipt—and then shipped the same day. This innovative approach to concurrent engineering created quite a stir. Dozens of teams from companies, manufacturing associations, and others made the pilgrimage to Boynton Beach, Florida, to see this process in action. These teams inadvertently became part of Motorola's unofficial pager sales force.

Expect to see many more examples of mass-customized products in the future. Ford Motor Company, taking a cue from the booming after-market for spoilers, air scoops, and other body moldings, is planning to provide such styling options as part of the production process, thus cashing in on young buyers seeking a particular "look." The combination of custom-crafted products and instant gratification—at conventional price levels—is a powerful elixir that will create bigger and better markets. It is already sending conventional retailers into a scramble to cut costs and provide other incentives so that customers won't defect.[17]

One of management's key responsibilities when tackling production process improvements is to attend to the "soft" issues. Your process engineers tend to focus on the value that agility, cost cutting, and cycle time reductions can deliver. Nothing wrong with that—in fact, it's primary. But recognize that fostering teamwork and creativity among your people creates true agility. They must take collective responsibility for continually improving the way work is performed and how customers are served. Quick restructuring, cost cutting, and downsizing are not good roads to long-term prosperity. Rather, investments in training, process measurement and improvement, better use of information, and a thorough commitment to customer delight are far more powerful means to sustain competitiveness.

3.4: IDEAS FOR ACTION

1. Commission a well-rounded senior-level task force to develop (or refine) your manufacturing strategy, as outlined in Section 3.1. Act upon significant needs that emerge.
2. Are your production systems geared best to the kind of manufacturing operations you run? Can you find gains in implementing lean or agile production philosophies? Are you using enlightened line, cellular, flexible, or job shop manufacturing approaches appropriately?
3. Revisit your supply chain with an eye toward making it more dependable and more nimble. Look for opportunities for formal partnerships, intranet and e-business tools, EDI, vendor-managed inventories, and better ways to forecast demand. Are there opportunities to shorten (disintermediate) your go-to-market channels?

4. Examine your production operations for opportunities to improve communication linkages to product engineering and R&D—and to the other "spokes," for that matter.
5. Take up the use of process simulation tools to model and improve your production processes. Provide suitable training in the use and application of these tools for advancing your concurrent engineering practices.
6. If you haven't done so already, take a leisurely and critical tour of your production operations. Ask lots of questions and come up with a list of improvement opportunities.

Chapter 4

Systems

Making Information Technology Work

At the heart of most waterwheel technology has been the simple "hub-and-spoke" design. This arrangement provided sturdy support to the outer rim and to the perimeter vanes that caught the incoming water, thus propelling the wheel to turn. This design evolved as being lighter and easier to repair than a solid disc wheel. It was an efficient design and used widely. Many thousands of these durable waterwheels are still at work today throughout the world.

This same hub-and-spoke architecture is reflected today in, of all things, information management. The heart of this network is a server—a computer that warehouses information in a way that makes it easy to locate and send on request any piece of information, in any desired format. In our analogy the wheel's hub plays the role of the information server, dispatching data out along a sending spoke, then around the wheel rim, and back again along the receiving spoke. In this scheme the spokes, or "information pathways," work together because they are linked by their common access to the central data repository, the server. It's a simple and effective client-server network. It's also fault tolerant: just as with the design of the waterwheel, if one spoke fails, the load can be redistributed among the remaining spokes, and the work can continue uninterrupted.

This same architectural concept applies to new product creation. All business processes feed on information, enabled by this or a variation of this network—as was depicted in Figure 2.1. Information exchange requires full cooperation among the business "spokes." Our New Product Creation Wheel serves as a metaphor for information-driven product creation processes. It provides robust and flexible information pathways and thereby enables product creation to thrive in a flexible environment—a huge improvement over traditional serial, one-at-a-time processes and their attendant queues, bottlenecks, and dead times.

In this chapter I'll give you a practical overview of information technology (IT), particularly as it relates to new product creation. I'll spare you from the bits and bytes of the technology. I'll also spare you the five-mile-high "big picture" of IT that many marketers like to talk about. Instead, I'll offer some useful information that may serve you well in thinking about strategy and benefits. First, we'll have a look at enterprise resource planning applications, then at its father, manufacturing execution systems, and then at its close cousin, product data management systems. We'll look also at important issues surrounding computer-integrated manufacturing (CIM), factory automation, and systems integration, which are central to developing valuable products. I'll discuss the role of consultants in helping implement IT systems. Then I'll conclude with what I regard as one of the most potent business applications of IT, knowledge management.

4.1: INFORMATION SYSTEMS—YOUR KEY TO BUSINESS EXCELLENCE

The stakes and investments in IT are huge. How huge? Manny Fernandez, CEO of the GartnerGroup, estimates that in the mid-1990s a typical company invested about 1.5 percent of sales in IT. He estimates that by 2003 this figure will be in the range of 12 to 14 percent. IT investments by then will commonly exceed the company's R&D budget. Clearly, information technology will be a major factor in shaping a company's approach to product creation.

With the escalation in IT spending, a company should expect to reap significant business benefits, but no benefits can be won unless two conditions are met. First, the CEO must accept direct accountability for the expected benefits from IT spending. Such investments must be seen as *strategic*, not only tactical. IT is an instrument for reshaping the company's business strategy over the next three to five years. Some of the questions you must ask are, How can technology keep and attract more customers?

How can it be used to gain deeper insight into the real needs for new products in the marketplace? How can it be used to garner and act upon competitive intelligence? Answers to such questions will prompt the right IT investments to capture strategic advantage.

Today most companies earmark some 85 percent of their IT budget to "utility" functions: expanding and upgrading systems for internal information and reporting purposes, much of which is accomplished through outsourcing. Only about 3 percent is earmarked for new strategic initiatives, such as gaining competitive advantage.[1] But many leaders expect a correction of this imbalance as we become more conscious of the need for better information about markets and customers.

Which leads to the second condition that must be met. The *real* power of IT lies in its ability to do more than merely store information and handle transactions. It can help you uncover new and better ways of doing business. IT must therefore be directed in a way that enables your company to deliver this power, to leapfrog your competitors. The relevant questions here are, How can IT restructure the traditional supply chain and use e-business to grow the market and increase share? How can knowledge be catalogued and retrieved so as to capitalize upon successful practices of the past? How can data and text mining be used to customize market approaches?

More CEOs are embracing and taking personal ownership of information technology to get answers to these questions. They want assurances that value from the heavy IT investments is being realized. We'll also see more company boards involved in oversight of IT strategy-setting to make sure the investments they approve will actually create better futures for their companies.

Indeed, the IT market is huge. Companies worldwide are investing well over a *trillion* dollars annually in information systems—including network equipment, hardware, software, technical support, and training. U.S. companies account for some 80 percent of the total, according to the Information Technology Industry Council. And with the IT industry growing at about 11 percent a year (and expected to accelerate), this industry sector will easily double midway through the first decade of the 21st century.

Enterprise Resources Planning Systems—Living with a Big Gorilla

Enterprise Resources Planning (ERP) systems are credited today for many business performance improvements. They orchestrate much of a corporation's IT infrastructure: networks, operating systems, telecom, and so on. It's difficult to overstate the enormous influence they're having on revolutionizing the way mid-sized and large companies do business, by integrating financial, supply-chain, and customer information efficiently. These systems have taken business processes out of the file cabinet and into client-server environments, where they orchestrate business transactions not only within the enterprise but also all along the value chain. These systems have made modest companies efficient ones and competitive enterprises veritably hawkish. On the other hand, package suppliers and integrators have too often oversold their wares by not delivering on their promises. System costs commonly exceed initial estimates—in many cases by very substantial amounts. Yet on a net basis ERP systems are essential. You simply can't afford the cost of *not* having an integrated IT system to support your business. Moreover, you must commit to moving that system forward and improving its power to serve you better. It's hard to imagine any significant enterprise creating valuable products without them. And the industrial world will be even more dependent upon ERP systems well into the future.

How the Big Gorilla Got That Way

Like human beings, modern ERP systems also evolved—not over millennia, however, but a mere quarter century. IT began in the late 1960s with nascent plantwide information systems, in particular the automation of basic accounting processes. In the early 1970s came the first systems for materials requirements planning—MRP. Packaged MRP software systems back then proved their ability to plan, track, and control all "material" in the master schedule. The schedule determined what materials (raw materials, components, subassemblies, and so on) were needed and when, then matched those requirements against plant capacity, allowing the MRP system to schedule production—a major improvement over manual systems. For the first time an automated system determined production needs based upon customer orders—and enabled companies to satisfy those requirements by managing inventories and purchases accordingly.

Soon after, MRP yielded to an even more powerful tool, manufacturing requirements planning—dubbed MRPII to distinguish it from its "materials" ancestor. MRPII expanded the capabilities of MRP, permitting the planning and controlling of all *manufacturing* resources—not just materials—within an industrial company. These systems began with sales and operations planning and scheduled work by electronically laboring through demand planning, master scheduling, capacity planning, and supplier and plant scheduling, finally driving production execution. This added capability represented a great leap forward in forecasting and scheduling production accurately. MRPII systems still remain the reliable production backbone for most small and mid-sized manufacturing companies.

A further evolutionary step was the development of manufacturing execution systems (MES), which extended MRPII functionality by *actively* tracking production, specifications, engineering change notices, materials, labor, machine utilization, and scrappage. MES provided a key link between production and the production floor process control systems. It empowered managers, engineers, and operators with the tools to execute a production plan based on actual, momentary capabilities by using finite scheduling to take into account instantly the equipment capacity, the status of current orders, and work in process.

The late 1980s brought the emergence of enterprise resources planning, ERP. These systems were able to do all that MRPII systems did, but on an *enterprise* basis, not just within production site operations. ERP was able to integrate all production forecasting and scheduling requirements throughout the entire business structure. Rather than simply "running production," ERP enabled the notion, at least in a primitive way, of "running the company." Today MES packages can be bundled into ERP systems or can be separately acquired and integrated; they complement each other. Incidentally, the term ERP is a bit of a misnomer. Only about 5 percent of the software code is dedicated to "planning." The great majority supports process execution and management.

Today a few large package providers—SAP, Baan, PeopleSoft, J. D. Edwards and Oracle—dominate the ERP market, accounting for 64 percent of total revenues.[2] At this writing, SAP leads the market in share, owning some 9,000 customers in 90 countries. These packages are highly complex and typically require one to four years to implement, at costs often in the tens of millions of dollars. Moreover, these giant systems often are structured not to conform fully to the enterprise's particular business processes. To some extent, the processes need to be customized so that they can be "managed" by the ERP system. Of course, the danger is that the tail will wag the dog. Thomas Davenport of Boston University's School of Management cautions that some companies may lose a portion of their uniqueness and competitive advantages by squeezing themselves into a particular ERP package.

But for our purposes we'll sidestep these (important) feature differences. Instead, we'll look at generic ERP systems in terms of what they are and what they can do.

THE BASICS OF ERP

Figure 4.1 shows the architecture of a generic ERP system. The heart of the system is the planning and control module. This piece manages all internal operations, from sales and customer service information, through inventory control and capacity planning, down to the many details of shop floor management. And it does so in real time. It digests the massive data continuously fed into it from multiple remote sources. It transforms those inputs into instant information updates and forecasts, synchronizing and managing the flow of materials electronically throughout the entire supply chain. One example: Some production lines are designed to accommodate "late-point product identification" (LPPI) so those platform products can be customized to the customer's particular requirements at the very last stage of manufacture. This practice complicates materials and lead-time planning but offers huge benefits. Late-point identification would be all but impossible without real-time scheduling and inventory control—without, in other words, ERP.

The heroes in this entire system are the finite scheduling algorithms. Earlier ERP packages had to assume, for scheduling purposes, infinite inventory and production capacity. Nothing is infinite, but back then the mathematical algorithms and fast microprocessors to run them were not available to enable realistic forecasting. As a result, the forecasts often were seriously flawed.

Flanking the planning and control module in Figure 4.1 are the financial and human resources management support modules. They interact with the planning and control module for administrative updates. ERP allows payroll, general ledger, accounts receivable and payable, and other administrative functions to be in lockstep with current as well as forecasted business conditions, enabling staff functions to make better decisions about future requirements and plan for them earlier.

Feeding the finite scheduling function in Figure 4.1 is the supply chain management (SCM) system—which is commonly bundled with ERP systems. After all, SCM requirements draw from many of the core ERP functions: advanced manufacturing planning and scheduling, demand planning, supply planning, and transportation management. But before

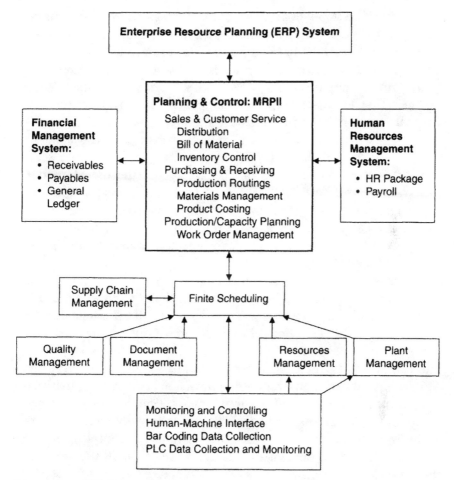

FIGURE 4.1   ERP FUNCTIONALITY ARCHITECTURE

this nexus between SCM and ERP began to develop, a cadre of IT package vendors offered stand-alone SCM packages. Now some of the leading ERP vendors, like Oracle and SAP, have forged alliances with SCM vendors such as Manugistics and i2 Technologies to provide bundled products. And so it is with quality, document resources, and plant management tools. They are available as modular packages but are more effective when integrated with the entire ERP system.

One SCM tool that is proving particularly valuable within large enterprises is strategic procurement. An example: It's not unusual to find a particular component carrying different part numbers in various business sectors that have stand-alone ERP systems. Strategic sourcing systems can ferret out these common parts and consolidate parts procurement across business units, resulting in significant savings through added purchasing leverage. But these systems are capable of much more. When coupled with data-mining techniques and Internet tools, strategic sourcing can identify and locate the lowest-cost, available components from suppliers or from internal inventories. And through the use of radio- and satellite-based technologies, strategic procurement can track materials and consignments as they move through the supply chain.

Another trend in supply chain management is the use of vendor-managed inventories, a topic discussed in Chapter 3. This isn't really a novel idea—automakers have practiced supply chain management (SCM) with their dealers for decades. But mega-store chains like Wal-Mart have honed this practice to a fine edge by pitting competitors against each other for prime shelf space. Other business sectors that have until recently been slow to engage these techniques are rapidly adopting them. Now with the use of extranet technologies for cross-enterprise coordination and with the tools of strategic sourcing, industry is well posed to exploit the possibilities.

Choosing an ERP system is a difficult, drawn-out process. You have many options, but the cornerstone of the decision process is a dedicated internal team that represents internal users, finance, and IT professionals. ERP systems now come in a variety of flavors. And because the IT market is so dynamic and is expanding rapidly, vendors are continually adding new functions to their products and finding other ways to differentiate themselves from competitors. Companies that have plans to implement full-featured ERP systems (and virtually all companies should!) need to make their selections with great care and deliberation. Large mainframe ERP systems are not for everyone; many equally featured mid-sized ERP systems may be more suitable and cost-effective for smaller companies, single or multisite. Some run on PCs and can be linked together through client-server networks. They can also be connected to a central mainframe system to provide for local transactions and planning, as well as enterprise-wide information sharing.

Such decisions are crucial and can lead to costly misjudgments if not carefully examined. Make choices in view of the way your company is run and measured financially. As an example, when giant ABB was evaluating its ERP needs, the decision rested largely on its requirement for activity based costing (ABC). ABC (further discussed in Chapter 8) is a system for accurately determining true (as distinguished from allocated) costs—and therefore prices—of parts and systems ABB delivers. It's a critical component of ABB's business strategy, and ABB ended its evaluation process by selecting what was then the latest client-server version of SAP, R/3, in part because it was capable of providing ABC information.

MAKING ERP WORK FOR YOU

Yes, you have many opportunities available through the power of ERP systems. But the devil is in the details. If you expect to leverage this technology to best advantage, invest in close, executive level oversight. I really mean CEO level. This individual must first have a clear vision of your company's future, then provide for managing the time commitments and project costs involved. In the IT world, getting from point A to point B is usually not a straight path. There *will* be disappointments and setbacks. So common is this experience that it has its own sobriquet, the "valley of despair," which shows itself by creating confusion, doubt, and inefficiency at the beginning. But with careful planning, you can minimize the valley's depth and climb out quickly. The Deloitte & Touche Consulting Group recommends the following list of best practices for implementing an ERP system:[3]

- Focus on capabilities and benefits, not rushing to "go live."
- Align the organization with its strategic destination.
- As changes begin, achieve balance among people, process, and technology across all areas.
- Use the business case as a management tool.
- Apply planning and program management practices throughout the program life cycle.
- Transition project roles into new and stable "ways of life."
- Build and leverage process expertise.
- Extend capabilities beyond the ERP platform.
- Promote postimplementation commonality.
- Assign clear ownership of benefits.
- Define appropriate metrics and measure them.

One more point on this theme of minimizing chaos while creating change: there are legitimate reasons for hesitating to implement costly, obsolescence-prone IT systems. Benefits must be weighed against costs and risks. You may not have the right internal sources available to pull it off.

Yes, you can have outside consultants shoulder the load, but there are cautions here, too (as discussed later in this chapter). The overriding success factor is your ability to marshal a distinctive culture change within your company. It will affect people's jobs; it will affect the way they go about their jobs. This aspect alone will take resources and patience; so don't go into it unless you're prepared to support it.

Beyond the cultural aspects, other concerns may pop up that managers must face when implementing ERP systems. Among the most often cited are:[4]

- Lack of in-house expertise (55 percent)
- Executive management that does not grasp benefits (38 percent)
- Inadequate planning or a lack of vision (35 percent)
- Outdated cost justification methods (30 percent)
- Fear of failure (25 percent)

Be prepared for surprises and discouragement, and minimize grief by actively involving your internal customers in the process.

Trends in the IT Market

Many business analysts believe that the quick rewards from ERP systems have already been harvested. Mid-sized and large companies by now are well along in streamlining their internal operations, forcing SAP and rivals to target smaller customers. And a burgeoning product market for smaller ERP systems does exist. These systems are mostly targeted at small and mid-sized companies and used as plant-level "managers" under a main supervisory, or "corporate," ERP system. So competition can only increase in the years ahead. Price competition among the major vendors already has become intense in some applications, such as the HR software and government and university markets. Meanwhile, SAP, Oracle PeopleSoft, and other tier-one ERP vendors are moving into newer markets that are growing more quickly, including front-office tasks such as sales, marketing, and customer service.[5]

The big need, still largely unfulfilled, is for ERP systems equipped with customer-relationship management (CRM) and related sales-force automation tools. This functionality is generally not integrated into the current ERP base yet is absolutely vital to business competitiveness. Squarely in the lap of ERP vendors, the challenge is to address the "backlash against the inadequacies of monolithic application packages."[6] Some, including Oracle, are leveraging themselves by using the Internet computing platform in conjunction with client-server systems to provide CRM and business intelligence.

A growing trend in the IT market is to offer more choice and flexibility in ERP systems. Some vendors are offering a central structure, or "spine," that might be a fully functional MRPII or a simple financial package. By connecting a variety of specialized packages to this spine, an ERP then achieves a "plug and play" capability that offers both power and customization. It shifts the role of implementers and service providers away from the "spine" vendor and to the system integrator. Of course, this approach calls for the development of industry software and hardware standards, which will take time. Whatever the future of ERP, prosperous system providers will be those who can cost-effectively evolve the product in harmony with the growth and changes of particular business segments.

Another IT trend for managing business is the use of middleware—the software that resides between the mainframe and server systems, and the custom applications that drive specific system outputs. This product market is emerging in response to the explosion of distributed computing through the Internet. Middleware products like CORBA and MT/COM are providing reliable infrastructures for development of business applications. Such products are also extending their support to Java and http programming languages, stepping out in the forefront of distributed computing. Java provides for the transport of software code to any recognized operating system. Because it's very nearly "platform free," Java, Linux, and similar languages have significantly simplified and enabled the development and deployment of transaction-based enterprise applications.

However, the middleware market is still immature, so exercise caution. Rules for its use, as well as key players, have not settled out. And because the law has not caught up with technology innovations, serious disputes can erupt over who has ownership and control of the middleware. Among the issues are, who has exclusive rights over data access? Who establishes policy issues, and who defines access rules?

Still another trend is toward outsourcing IT functions, which correlates with other shifts toward doing only those things in house that support an enterprise's core competencies. The consulting firm G2R estimates that the growth in outsourcing IT administration to service providers is growing at about 20 percent per year and already is a $30 billion business in the United States. More and more firms are finding that "doing your own" ERP system and shop floor system upgrades saps organizational energy and leads to mistakes and uncontrollable costs.

E-Business

E-business is the trend of trends. Accordingly, there's a booming initiative to incorporate and exploit e-business and Web-enabled functions directly into ERP systems. Major vendors are moving rapidly to incorporate e-business services to streamline customer-vendor transactions—the "front office" functions. These developments are bound to shake up the auto industry's long reliance upon electronic data interchange. Around since the '80s, EDI supports supply chain management through the efficient exchange of routine drawings, specifications, quotes, purchase orders, and other documents. But for EDI to compete against the threat of ubiquitous and powerful e-business systems, it must itself improve. For example, EDI doesn't provide true high-value applications across enterprises and up and down the supply chain. EDI is trying to respond to this challenge by moving toward private value-added networks—such as those being offered by AT&T and GE Information Systems. These technologies are developing rapidly and likely will change the landscape of application-to-application and business-to-business integration.

Indeed, Web-enabled supply chain management is poised to have a significant influence on industry's quest to disintermediate the supply chain. By connecting your producers directly to the ultimate customers, you reduce costs and have direct and immediate feedback from your customers. A friction-free supply chain. The middleman is expendable—unless, of course he can bring some specific value that you are unable to provide yourself. Web-enabled supply chain management affords the possibility to deliver new products and services directly to the market. Distance and geographic boundaries are irrelevant. This opportunity ought to be on the desk of every CEO really concerned about business strategy.

On the retail side, the enormous potential of the Internet for facilitating buyer-seller relationships is starting to emerge. The Web provides a low-cost distributed computing platform for business commerce. Its power is enhanced because of its capacity to handle security and to provide speed, ever-broader bandwidth, and reliability. Examples abound. L.L. Bean and hundreds of other direct-marketing enterprises offer virtual catalogs over the Internet. Schwab and other brokerages offer online investing services. AMP has its full catalog of over 80,000 products online. Such services are paying off as Web-surfing has become a national mania. Some 30 percent of U.S. adults are on the Internet daily, a figure that is sure to grow rapidly. Forrester Research, Inc., forecasts that by 2003, sales for e-commerce transactions will exceed $100 billion, or some 6 percent of consumer retail spending. Worldwide, 550 million people are already connected to the Web, buying new products and services. And by the way, this surge in Web-based consumerism is creating a huge demand for e-commerce consumer-interactive software.

One company happily selling its products and services via e-commerce is General Motors. GM is going head to head with competitors with its Web-based online autobuying service, GM BuyPower. Learning from the experience of its Saturn division that buyers loathe the ritual of price haggling when buying a car, GM set up BuyPower to eliminate that dance while providing more customer convenience and value. BuyPower gives consumers direct and instant access to model and equipment pricing information and to dealers carrying specific products. GM even provides its customers with information on competitive products and can arrange for a test drive and financing. Other auto makers are following suit. With more than a quarter of auto buyers routinely searching the Web for product information, this market will likely skyrocket. And the action is not limited to auto makers. Many other companies, including GE, Cisco, Dell, and AMP, are finding it quick and profitable to transact with suppliers over the Internet.

Security

Data and information security has become a leading issue as consumers jump feet first into the electronic Web of commerce. You can't afford system crashes that erase precious information. You can even less afford hacker intrusions that corrupt your system, steal your information, and harass your employees. This is complex, unpleasant, and expensive stuff. Yet security breeches do happen—more often than you might imagine. They constitute a silent poison that can infect and seriously damage your business. They can corrupt the integrity of your information via hacking, vandalism, eavesdropping, penetration, and impersonation. But there are tools and methods available to protect yourself from this threat.

If you haven't already, seek the protection you need. Systemwide data security and firewalls are essential for your private networks and intranet links. These safeguards achieve a number of very good things. By using encryption techniques to ensure message integrity, they provide for the digital equivalent of personal signatures to authenticate senders and receivers, buyers and sellers in online transactions. They enable the secure use of credit cards. Easily installed on Web browsers and on private computer server networks, these security measures are also being designed into the microprocessors that run computers.

Firewalls are the first line of defense. Software for real-time intrusion detection is another safeguard. An especially powerful line of protection is "ethical hacking," in which you bring in a small team of pros with the experience to crash through firewalls and other security measures. By trying to invade your data systems, the team can uncover any security lapses. IBM and other system providers use ethical hackers to detect, correct, and certify Web apps for their customers.

What does all this have to do with product creation? Everything! Always remember that the process is *sovereign*. Information technology, in the form of ERP and companion systems, has successfully enabled the management of complex, interrelated processes by routinely running production from the supply chain all the way through to order fulfillment.

And that's just the beginning. PRTM's Michael McGrath envisions a fundamental reshaping of the new product development management process. To come is the introduction of Web-centric architectures for enterprise software—common application platforms for document preparation, product prototyping, project scheduling, and e-mail as the necessary information infrastructure—a completely integrated and innovative product development system.[7]

4.2: PRODUCT DATA MANAGEMENT SYSTEMS

Another approach to integrated business information—an approach that has been upstaged by the runaway ERP train—is product data management systems, PDM. PDM products are becoming essential in the development of valuable new products. Although they don't enjoy the status that senior executives give to ERP systems, PDM systems have been taking on increasing importance since they began in the mid-1980s. Becoming essential for designing and developing new products, PDM systems free engineers from the burdensome paper-based system of component and system drawings—drawings that required multiple revisions and were distributed to multiple vendors. Instead, PDM creates a single, permanent repository for all product information—including design, components and materials, assembly methods, revision control, and manufacturing process—as the product proceeds through development. Facilitating not only product development, PDM is also invaluable for patent filings and other intellectual property purposes. It helps with product warranties and recalls by summoning up original, "as built" product designs.

Now highly evolved, PDM systems can bring together designs, simulations, and analyses for computer-aided manufacturing planning. They can create bills of materials for purchasing, vendor specifications and pricing, process plans, standards and customer requirements—all of which can be attached to drawings. They can reduce engineering change orders by getting the right people involved early for approvals and signoffs—thereby reducing surprises. Because of its ability to cut development cycles and part numbers as much as half while streamlining and improving the development process itself, PDM has earned credibility within engineering functions. Indeed, a PDM system should align itself with the particular product development process it supports. And, in fact, it has.

One caution regarding this terrific tool of PDM is security. Leakage of proprietary and competitive information to competitors, whether through hacking or other means, is a risk that needs to be controlled. The modern enterprise transcends business walls. The virtual enterprise—a web of interconnected companies within a supply chain—carries its own significant risks, among them the potential for pervasive information and intelligence espionage.

PDM has been a savior for hundreds of companies, including the venerable Otis Elevator Company. Otis needed better coordination among its various production and service units throughout the world, which included maintaining more than a million installed units, some of which are 100 years old. Now all of Otis's parts and process plans from day one have been scanned into its main PDM system and can be remotely accessed by laptop computers in the field. Result: correct decisions made in minutes rather than days. Otis has gone on to manage the life-cycle requirements of all its installed units. Now *that's* customer service! And similar stories abound from giant companies such as Boeing, Ford Motors, and Whirlpool, as well as San Jose–based Diamond Multimedia, a smallish (fewer than 1,000 employees) producer of computer games, sound cards, and Web pages.[8,9]

PDM has focused primarily on engineering productivity, not on overall business productivity. It's been justified largely on faith because many of its benefits are "soft." After all, engineering productivity *is* difficult to quantify. Yet PDMs continue to improve their capabilities. Over the horizon will come Web-enabled intranet and extranet capabilities that will multiply our ability to seek out and coordinate with vendors, customers, and other business partners. PDM systems have the potential to support e-commerce, giving users access to electronic purchasing.

Already ERP and PDM systems have converged, as explained by Ed Miller, president of Ann Arbor–based Cimdata Corporation. "Product data structures in ERP generally define parts and how they are put together on the shop floor, so it is typically oriented toward materials, scheduling and production processes. PDM structures, on the other hand, are typically more functionally oriented, focusing on what the product does and how it is configured."[10] ERP vendors like Baan are beginning to bundle PDM capabilities on their products' front end. They recognize that product development is the foundation of any enterprise's fortunes. PDM vendors, on the other hand, are adding purchasing, manufacturing, and sales and marketing capabilities to their products. And they will continue to exert their influence in the ERP marketplace.

4.3: IT DRIVES CIM AND FACTORY AUTOMATION

One of the key components for product creation is the intelligent use of integrated manufacturing systems. Why is it key? First, computer-integrated manufacturing (CIM) systems are vital to meet the high quality standards that today's competitive markets demand. Not only does poor quality steal from profit margins, but it turns customers away from you and toward your competitors. Second, CIM is essential for shortening the product development cycle. Going from product conception to prototype to drawings and specifications, then to production planning and setup requires seamless automation handoffs along the entire process. Time is money; automation allows you the opportunity to have more of both. And third, CIM technologies liberate the talents of the workforce to do the mind work needed for production, relegating the dull, repetitive work to automation.

I'll assume you are at least acquainted with CIM practices; you may even have deep knowledge of them. So I won't burden you with the details. Let's agree that CIM is part of a highly automated production environment, with input links from design engineering and outputs to various market channels. In general, CIM comprises:

- Production design: product data management information
- Production planning: planning and creation of the production process
- Production control: modeling, simulation, and scheduling
- Production equipment: the computer-driven tools of production
- Production processes: data-driven equipment units.

Tying all this together are myriad tools, including networked sensors and controllers, input/output devices, test equipment, robotics and specialized unit processing machinery, and bar codes and similar identification appliances. These aids, in turn, are tied into the ERP systems that drive the enterprise, as shown earlier in Figure 4.1.

You can approach and design production processes in several ways, some of which are discussed in Chapter 3, in "Production Methods: Matching Your Approach with Your Business." Generally speaking, there's a basic distinction between discrete and process automation. The former describes distinct units of production, whereas the latter refers to continuous, indivisible flow of materials. They're treated separately because their approaches to control, test, and packaging are somewhat different. But more recently the tendency has been to regard all production processes as batchlike for purposes of process control. The reason is practical. Batch processing and control are inherently superior when it comes to security, redundancy, data acquisition, forecasting and trending, and of course, data warehousing. In fact, major process automation companies are leading this movement. Discrete processing and machine tool control now are in decline in the United States. Companies like Allen-Bradley are now concentrating on growing their markets in batch processing and process control. Likewise, Honeywell is moving toward discrete control yet is keeping its process capabilities, such as material handling.

4.4: MANAGING YOUR CONSULTANTS

Management and IT consultants share a common public image. They're the targets of more criticism and scorn—or praise—than just about any other profession. But what really counts is that outside consultants can be of great value *if* you use them wisely. They can provide expert guidance that is objective—a perspective you can't always get from your own staff.

Consultants can also be cost-effective: you don't have to carry them on your payroll; they're there when you need them and gone when you don't. Most consulting engagements end up delivering good results and goodwill. Occasionally, however, they don't. Those that fail do so mostly because you, the client, failed to select the consultant properly and to be engaged with and manage the consulting team effectively. You have to be a smart and involved customer to expect a successful result.

Some years ago I wrote a short article, "Managing the Consultant," in a professional magazine.[11] The seven tips I discussed then are just as valid today as 20 years ago:

- *Choose your consultant carefully.* Selection should be based on prior personal experience or, alternatively, probing discussions with the consultant's recent clients.
- *Appoint a single senior executive to coordinate closely with the consultant.* The consultant and his or her team will interact with many, but overall direction must come from a single, involved executive.
- *Discuss costs frankly and in advance of the engagement.* Discuss the relative merits of various cost approaches: overall fixed price, fixed priced with redeterminable phases, or time and materials. And beware of "scope creep"—when you may be drawn into an engagement only to find that some elements you presumed to be included in the project cost weren't. Also discuss rates, warranties, and contingency policies.
- *Give the consultant specific objectives and direction.* The work scope must be crystal clear, whether it's a general assessment or a particular project. Be very frank in your relationship with your consultant.
- *Don't expect the consultant to solve all your problems.* Help your consultant when navigating political waters and keep your expectations in line with the work statement.
- *Expect specific outputs from the consultant.* A consultant's recommendations must be in writing and actionable. System test and "going live" must follow predetermined protocols and yield agreed-upon results.
- *Respect the consultant's ethical code.* Don't pump your consultant for proprietary information.

In addition, there are special considerations when consultants assist in implementing large ERP or similar enterprise-wide systems. A study from the Harvard Business School[12] urges that such implementations be approached in stages, as in an evolutionary process. They make an analogy with entering a joint venture with another company; the end point evolves rather than being fixed at the outset. Each stage, from preliminary data collection through to production rollout, should be taken on as a limited project with defined costs, deliverables, and with full management awareness. Assign a subject expert on your staff to oversee the details of the entire project closely. This person must be sufficiently engaged to evaluate accurately whether the process is on track.

This close oversight reduces risks on both sides. It also allays the fear that most (two of every three) executives harbor—fear that an ERP implementation may actually cause business operations to suffer. Such apprehension is well grounded—and is a scathing indictment of management and IT consultants who routinely promise more than they deliver, and of business executives who ask for and expect the moon. Some 70 percent of the investment that companies make in IT applications either overrun by a factor of two (yes, 200 percent!) or are simply not completed.[13] It should be obvious that technology is to serve the company, not be its master. Yet in too many cases ERP systems implementers expect the client to adapt to the system's approach rather than the other way around. When it comes to consultants, don't let the tail wag the dog.

4.5: What's on the Horizon—From Data and Information to *Knowledge!*

Business knowledge exists at many levels. At the most primitive level is the *bare data:* surveys, reports, logs, and such. Simple statements of fact: "Our Acme product has 25 percent market share." This statement may be completely accurate and potentially useful but doesn't enable you to do anything with it. The next level of business intelligence sophistication is *information*. Information is data that can be combined to create new facts and insights; "Acme is holding market share in the East but steadily slipping in the West." This information is richer than mere data, and you can begin to act upon it.

The next step leads to *knowledge*—insights developed only through deeper analysis and understanding of the business issue. "Results of our nationwide focus group program indicate that we should stay the course in the East but offer Acme products in both scented and unscented versions in the West." Finally, the highest level of business intelligence is *wisdom*—a rich understanding of the whole business environment that allows a company to engineer and deliver a more beneficial future. "We at Acme foresee that Web-based information will change the entire market dynamic, and we must therefore move Acme to a customizable platform product that can be delivered to order via the Internet."

Your goal, as a company, is to move up the continuum from data to wisdom. You can achieve this only if you manage your knowledge.

Most companies understand that their greatest assets are their people and the knowledge they create. They also realize that managing knowledge is both important and difficult. People come and go, and the wisdom and insight they acquire too often goes with them. Ideally, such knowledge should be passed on to apprentices, but many factors interfere with the orderly process of mentorship. In addition to knowledge created within, knowledge comes from outside sources. Knowing your customers' tastes and expectations is vital and must be "managed" to exploit this information effectively. Moreover, knowledge gathered for competitive intelligence assessments needs to be stored and made accessible to those who need it.

Knowledge Management

The sheer volume of knowledge being acquired compounds year after year. Even if all of it were to be archived in databases (and in truth, very little is), how could it be accessed? How can you call up a packet of knowledge and not get a data dump? Or get something that's precise but absolutely useless? And what should be weeded out, and when? These are the central challenges of knowledge management (KM).

Knowledge management, at its most basic level, is a collection of practices and technology tools that enable knowledge generation, codification, and transfer on demand:

- *K Generation:* Creation, acquisition, and synthesis of potentially valuable knowledge—internally, from suppliers and customers, from competitors, and from other business trends.
- *K Codification:* Methods for accessing knowledge and transferring it in formats that make it easy to access.
- *K Transfer:* Getting valuable knowledge packages in useful formats to individuals and groups that need it.

Rooted in the quality movement of the '50s, KM helps the human role in the workplace. It draws from the evolution of information resource management and the growing awareness that people are a company's most valuable asset. KM as a management tool really began in the early '80s when technology made it possible to store information almost without limit, and is now becoming a vital force for improving operational efficiency and competitive position. As evidence, in 1997 Ernst & Young surveyed a number of CEOs and found that more than three of every four believe:

- KM is vital to them because their businesses are knowledge intensive.
- KM can be important in gaining competitive advantage.
- KM will be vital for capturing information about customers' needs and preferences.

Given the growing importance of managing knowledge, it's no surprise that more and more Fortune 100 companies are establishing a new role: chief knowledge officer. This position sponsors and structures formal KM processes and projects. The CKO (or equivalent title and responsibility) is the chief KM champion: this person teaches and preaches the whys and hows of the emerging practice.[14]

Yet KM is not really about technology. Yes, all the apparatus of modern information technology systems can be brought to bear on the implementation side. But technology is the servant, not the master. The obstacles against creating a useful KM process are not technological. Rather, they're bound up in the company's mission and culture.

Most companies and most people regard knowledge as power. You share the power; you diminish your own power. So keep your knowledge close to your vest, and you'll keep your job. If there's little incentive to share insights, contacts, skills, and wisdom, all the systems that money can buy won't help you create a lasting KM environment. To create such an environment, you must first recraft your company's culture to one that expects and awards the free exchange of knowledge. Form follows function: start with the culture, then implement it with systems to serve your needs. The hardest part usually is the cultural environment; it must be made ready before your company can create the real teamwork needed to make KM work. Your goal is simple: to create a triumphant company— one that is agile in collecting, storing, distributing, and using valuable knowledge on demand.

Getting Started

To get started with knowledge management, here's a four-step checklist:

1. Identify a specific area of your business that you believe most needs improvement—or that could be made more effective and provide a differential advantage over your competitors. It might be field and product support, competitive intelligence, or sales and marketing, or some other process. Then pull together a team to examine and critique the present process: inputs, process work, and outputs. Have on this team a senior person who has access to top decision-makers so that the project won't stall for reasons of visibility. Look beyond incremental process improvements that can or should be made in any case. Get your team to think, "OK, but what if . . . ?"

2. Now comes the critical part. Take these "what ifs" above and transform them into a conceptual model of the specific benefits your current process could deliver if only . . . Now you're crafting a business strategy—one that can deliver differential advantage. Look at that strategy: Is it practical? Will it provide unintended consequences, good or bad? Is it attractive enough to warrant the effort? Look at measuring your current "return on knowledge," and set a target for what it should be in the future.

3. Now comes your process transformation—or re-engineering task. Do this carefully, taking into account all the factors that will change, and how. What kind of knowledge is needed, by which people and functions? Do you already have some or all of it? How will you capture, transform, and communicate important knowledge? Will this new process require new systems equipment, Internet or groupware communication tools? How can your IT systems provide for your needs? Complete this phase with a business plan that includes costs, benefits, process changes, and measures of success.

4. Now comes implementation. Appoint a person or task force to manage the project. Seek outside expertise unless you really have it in house. Your task force should formally train all persons who will be affected by this new business process. Give careful thought to cultural matters. If you have a boundary-free environment in which teamwork and collaboration flourish, bully for you. But if, like many companies, you have turf issues, intransigence, or other forms of personal-protection politics, you'll need to provide *every*

employee with a heavy dose of continuing training and education. Yes, it's expensive, but it's something you need even without a KM initiative.

Perhaps you need a more ambitious technology agenda—one that actually archives internal and external knowledge continuously. Then you'll need to capture *explicit* knowledge—that which is codified and archived somewhere—as well as the more difficult *tacit* knowledge—what people know from their insights and experience. This central KM issue requires a well-drawn attack plan.

You'll probably also want to provide for knowledge-sharing that is specific to new product creation and involve R&D, design, production, and marketing. Document management now is merging with project collaboration, work-flow design, real-time team scheduling, and search engines to provide a rich knowledge-sharing environment. Maybe you'll need improved capabilities for competitive intelligence-gathering, tools for business simulation, modeling, forecasting, and decision support. Maybe you'll need KM to manage customer information: demographic and lifestyle information, purchasing behavior, and the strategic use of e-commerce.

Start with a sharp focus. Let your needs drive your technology selections. Some technologies include search and retrieval tools, imaging, scanning and speech recognition systems, software agents, and data storage systems. Whatever your needs, your plan should be *evolutionary*—staged to achieve higher levels of KM in the out years. Select business information and document management technologies to tie in to and support your key business practices.

One of first companies to implement a KM system was the Memphis-based specialty chemical company Buckman Laboratories. Buckman began experimenting with "knowledge engineering" even before knowledge management became a buzzword. They've found over the years that matching up cross-functional teams with online data sources, discussion forums, and CRM databases can create markets, reduce time to market for new products, and increase sales to existing customers—while sharing product and other information. Buckman is quick to say that they've not mastered the potential of KM. It is part of their operating culture, and they proudly admit that if their KM system were to shut down, there would be wholesale revolution across the company. On the other hand, there's still more to learn. They've found that KM doesn't wield as long a lever as they'd like when it comes to speeding up the innovation process. But they're working on it.

Congratulations! You've now begun the hard work, and you'll be positioned to roll out and implement your KM implementation plan. You'll find the payoff well worth the investment.

4.6: IDEAS FOR ACTION

1. Make information technology systems a part of your intellectual capital with board-level oversight. If you haven't done so already, include your CIO as part of your operating committee. And IT should be part of the operating committee's agenda.
2. Develop a five-year strategic plan for your IT systems and infrastructure. Tie this plan closely to your new product evolution process and to your markets.
3. Your CIO should have a "customer council" to look for ways to share information that's really needed, such as quality and customer reports.
4. If you haven't already, deputize an individual with the skills to plan and lead your competitive intelligence mission. Charter this position and establish clear expectations and results.
5. Investigate Web-enabled supply chain management approaches for your business. How can you gain by making certain purchases over the Internet?
6. Work to empower your ERP application suite to include customer-relationship management.
7. Consider creating wider use of groupware for communication and coordination within your organization.
8. Examine, along with your suppliers, how e-business technology can shorten and stiffen your supply chain. Partner with them to develop "win-win" approaches.
9. Make sure your company is in step with Web-based e-business as part of your go-to-market strategy.
10. Have your engineering groups come together on a product data management system that can help streamline your product creation process.
11. Empower your production operations with a voice in developing and executing your IT strategy. Too often they are told, not asked; this results in missteps.

12. Decide now that you'll develop a plan for implementing a knowledge management system that suits your business. Involve your entire operating committee, including support functions, and your board in choosing your initial business improvement target.

Chapter 5

Leadership
Form Follows Culture

The waterwheel has been at the center of transforming societies for some two millennia. We've touched on its importance as a water-driven *engine*—delivering power from river waters to make staples ranging from flour to iron and glass. But the waterwheel has also long been employed in another way, to *produce* water for drinking and watering crops. It does so by taking in the water not from the *top*, as in the overshot wheel, but from the bottom. This configuration is known as a noria and dates back to ancient Egypt. Buckets are affixed around the wheel's circumference. The flowing water fills the buckets from *underneath*, and the water is carried to the top of the wheel, where the buckets then empty onto higher ground, thereby flooding it. I can't overstate the significance of this simple and ancient device. It has transformed entire societies by providing the conditions for modern farming practices.

It took teamwork and leadership to build a noria. It was more than a construction job. It required a vision of water flow, how to direct it, and what crops could be cultivated with the new water. The visionary had to harness the talents of many men to site, design, and build the noria. It had to be sturdy enough to withstand floods. Land had to be tilled to direct the water to the most fertile areas. Such a project demanded plans, people, and commitment—and someone to carry it through. The project leader had the leadership role not because of his title or office but because of his skills at gathering and directing a team of capable people. People who conceived and led such large civil projects were members of a new breed who led not because of wealth or title but because they could marshal the resources necessary to carry out and complete a complex project.

Nothing really changes without leadership. Improvements in the water-wheel (or noria) over the centuries literally remade regions throughout the world—regions that hadn't really advanced since the last ice age. And so it is with organizations. They require leadership and all the other supporting spokes to achieve the level of competitiveness and financial strength needed to be competitive.

The concept of leadership begins with a simple maxim that I believe speaks volumes. Renowned Chicago architect Louis Sullivan summed up a century ago his approach to creating buildings: "Form follows function." He meant that the size, spatial arrangements within, and overall style were a consequence of the structure's basic purpose. I've found this maxim especially useful in organizational leadership.

In this chapter I'll discuss that fuzzy but all-important notion of organizational "leadership" as regards product creation. It comes in many guises, many styles. However, what's important is not nearly so much the style but the connection between an organization's culture and the approach leadership takes. This approach is subtle; it has nothing to do with a leader's personality. What really counts is having and promoting a vision so people will want to follow it naturally. The quality of a company's leadership and its management can easily make or break an organization. An organization's *form* must follow the leadership *function*, which is to set a vision and implement a plan to achieve that vision. It's the right pairing of leadership with organizational management that creates great companies.

5.1: THE ADAPTIVE ORGANIZATION

A key objective of your company ought to be to create *real* teamwork and a culture of shared knowledge to serve the creation of new products. But you must first understand and address the prevailing cultural and incentive issues in your company before you can expect to establish true teamwork. Your goal is simple: triumphant companies are those that freely share valuable knowledge with those who need it. Teamwork starts with culture and is enabled by leadership. And where the prevailing culture works against agility and excellence, leaders must step in and reshape the culture. Indeed, the single biggest need of most companies today is leadership.

This simple idea underscores what is absolutely basic to this book. No new products, regardless of the money you throw at them, can ever be efficiently and cost-effectively brought to fruition without a culture that supports your company's goals. *Truly* supports. No lip service, no halfhearted boosterism, and no superficial programs. Everyone, from those in the highest leadership positions to the lowliest of employees, must be on the same corporate culture page if your company is to excel in creating new products.

Of course, technology and process are vital ingredients for high-performing organizations, but how the organization itself functions is equally, if not more, vital. I want to paint for you a vision of new organizational styles that are rapidly replacing old habits. But before I do so, you need to understand two things: First, not all manufacturing goes on within mega global organizations. There are a few giants, of course, headed by General Electric with annual revenues approaching $200 billion. However, manufacturing's rank and file are the some 400,000 *other* companies that make up some 14 percent of the entire labor force. In aggregate, the manufacturing industry accounts, directly or indirectly, for about 18 percent of the total U.S. gross domestic product. And the majority of manufacturers are small companies, 90 percent of which employ fewer than 100 workers. Most of these small companies are "mom and pop" or other privately owned suppliers of parts, components, or equipment to larger manufacturers. Small companies attract little notice *because* they are small and often located off the beaten path. And they are run very differently from the big ones. Organizational styles vary widely and especially vary with size. Up to now, big companies have usually been driven by policies and procedures and by vertical chains of command. At the other end of the scale, small companies have usually operated at the behest of the owner/manager, who made the rules and directed all the employees decisively. In both cases few employees were ever empowered to think and act creatively.

Second, the service sector is growing incredibly fast and is fusing with the goods-producing sector. In the United States, services have been growing faster than manufacturing and by 1990 had surpassed manufacturing both in jobs and in sales. Services are clearly becoming more important to our economy. Manufacturing, on the other hand, continues to employ fewer and fewer people, although it continues to produce more and more globally competitive goods.

Furthermore, the distinction between manufacturing and services is becoming ever more blurred. Traditional manufacturers see themselves as providing their customers with products wrapped in value-added services.

Beyond just making a product, manufacturers frequently assist in selling the product and can even upgrade, repair, and service the product over its useful life. Moreover, manufacturers increasingly are taking life-cycle ownership of their products in compliance with environmental principles and regulations. The customer buys a product that is "wrapped in service," just as service providers offer their customers packaged, often customized "products." The two aspects of production and service have become intertwined. If the manufacturer doesn't meet the customers' expectations on either count, the manufacturer forfeits customer loyalty. That's how jobs and fortunes are lost.

In sum, then, the two important facts about manufacturing are that it comes in various sizes (mostly small) and levels of sophistication and it's becoming more and more entwined with support services. Keep these two points in mind as we review how production enterprises were once organized and how they *should* be.

The Old Rules of Organization

For some 200 years companies of any substantial size have forged their workforces to comply with the following four principles and assumptions:

- *Scalar Principle:* Authority and responsibility flow in an unbroken chain from the chief executive to everyone else in the organization. This chain establishes a hierarchy of authority roles within the organization.
- *Unity of Authority Principle:* Every worker in the organization must report to, and take direction from, one and only one person.
- *Exception Principle:* Only the unique, far-reaching decisions are to be made by senior management. Decisions of a recurring nature can and should be made by employees further down the authority line who are more directly affected by such decisions.
- *Span of Control Principle:* There's a limit to the number of employees a manager can supervise effectively. Depending upon the particular circumstances, this "span of control" may vary from a few, particularly at the top of the authority line, to 50 or more at lower levels.

Such pioneer organizational teachers as Frederick Taylor, Max Weber, and their disciples promoted these principles. They saw the enterprise as consisting of a collection of individuals. If each individual had a clear understanding of his or her duties and responsibilities and performed accordingly, it followed (so the argument went) that the overall performance of the enterprise would be "optimized." Right? *Wrong!*

Modern thinking and experience have shown the above four principles to be largely ineffective. Vertically structured organizations as conceived by Henry Ford and implemented by countless enterprises impede the flow of knowledge within the organization. Obedience to organizational protocols exacts a high price by thwarting quickness and agility in doing everyday things—a fatal flaw when applied to modern information-driven companies. Information must flow swiftly both vertically and laterally within the company if that company is to compete on time-based principles.

A basic truth of life—whether in the technology or the humanistic domain—is *no system is optimized simply by perfecting each component individually, in isolation from the whole.* Optimal performance results only by accounting for all interconnections between system components. Evidence of this truth abounds. One example is the legendary inefficiency of bureaucratic business systems in which departments don't freely share information with each other. In another example, the educational community has been deficient by ignoring the cross connections between such subjects as mathematics, music, and history that make for a richer educational foundation. These and countless other examples convincingly prove that optimizing a system's individual components—rather than the whole—inevitably leads to overall suboptimal performance.

Anyone who has ever watched a well-played football game understands intuitively the principle of suboptimal performance. Without total teamwork and personal sacrifice to give teammates a better opportunity to block or score, football is less like an orchestra and more like an exercise in cacophony. At its best the game depends on a strategy, a leader among equals (quarterback), and adaptive strategies of the moment. Gone are the days when football was micromanaged by the coach from the sidelines. Replacing these approaches are more effective, *team-oriented* strategies. Industrial organizations are now starting to catch on, emulating the football metaphor. They're also starting to catch on to another basic truth. Managers are turning away earlier assumptions that denied employees' intelligence, allegiance, and desire to work together cooperatively. Yet much remains to be done.

A LESSON FROM STOVEPIPE

Effective enterprises have already begun to shed their former organizational "silos" in favor of less rigid styles. To demonstrate how inefficient vertically structured organizations can be, consider StovePipe Industries. Mitch, a production supervisor at StovePipe, is concerned about a recurring problem with an electrical power module that his line operators assemble. It seems that several module failures have occurred recently at the final test station and have all been traced back to a particular electrical connector. Mitch would like to find and approve another connector vendor, someone who can provide a more reliable product at the same price and, as long as he is at it, one that possibly will be easier to install in the assembly process as well. In an ideal world Mitch could work directly with Pam, the design engineer responsible for the module. But things just aren't done that way at StovePipe; everyone works through the organizational chain of command. It's a "by the book" company, and Pam is part of a different functional organization.

So Mitch chats instead with Ida, his boss and director of power supply manufacturing. She has some reservations with second-sourcing this component but agrees to talk it over with her boss, Xavier, VP of production operations. Xavier, however, is out of the country for two weeks, so Ida e-mails him, summarizing the issue and her discussion with Mitch. Unfortunately, Ida mistakenly characterizes the problem as being the electrical splitter, not the connector. The next Monday, Xavier reads the message in

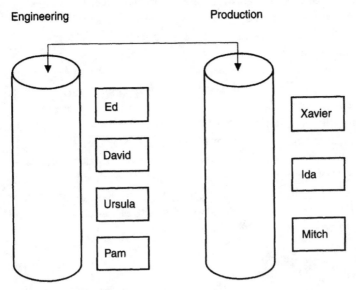

FIGURE 5.1   THE SILOS OF STOVEPIPE

Singapore and is upset because the supplier of the electrical splitter component, Acme Products, has been one of StovePipe's preferred suppliers for five straight years. StovePipe has never had a problem with Acme before.

The following week Xavier returns to the United States and two days later—at the executive staff meeting—discusses this "crisis" with his counterpart, Ed, the executive VP of product engineering. Ed deftly hands the issue off to David, director of power equipment engineering (and head of Pam's functional organization), who in turn calls a meeting with the Acme sales executive. The sales exec is surprised because he's not heard of this problem before. Furthermore, he can make no sense of the nature of the problem the way it's being explained to him. But present also at that meeting is Ursula, David's design manager. She sees this issue as potentially seriously political, a problem that could make her look bad. She soon decides to discuss it with her subordinate, Pam, the design engineer; Pam is responsible for specifying and sourcing both the connector and the splitter. Ursula urges Pam to get to the root of the problem, ASAP. Quick-minded Pam promptly asks, "Are you sure it's a splitter problem, not a connector problem?" Aha!

The issue is ultimately resolved when the two directors, Ida and David, decide to hammer out a solution themselves and have it approved, respectively, by Xavier and Ed. Three months later the fix is implemented. The engineering tolerance specification for the connector was simply tightened up a bit, and there were no further incidents.

You don't need this kind of "problem-solving." But it's all too common even in some of today's enlightened organizations. Think of the time and human effort wasted, not to mention the political capital misspent in trying to communicate up one stovepipe hierarchy, over to another, down that stovepipe and then outside the organization to the supplier(s). Wouldn't it be ideal if Mitch and Pam could simply talk the issue through and then come up with an action plan to which they both are committed and responsible?

The New Organizational Rules

Unlike StovePipe, today's effective organizations operate more by processes and less by functions. Business functions—human resources, finance and accounting, R&D, engineering, production, sales and marketing, legal, and others—are vital ingredients of the organization. They are repositories of specialized skills and knowledge—the spokes of our waterwheel. Together, these functions enable the enterprise to perform. But that's not to say the enterprise should be *organized* by function. The organization should mirror the *internal processes that deliver value to the customer*. Processes tend to be horizontal—they flow across functions from the time a customer places an order all the way through to the point that the product is in the hands of that customer. An organization *really* should operate with a flow of work-product that is supported along the way by functional specialists. In fact, if functions align with the actual business processes, the result is faster throughput of work-product, fewer errors and redundancies, and lower cost—all of which deliver value to the customer.

EMPLOYEES COME FIRST

So what will this new approach mean to the individual? The successful employee of the future will be able to:

- Feel and act empowered to take initiative and exercise appropriate powers regularly
- Take reasonable risks without fear of reprisal if things don't go well
- Carry an inventory of fresh skills and knowledge despite his or her age
- Be perceived by others—if only within a narrow domain—as a leader, a mentor, and a practitioner of excellence
- Exhibit integrity with commitments and people
- Look beyond his or her specific function, to improve the linkage with other functions
- Coordinate—both inside and outside the company—to exchange ideas with people in similar responsibilities.

People are important, yes, but they also need to *feel* important. Even today, as sophisticated as we've become, measuring people's importance is simple: the higher up in the organization you are, the more important you are. Despite all the recent clamor about management encouraging employees to take initiative, little *real* progress has been made. The sad fact is that more than half the workforce today believes management doesn't encourage or care about employees' ideas.

Looking ahead, however, with flatter "horizontal" organizations and shorter reporting chains, an employee's sense of importance will increase if she or he can influence others *across* the organization. Certainly the opportunities are abundant. However, people must take the initiative to broaden their influence across the organization. People must focus more on becoming scions of the company rather isolating themselves within their work circles. This point brings us to the subject of leadership, the focus of this chapter.

5.2: JUST WHAT *IS* LEADERSHIP?

Making needed things happen requires more than plans and activities. Accomplishing the right goals in a complex organization requires leadership. Indeed, leadership is perhaps *the most essential ingredient* for successful product creation. It is the ultimate differentiator among competitors.

"Leadership" is the business world's most common buzzword. We use it casually and in wide-ranging contexts. It's a special quality manifested only in some individuals. Leadership and leaders are celebrated in this society as much as stardom. Most people learn about this quality firsthand by interacting with other kids in grade school and on the playground, then by observing student officers and athletes in high school and college; and finally by acknowledging leaders in business, theology, the arts, politics, and so on. Leadership is a slippery kind of thing, one that's hard to measure. It's one of those "I can't define it, but I know it when I see it" things.

Understanding effective leadership and management styles is extremely useful for those involved with new product creation. Those who "get" the concept can turn their insight inward so that they themselves may become even better leaders and managers. Yet as important as leadership is to business today, only a few really useful ideas are worth discussing, and they're the ones I'll discuss here.

Just what is the essence of leadership? Most often it's seen in a visionary person—one who makes a difference as his or her life's role plays out, particularly parents, mentors, and volunteers; politicians and activists. Most leaders are regarded as powerful persons, such as General George Patton, Chrysler's Lee Iacocca, and GE's Jack Welch. Yet not all leaders grab the spotlight as visible icons with a large following. Many are quiet leaders, people like Mahatma Gandhi, Martin Luther King, Jr., Motorola's Bob Galvin, and countless others who seek to create environments in which others also can lead. The fact is leaders come in all kinds of packages. One's vision, ideas, and ability to engineer and sell a better future is the essence of leadership. Style in itself means little. Real leaders accomplish uncommon goals. They're not leaders because they try; they become so because they make good things happen through change.

Although leadership is to some extent "born," a person can acquire it through experience and mentorship. And it can be developed and strengthened with time. Leadership is a talent, and like all talents it can be elevated with time and effort. You may not be a good golfer, but you certainly can become a better one the more you practice the game.

Here's another dimension of leadership. A general notion exists that everyone, at any level, can become a leader. This idea has been around since Follett wrote about it in the '20s and Maslow in the '60s. Think of it as "distributed leadership," as consisting of degrees of leadership. Most people display some degree of leadership in their daily lives: in their communities, in families and among friends, within social circles, on campuses, in the arts, at work and play. Grassroots leadership also is powerfully at work with the emergence of workplace empowerment and horizontal organizations. And it's thriving in the business of product creation. For example, no longer do large government and corporate labs have a corner on product innovations. Creation and execution are more likely today to be done by small, energized teams that work collaboratively with a network of colleagues. And they do it faster, more creatively, and at less cost than their bigger cousins do. As *Wall Street Journal's* Tom Petzinger, Jr., points out, small teams of creative people often overtake capital as the critical factor in innovation. There's a message here for product development processes. Leadership, especially within large companies and their R&D organizations, best enables new product development by promoting a culture of many small and interconnected collaborations, and by providing teams with the tools and middleware to rank-and-file leaders so they can communicate with each other.

Lessons from the Legend: Attila the Hun

Leadership does not equate with goodness. History gives us as many despot leaders as it does righteous ones. I've been especially intrigued with leadership style of one of history's most heinous knaves—Attila the Hun. By any measure, Attila was a monster. In the mid-fifth century during his 20-year reign of terror, he and his tribes pillaged and raped much of what is now central and western Europe. He and his brother ruled the many tribes of nomadic Huns. He then murdered his brother so he could run the whole show.

Despite his ignominious style of conquest, Attila was a brilliant leader who earned the respect and loyalty of his subjects. Biographer Wess Roberts has developed a profile of his leadership style.[1] However despicable, Attila was instinctively a wise man. Some of his principles are summarized in Table 5.1; the military hierarchy is Hun (a member of any of several nomadic tribes of the era that roamed from central to western Europe), chieftain (any of the Huns' cadre of leadership), and king (leader of all Huns; that is, Attila).

How does Attila's creed play out today? Awfully darn well! Business leadership will depend strongly on motivating and empowering people at all levels to make decisions—decisions that affect the work of their teammates and other associates. Communications is more complex than in the past. Rapid coordination across various levels is vital. Remember the notion of the "high communicator" popularized in the '60s and '70s? This idea was that every organization needed a few people—high communicators—who were information junkies. These individuals tended to read everything, file everything, know everybody, and freely give information to anyone who asked. Anyone who needed to know something just dialed up Joe, and Joe (and only Joe) would be able and willing to help out. People like Joe were valuable assets—and still are!

This idea is now given new life. The notion of an isolated communicator has been extended to a *network* of such people—people collectively who

TABLE 5.1   ATTILA THE HUN'S PHILOSOPHY OF LEADERSHIP

Advice and Counsel
A king with chieftains who always agree with him reaps the counsel of mediocrity.

Decision-making
The ability to make difficult decisions separates chieftains from Huns.

Delegation
A wise chieftain always gives tough assignments to Huns who can rise to the occasion.

Developing Chieftains
Strong chieftains always have strong weaknesses. A king's duty is to make a chieftain's strengths prevail.

Goals
Chieftains should always aim high, going after things that will make a difference rather than seeking the safe path of mediocrity.

Leaders and Leadership
Strong chieftains stimulate and inspire the performance of their Huns.

Personal Achievement
There is more nobility in being a good Hun than in being a poor chieftain.

Problems and Solutions
Huns should be taught to focus on opportunities rather than problems.

operate at *all levels* of the organization. It plays off the theme of the 1993 movie *Six Degrees of Separation,* whose premise was that everyone in the world is connected to one another by a chain of no more than about six people. Just find the *right* six people and you can connect with anyone, anywhere. Within the context of the business organization, with just one or two of the right "Joes'" at every organizational level, *everyone* can have quick access to needed information. It turns a large company into a smaller, more information-efficient one. It allows anyone to cut across traditional organizational boundaries to speed dramatically the flow of information within a company. It's a step—a small step—in the direction of creating a knowledge management environment.

Leadership, then, comes not only from individuals but from *teams* as well. I call it *collective* leadership. To me, basketball's Phil Jackson, who led the Chicago Bulls to six world championships, best exemplifies this concept. He taught his players that everyone simply had to work for the benefit of the collective team. And it worked. According to Jackson, "What appealed to me about the system was that it empowered everybody on the team by making them more involved in the offense, and demanded that they subjugated their individual needs to those of the group. This is the struggle every leader faces: how to get high achievers on a team to give themselves over wholeheartedly to the group effort. In other words, how to teach them 'selflessness.'"[2] In this situation, who is the leader, Jackson or the team?

Distinguishing Leadership from Management

The term "leadership" is sometimes regarded as synonymous with "management." But, in fact, they're very different. Some leaders are wretched managers; they lack the day-to-day attention to detail that is the stock in trade of good managers. But they may excel as visionaries and as change agents. Some good managers, on the other hand, aren't necessarily adept at the things that mark effective leaders—things like vision setting, capitalizing upon a crisis, challenging the existing order of things, or creating a new and better future for the company. Good managers excel at *process;* good leaders excel at creating new *prospects;* legendary leaders excel at both.

"Chainsaw" Al Dunlap, the controversial turnaround specialist, is a case in point. During his forays as an executive in various forest, packaging, and consumer products companies, including Scott Paper and Sunbeam, he did indeed breathe new life into struggling companies. His track record bespoke of his leadership skills, despite his extreme "take no prisoners" tactics. Although he was despised by many as being arrogant and heartless, he was a leader that made drastic changes rapidly. Dunlap was one of the best at radically improving business performance but, like many leaders, lacked the attention to the details of the business—which was his ultimate undoing. He was unseated as CEO of Sunbeam in 1998 because of allegations of financial book-cooking, of which he apparently was unaware—but certainly should have been. The lesson here is that good leaders aren't necessarily good managers and need competent, trusted managers to run day-to-day business processes.

Leadership talents are generally distinct from management effectiveness. Both are needed in the business of product creation. Leadership sets the vision, the product, and competitive environment and secures and mobilizes the needed assets. Managers implement and refine sound business processes. Leadership is all about vision and goal-setting. Management is about execution—doing the right things in the best way and trusting and frequently communicating with employees—and about tolerating mistakes and learning from them.

Among the many aspects of leadership is "coaching." Like Phil Jackson, a good coach is someone skilled at communicating with, motivating, and empowering people. The best coach I've ever seen in action is Jerre Stead, of the giant computer distributor Ingram Micro. He's a master coach; even his business card reads not CEO but "Head Coach." Here are some of the attributes of a truly good coach, such as Jerre:

- Constantly is "in touch" with everyone: by talking to groups, by pressing the flesh with associates near and far, by wide use of Internet messaging—and just by being positive, truthful, caring, and upbeat.
- Sets clear directions about strategy, individual responsibility, and individual performance measurements and rewards.
- Provides the training and education—as well as the tools—that enable all employees to perform at their best.

Incidentally, Jerre also is legendary for his attitude about keeping customers foremost in mind. He expects every employee to walk out of any business meeting if, within 15 minutes, the word "customer" doesn't come up.

Table 5.2 illustrates the differentiators that set managers apart from leaders.[3]

By the way, as important a quality as it is, leadership almost never is taken up in college programs. The sole exception is in military academies, where leadership training is a cornerstone of their programs. Isn't it interesting that the Army, Navy, Air Force, Coast Guard, and similar academies

TABLE 5.2   LEADERS AND MANAGERS

The Leader ...	The Manager ...
Does the right things	Does things right
Has a long-term perspective	Focuses on the short-term
Assumes responsibility	Accepts accountability
Challenges the status quo	Accepts it
Asks what and why	Asks how and when
Focuses on people	Focuses on structure and systems
Develops and innovates	Maintains and administers
Thrives on change	Copes with complexity
Is driven by his or her inner being	Complies with the existing order
Inspires trust	Relies on control
Eyes the horizon	Eyes the bottom line

have much higher success in developing leaders than other institutions of higher learning? Yes, leadership *can* be learned! It's also interesting that the competition for managers with a military academy background has become intense; business sees a correlation between leadership training and career success.

OK, so leadership and management are generally independent talents. But good leaders and managers both share one quality: trusting their instincts. Seasoned executives—both leaders and managers—must regularly rely on instinct when making decisions, particularly in situations having many complex and conflicting aspects. These people have the ability to draw upon their experiences to help them make generally good decisions, even in risky situations. And just as important, these same leaders and managers instinctively know in what situations they should *not* listen to their inner voice. Life experiences, as rich as they may be, don't provide a basis to confront every difficult situation. These leaders and managers find it better to defer a decision or to seek the counsel of a trusted friend. Knowing when to run with the ball and when to punt is a key attribute of good leaders and managers.

5.3: LEADING NEW PRODUCT DEVELOPMENT: NAVIGATING WITHIN THE AMORPHOUS ORGANIZATION

What are the leadership, management, and organizational skills needed for developing valuable products as the new century unfolds? The truly successful product-oriented company will have to change in the following 10 areas:[4]

1. *Agility:* A leader's vision must be large enough to accommodate near-term changes in business opportunities and competitive threats. Leaders at all levels must respond rapidly to unforeseen opportunities and threats. Managers must have quick access to information to assess the conditions under which the company could fail, as well as the data to measure their ongoing success.

2. *Organizational Structures:* When there are fewer management layers and even more emphasis on teamwork and flexible work schedules, human capital displaces financial assets. Managers must know clearly and specifically how they are being measured, as should all employees—the notion of *distributed leadership.*

3. *Interdependencies:* Because of the constant search for new customers, suppliers, and alliances and the need to fine-tune existing relationships, each player must understand that to succeed, all others must also succeed—à la Phil Jackson and the Chicago Bulls and the Los Angeles Lakers.

4. *Process Focus:* Always remember, the *process* is sovereign. In new product development and everything that supports it, everyone needs to practice customer intimacy to succeed. Managers are to improve continually their business processes. They need to create a sense of urgency and focus always on the main mission: implementation.

5. *The Learning/Knowledge Organization:* Information networks will displace traditional print and voice sources for knowledge. The new leadership will depend ever more strongly on personal communication skills and on linking communications across every level of the organization. The techniques aren't all here yet, but groupware tools are developing. So companies can get a running start by putting the infrastructure in place and ensuring that everyone can use it.

6. *Cultural Values:* Leaders must have a clear set of values to which all are expected to adhere. Leaders should be results-oriented and embrace these ideals naturally. They must establish a common culture within the company that expects cooperation over competition, initiative over decrees, and that considers people as the organization's most valuable asset. This often requires a continuing dose of change management.

7. *Communications:* Leadership must continually speak honestly, candidly, and openly to the whole organization through various media and approaches and provide all employees with a real understanding of how the organization is performing, against what measures, and against major competitors.

8. *Empowerment.* The new organization will use the word "no" sparingly. It will empower everyone with the tools, the permission, and the responsibility to make good decisions, ensuring that all are equipped with the knowledge to understand fully the consequences for their decisions on the company and for colleagues.

9. *Up-Skilling:* A plan to double—maybe triple—investments in training and education is a benchmark of future organizational success. Every employee ought to receive four weeks or more of bona fide training each year. The levels of training investment (percent of payroll or of sales) your competitors and other admirable companies spend per year should fuel training decisions and drive the delivery systems needed to match the particular needs of each individual.

10. *Rewards Sharing:* A successful company will expect more of everyone. Employees will always be the most valuable assets. The generous rewards will be distributed to everyone on the teams, with particular emphasis on longevity and innovative inellectual property.

William Shakespeare once wrote, "When the sea is calm all ships alike show mastership in floating." The competitive sea ahead will be a good deal choppier than in the past; it's leadership and management that will determine who masters the waters and who goes under.

Why? Competition, globalization, and emerging markets are changing the new product landscape. But organizations' styles themselves are changing as they experiment with empowered teams, outsourcing partnerships and alliances, new ways of structuring the supply chain, e-business, and workforces that are more skilled—and more mobile—than in the past. These evolutionary forces create added complexity—complexity that requires more than good management; it calls for different organizational structures than those epitomized by the conglomerate organizations of the '60s and later.

One model that is emerging is the "inside-out" company. The term "inside-out" describes companies that are constantly reinventing themselves—turning themselves inside out again and again. The idea is that if outside change is faster than organizational improvement can keep up with, the only alternative is to reinvent the company periodically. Inside-out companies will replace organizational stability with constant and abrupt change. Information and knowledge networks will replace reliance on human hierarchies. Self-sufficiency will occur not by ownership of production tools but through partnership interdependencies. These companies create egalitarian rather than hierarchical cultures—to encourage teamwork, cooperation, and loyalty among all employees. These companies focus on product creation as their central business mission and breed cultures that emphasize nimbleness, technology, intellectual property, and customer intimacy as the key ingredients for success.

One company that epitomizes the inside-out model is Cisco Systems, a San Jose–based provider of networking tools and equipment for the Internet. Cisco, founded in 1984, excels at reaching outside its walls to source talent, services, products, and partnerships. CEO John Chambers harnessed all the talents of his 13,000 associates to provide tools and services that will, in his words, "change the way people live and work, play and learn."

And Cisco has been highly successful. It has quadrupled its output, with no added brick and mortar, by outsourcing 70 percent of its production to outside partners. It has reduced the time it takes to bring a new product to market from 18 months to just 6 months. And the marketplace has embraced this way of doing business: in 1998 Cisco had a market capitalization about 12 times its annual revenues (of some $8 billion). Certainly one of the keys to Cisco's success is that it leverages its business expertise as a leader in network applications by its own pervasive use of Internet and e-business. More than half of its sales are made on the Internet, which is also the site of its product and customer support functions, making Cisco more responsive, more agile, and more cost-effective.[5]

But the other key is *leadership*. Chambers is a man driven by the need for human contact. He spends more than half his working time with customers. The rest is divided between his network of partners and, of course, his employees. He constantly and personally communicates with his associates at all kinds of gatherings: quarterly meetings, birthday breakfasts, picnics and other socials. He makes himself real and available, and it pays off in loyalty and overall employee morale. He exemplifies leadership.

Culture change is one of the stumbling blocks to creating an inside-out company from a traditionally managed one. It's very hard work to modify—let alone turn inside out—a company's established values. Such a task requires a clear vision of the company's aspirations: a vision in which the customer occupies center stage. It requires leaders—a *team* of leaders— who focus relentlessly on the process of change. The leadership team must actively engage all employees and partners in the process of change by articulating the vision and its implementation. And it takes time. As the change takes place, senior management must share the rewards with all employees through bonuses and stock options.

It takes patience and time to stabilize this kind of change. In my studies of cultural inertia and cultural change, I've developed a rule of thumb. I've looked at the time it takes for companies to change—*systemically* change—their culture: their vision, values, principles, and customs. It turns out, not surprisingly, that change takes longer for larger companies. I've found that the time (in months) required to set in place a new organizational culture is approximately (number of employees/10)$^{0.5}$. For example, it takes a company of 2,000 employees about 14 months; of 4,000 employees about 20 months; and of 20,000 employees about 44 months. Of course, these are just relative guidelines, and results depend upon the intensity of the effort and other factors. This "rule" is analogous to "Moore's rule" (after Intel's Gordon Moore) for semiconductors: computer processing speed doubles about every 18 months because of the constant miniaturization of semiconductors.

It *is* harder to turn an ocean liner than a sailboat. That's precisely why small, agile companies—and partnerships among groups of smaller companies—are more adept at adjusting to changing business conditions. They're more amorphous and nimble. They're the future!

Former Intel CEO Andy Grove practices what he preaches to up-and-coming CEOs: "Work on strategy every day." When Novell's CEO, Eric Schmidt, took the reins in 1997, Grove advised him to do nothing for six weeks, then change *everything*. Schmidt took the advice and began his first days seeking the counsel of Novell's most respected managers. With their suggestions he developed his game plan and went on to engineer a highly successful turnaround.

Here's another leadership lesson from Andy. In 1985 Intel was forced to abandon its dynamic random access memory (DRAM) business because of oversupply capacity, largely in Asia. As a result, Grove reduced Intel's workforce by some 30 percent, closing eight plants in the process. Determined never again to be a victim of uncontrollable business conditions, he reinvented Intel around the idea that employees should "own their own employability." He made a covenant with his employees, a promise that Intel would make every effort to anticipate and prepare employees for sudden negative changes in business conditions. This covenant involved several initiatives; chief among them were continual communications from the CEO about business gains and threats and their implications, an increase in Intel's investment in training and education (now more than 6 percent of payroll and some 3,000 course offerings), and a thorough annual employee appraisal process. In the event that workforce reduction should become essential, those affected will be put into a special "pool." Each person in the pool will be given four to six months to search for another job within the company, seek additional training to qualify for a new position, or take a temporary assignment that doesn't count against their time in the pool. This honest and practical partnership approach to coping with changing business climates has been a winner for both employees and the company. Leadership? Of the highest order!

Many young, dynamic companies are throwing out the usual rules of company behavior. Synopsys, a California company that develops tools for testing microprocessor designs, embraces teamwork in all areas. Team members are intentionally given no clear path of progression, no "checklist" of things to accomplish before being promoted. What's the consequence of this vagary? How about improved performance? Those who don't strive to outperform others and take personal charge of their careers eventually find other pastures. The rest continue to sharpen their leadership skills and grow with the company. It's a self-selecting culture.

Alex Cutler, president and COO of Cleveland-based Eaton Corporation, has established a similar kind of culture. Admitting that such a change is demanding, Cutler says, "The admission ticket for this kind of responsibility is accountability—and not everyone wants accountability."[6] Some people think they want to be self-directed, only to discover they can't live up to their part of the bargain.

Leadership comes into play in all aspects of a living organization—even in the recruiting arena, as Joe Liemandt, Trilogy Software's youthful CEO, has shown. He puts his recent college and MBA recruits through a rigorous three-month "boot camp" to center them on Trilogy's particular culture. Yes, he has a "Trilogy University," but he provides most of the training and educational events himself. It's tough, physical, and mind-bending work that demands risk-taking and goal-achieving exercises. Trilogy spends nearly 10 percent of sales on this training program—not to mention $10,000 per head on recruiting. But the return is good; he gets the best, loses almost nobody during the training, and ends up with inspired, high-octane employees.[7]

Measuring Your Personal Leadership Quotient

In various places throughout this book, I talk about the importance of measurement. Whatever the process—product development, continuous quality improvement, production, administration—suitable metrics must be attached to measure performance improvement. Well-defined processes, such as assembly operations or sales activities, are more easily measured than, say, R&D or industrial design functions. And measuring leadership is even more elusive.

My attitude is laissez-faire: you're better off not taking leadership measurement too seriously. Sure, you can draw up a short list of financial, market, productivity, employee turnover, and other metrics. And you can set goals for these measures in the years ahead. This is useful and maybe even important. But if you pay too much attention to such a list, you may overlook the more significant point: What decisive steps are being taken to strengthen the organization's competitiveness, to reduce its vulnerability to unexpected turns in the marketplace, and to harness the loyalty and creativity of the workforce? If you do only the former, you're measuring management capacity, not leadership.

Nevertheless, I'll offer you a short, *personal* assessment. Here's a "test" that will help you to measure/evaluate your own leadership quotient— your LQ. It won't give you a precise number, but it will provide you with a general indication of how effective your leadership style is. To that extent it can be helpful.

For each of the following 10 questions, score yourself +1 for yes, 0 for neutral, and –1 for no. Try to be brutally objective or else you'll end up with

TABLE 5.3   DETERMINING YOUR LEADERSHIP QUOTIENT

1. Do you have a clear business vision for the future of your organization and a set of core goals that you share and discuss with your team?
2. Do all your team members clearly understand your vision and goals, and do they translate them into their personal agendas and what they expect from you?
3. Do you invest a third or more of your working time actually teaching and coaching your vision/goals to your customers and your team members?
4. Does your leadership "style" align closely with that of the overall existing organizational culture?
5. Do you consider yourself a better leader than manager?
6. Do your team members easily and frequently confide in you and feel comfortable in doing so?
7. Do you encourage and support risk-taking by your team members, and are you tolerant of risks that end up as mistakes?
8. Do you accept and handle ambiguity well?
9. Do you personally "take the heat" when serious problems arise rather than allow others to take it for you?
10. Do you subscribe to the dictum that the ends are never justified by unfair or immoral means?

empty flattery. If you score a five or more, rate yourself as a rather strong leader. If you score zero or less, you may want to take steps to strengthen your leadership effectiveness. If you're between these ranges, you're probably effective both as a leader and as a manager.

5.4: IDEAS FOR ACTION

1. Review your business vision for the future of your organization and set your supporting goals. Share them and talk about them with your entire team.
2. Provide the coaching necessary for your team members to translate your vision and goals into their personal agenda.
3. Does your leadership style align closely with the culture you'll need in the years ahead? If there's a gap, make it your mission to narrow it by forging a new culture that is better suited to achieving your goals.
4. Make it your responsibility that your team members clearly know what you *really* expect from them.
5. Aim to invest, say, a third of your working time actually teaching your vision and goals to your team members and your customers.
6. Do you consider yourself more a leader than a manager? Either way, make sure you have a balanced team offering both vision and execution.
7. Work to develop the trust your team members need so they can easily confide in you and feel comfortable in doing so.
8. Encourage and support individual risk-taking. Be tolerant of risks that end up as mistakes. Know that there are times when you should take the heat when big things go awry and times when lesser problems should lie squarely in the laps of your team members. Be wise enough to know the difference.
9. Spread the dictum that ends are never justified by unfair or corrupt means—and mean it!

Chapter 6

Long Live the Customer!

All the spokes of the waterwheel are essential, but none is more vital than the "customer" spoke. This spoke represents the distribution of goods and services that customers want. More than that, it also is the conduit that feeds information from customers to product developers.

There was a time when the customer didn't figure prominently in manufacturers' thinking. Until early in the 20th century, manufacturers had difficulty producing enough goods to satisfy a hungry nation. Just about everything was scarce, and in the absence of competition, prices could be set arbitrarily high. But all this changed after World War II and the emergence of a strong middle-class America. Customers became more choosy and demanding. By analogy, our New Product Creation Wheel is incredibly efficient at production. Customer satisfaction has become top priority as sellers compete for buyer attention. To paraphrase Walt Kelly's character Pogo, we've seen the customer and he is us!

Today companies create huge budgets to fund customer preference studies about products: about styling, features, convenience, image, brand recognition. Once again the customer is tightly in the product creation loop. Everyone now is searching for the voice of the customer. Manufacturers have found that enlisting customers in the pursuit of product creation is always productive. And we've learned an enormous amount about how to do this.

I recall as a small boy that my uncle's hardware store had a sign over the counter that read: "The Customer Is Always Right!" That sign puzzled me. It seemed, well, *backward*. In my child's mind I saw that the store had the goods; the store had the answers; customers came to the store to buy things they didn't have and to get answers to questions they did have. Seemed to me that the store was king, not the customer.

In later years, of course, I understood the truth of that sign. I learned that in the hardware business you must give the customer what he or she wants. I learned that if what the customer asks for won't really solve the problem, you are obligated to suggest a better alternative—even if that alternative means a diminished or lost sale. That way, you can be assured that the customer will come back again. The same wisdom applies to customers that are companies. As a supplier of products or services, you are obligated to provide the best possible advice to your customer. You do your best to act in his best interests. After all, you want your customer to stay your customer.

Meeting or exceeding customers' desires is a fundamental obligation of any business. After all, some 70 percent of all new products are driven by markets, not by new technology concepts. The process really is about customer pull, not technology push. Technology takes a supporting role, a role that enhances the product for the typical customer. But if you see signs of technology development for its own sake, kill or rethink the product concept!

The future will surely offer further acceleration of new, personalized products—products that are unimagined today. More choices and more competition for customers are increasing the tempo of modern business. Yet somehow many, many companies still hang on to the notion I held in my boyhood. I find it simply amazing that so much of our economy fails to recognize that the customer must always be treated as king. This chapter will highlight how to give your customers the royal treatment.

6.1: HOW TO GROW YOUR CUSTOMER BASE

Growing your business profitably comes down to mastering just two basic elements. On the cost side, you can cut costs, and you can streamline your supply and distribution channels. And on the revenue side, you can grow your profits by offering more attractive and valuable products and services. And you have three levers at your disposal for profitable growth:

1. Sell more goods/services to your current customers.
2. Increase your customer base.
3. Reduce defections (increase retention) of your customer base.

In fact, every strategy that a business can use for revenue growth—*every one*—ultimately comes down to pulling one or more of these three levers. So let's have a look at them.

Lever 1: Here the goal is to realize more revenues/profits from your existing customers through a variety of approaches. You can sell at higher price points, or you can hold the line on price and instead reduce your product costs. Being more efficient by streamlining your business processes will certainly reduce your costs, thereby increasing your margins. But another strategy is to sell more to your existing customers. Suppose you sell cars. You could try to sell/lease your customers a new car every two years rather than three. You could encourage them to upgrade their model and to buy a more comprehensive warranty policy. You might interest them in customizing accessories. You can offer other related products and services, such as accessories. Customers will pay for convenience and hassle avoidance, and you can exploit this opportunity by offering various personalized services.

Lever 2: Here the goal is to find and court new customers. In fact, you must anyway, just to stay even because of natural customer attrition. But to grow, you must do more than simply tread water. In other words, you need to fill new garages with your automobiles. You could explore new markets or export products or offer more product variety. You could woo new market segments by seeking and exploiting new-customer referrals and target marketing in innovative ways. You could put in place customer relationship management (CRM) tools to identify and track your customers' tastes and level of confidence with your products and services. As I mentioned in Chapter 4, enterprise resources planning vendors are finally getting the word that CRM is essential to business and that it ought to be integrated into their ERP products. Kodak recently did just that by entering the market of teenage girls. Kodak is seeking their advice, over the Internet, to design camera-case accessory products that will be marketed along with its disposable cameras.

Lever 3: This goal is to do even better at promoting customer loyalty. How? By focusing on the basics—superior products and services—and by earning a reputation that reinforces customer allegiance. The cost of attracting a new customer is far, far greater than the cost of keeping a current one. So it's overwhelmingly in your interest to do whatever it takes to keep your customers. Management guru Tom Peters estimates that some 70 percent of customer defections are triggered by their dissatisfaction with the "soft" issues in product or service delivery: lapses in courtesy, dependability, and just plain caring. Customer defections are a silent cancer that eats at your business and costs you market share because your customers almost never tell you the truth about their dissatisfaction. You won't even notice it; they'll just quietly slip away to your competition, finding another kind of automobile or working with another dealership. You won't get a second chance or an opportunity to correct your deficiencies. Moreover, the customer tells family, friends, and business associates why your products or services don't measure up. Their dissatisfaction leverages others. How likely are *those* people to become—or stay—your customers? Your loss is compounded because you lose not only your customer and his or her friends but also the next generation of potential customers. People have long memories.

All these levers—selling more to your existing customers, attracting new customers, and fostering better customer loyalty—have one thing in common: each lever depends upon consistently delivering superior products and services to your customers. Customers will buy your products and services, but they expect consistent value. Your opportunity is to bundle more value into your products—value as perceived by your customers. And how well you manage each of these levers depends upon how well you listen to and service your customers.

Pleasing Customers

To please your customers, start by regularly training your employees to understand "customer delight" and why and how to deliver it. "Delight" is not the ultimate goal—but it's an important milestone along the way. Set up the systems needed to capture your customers' wishes and interests— and their complaints. Complaints are *very* valuable to you. They're your opportunity to shine, to secure your customers' loyalty by the personal way you handle their dissatisfaction. Redouble your efforts to learn about your competitors' product and service offerings. Some companies use focus groups to collect valuable information about their customers' likes and dislikes. Developing and using such information requires that your human and your information systems work in concert. This combination of "high tech/high touch" for customers equips you with knowledge of their interests, their personal tastes, and other relevant information that you can exploit in your mission to delight your customer. Both tech and touch are important; one won't work without the other. Overreliance on high tech dismisses the importance of developing rapport with the customer; overreliance with high touch neglects your customer's personal relationship with your products and services. Employees may come and go, but customers are, you hope, forever!

Adding Value by Getting Closer with Customers

The emergence of customer information software (CIS) offers you another tool to help you draw closer to your customers. These systems, together with customer relationships management (CRM) software, are now being found in the enterprise resource planning (ERP) systems that we discussed in Chapter 4. These enterprise systems are used to run the back-end functions of manufacturing, finance, and human resources; CIS and CRM systems can do the same for the front end—customer relationships. Whereas ERP administers everything up through shipping products/services, CIS looks ahead by eliciting and capturing customer needs and interests. CIS systems help forecast and manage the fickle aspects of customer tastes, behaviors, trends, fads and fashions, and technology advances. They extend to sales force automation, telemarketing, customer support desks, and so on. They can help achieve shorter sales cycles, which brings obvious business benefits.

But just as with ERP, installing a CIS system may require that you either develop customized software that will conform to the way you do business or alter your business processes to be compatible with the software. Either course can be expensive and even risky. Whichever path you choose, these systems are becoming commonplace, adding value for building customer loyalty. It's well worth your while to get familiar with them.

Certainly one of the best ways to reach out and get close to your customers is by making effective use of the Web and the Internet. We think of the Internet as primarily a highly effective sales and information channel. And it certainly is. But it's also poised to help you and a whole new generation of smarter buyers to find real deals on commodity parts and supplies. What does this have to do with customer delight? Customers today are armed with plentiful information that was previously unavailable. There's a whole new generation of smarter buyers—which puts more pressure on customer loyalty. Customers now can easily access and slice and dice product features, costs, and delivery conditions. They won't hesitate to shift their business when it's in their economic interest to do so. This is the new reality. Competition from e-business will test your commitment and ability to keep your customers' loyalty. Your only defense is a commitment to deliver exceptional customer service.

The Internet also offers rich new help in sourcing. United Technologies, for example, began experimenting with the Internet by putting out a sourcing request on FreeMarkets Online—a Web marketplace for industrial goods. UTC's sourcing power realized a 40 percent discount over their planned cost. Similarly, GE is getting up to 20 percent price discounts by combining purchasing needs across business units and by leveraging its e-business power over the Internet.

Be aware, however, that these benefits don't always come free. Don't sacrifice the real advantages to maintaining working partnerships with your established suppliers. Look carefully before going to the Web-based auction block because of its possible downsides. Think of Web-based sourcing as just another business tool that you must use wisely.

Increasingly we'll see the Web as a tool for understanding how you can ratchet up the level of your customers' delight. You now have an opportunity to seize the power of the Web to get to know your customers—actual and potential. You easily can elicit their feedback, and you won't be alone; over 70 percent of U.S. manufacturers are *already* interacting with their customers over the Web.

And companies will use their Web sites for more than just advertising products and services. Your home portal can also efficiently handle product returns, survey customer needs and preferences, and offer personal advice and help with product selection. Take, for example, Cleveland-based Bailey Controls Company, a producer of instruments and control and information systems for power plants and industrial processes. It uses the Web to train its customers in using its control automation systems. Also, many truck and rail transportation companies use the Web to help them know the exact status and location of any customer's shipment and to manage inventory levels. And PeopleSoft is using its Web site to "vote" on new features or changes in its ERP products.

However, beware of taking too seriously the casual ideas your customers may toss off on your home page, in one-to-one encounters, or in focused group discussions. Such comments are often just soft ideas with no real intention behind them. All customers carry around their expectations for the products and services they use. But unless you understand their *primal* expectations, you may find that either you're offering what they don't need or they need what you aren't offering.

Already the Internet is a potent force for providing superior service and value. The influence e-commerce is having upon both new product and service providers and their customers is stunning. Author Walid Mougayar compares the current retail system to one under e-commerce. This example illustrates the costs embedded in the supply chain—costs that must either deliver added value to the customer or go away:[1]

CONVENTIONAL

Retailer—$1.00   *Total markup = 133%*
Distributor—$0.50
Wholesaler—$0.46
Manufacturer—$0.43

ELIMINATING THE WHOLESALER

Retailer—$1.00   *Total markup = 122%*
Distributor—$0.50
Manufacturer—$0.45

ELIMINATING THE DISTRIBUTOR

Retailer—$1.00   *Total markup = 100%*
Manufacturer—$0.50

Disintermediation—eliminating some of the middlemen—can bring substantial benefits to customers and manufacturers alike. It can create and share real value with your customers, taking a third of the cost—not to mention the time—out of the chain. But this shared value isn't free. It requires that you develop more effective channels to communicate directly with your customers. Your wholesalers and retailers are no longer in the middle to pass on their interpretations of what your end customer really, *really* wants.

Zeroing out your low-value-added middlemen also affords better information fidelity when communicating with your customers. Fewer middlemen means getting closer to your customers and their needs—which should top your "highest priority" list. The driving force behind Motorola's July 1998 announcement of sweeping organizational changes was primarily to get closer to customers. Its "warring tribes" culture had been effective in earlier times for building engineering excellence via internal competition. But over time the divisive atmosphere became responsible for higher manufacturing costs and slower product development cycles. Motorola saw that its future must focus on strengthening internal cooperation and harnessing Internet commerce to connect directly with customers. It simply needed to turn away from being product-driven and to become customer-driven.

On the other hand, value-added wholesalers and distributors certainly shoulder their weight by carrying inventories and by delivering individual services that manufacturers find difficult to do themselves. But those that can't—or won't—add value will soon find themselves obsolete. They are simply too expensive.

6.2: Value—The Aim of Every Customer

I mentioned in Chapter 5 the saga of Al Dunlap and his fall from grace in 1998 as chairman and CEO of Sunbeam. Dunlap was a turnaround master. He'd successfully breathed new life into Scott Paper and other companies. Widely vilified for his ruthless downsizing, hollowing-out, and consolidation approaches, he literally wrote the book[2] on restructuring companies so they become more competitive. His method worked for a time but ultimately failed, in part because his turnaround formula didn't understand and deliver on his customers' and retailers' expectations. Indifference doesn't get you very far. You must win the hearts and minds of the managers who implement the plans and of the customers who must see the benefit to them. Building muscle in a company does not automatically build customer loyalty. Real leadership means being able to listen as well as command.[3]

Just in case there is anyone out there who needs convincing that investing in customers pays handsome dividends, here are a few more facts:

- It costs ten times as much to bring in a new customer as to keep an existing one.
- For every customer who complains, 25 are silent.
- Ninety percent of dissatisfied customers won't buy from you again.
- A loyal customer generates a 40 percent compound rate of profit over a five-year period.

The message is clear. Listen attentively to your customers and get them to talk honestly about the quality of your products and services. Unless you actively solicit their ideas, feedback, and criticisms, you'll simply be out of the information loop. The high cost of losing customers and replacing them is a cost you can't afford to bear. On the other hand, the total value that a loyal customer brings you is great indeed.

But look out. Pledging allegiance to customer service does have its disadvantages. First, it can make you complacent. You may pride yourself—rightfully—on the way you help a customer with a problem, but most customers don't often give voice to their concerns. You only hear of the *big* problems—not the little annoyances that lead customers to find friendlier suppliers. And by the time you do hear from annoyed customers, it may take heroic measures to keep them in the fold. Merely handling their voiced complaints won't get you very far.

But another, more subtle and serious danger lurks. When have you done enough? The fact is "customer service" can't be measured with absolute precision; reliable methods don't yet exist. Oh sure, you can use questionnaires; you can conduct interviews; you can read the reports from your field salespeople—all good and important things to do. But these familiar mechanisms simply don't get to the key question: Who, specifically and really, are your customers? Going back to the example of the automobile buyer, who actually *influences* and who actually *makes* the decision to buy a particular car from a particular dealer? What are their criteria? How confident are they of their buying decision? And how could you serve them better? You can administer questionnaires, but there's more to customer service than mere feedback. There are few dependable methods to translate this kind of customer feedback into effective business process improvements. With so much at stake, you need something better.

So good customer service doesn't always deliver the goods; if it did, you'd lose fewer customers. What, then? Enter the era of customer *satisfaction* and customer *delight.* Satisfaction and delight represent sincere efforts to bring additional value to customers by consistently delivering responsive, friendly service. Nothing wrong with that. Yet even this touchstone won't set you apart. After all, customer satisfaction is *expected,* and "delight" is more brag than substance. Neither one is the quality differentiator that will take you to the top. Customer expectations of good service always increase with time. What was "wow" yesterday is expected today. In the past, customer "satisfaction" and "delight" may have made faithful customers, but today they're the norm. The bar has been raised—it simply takes more to keep your customers loyal.

The unfortunate fact is that overall customer satisfaction in the mid-1990s started to decline. No industrial sector escaped this illness. It happened despite increased emphasis on total quality management. One would think that quality should somehow correlate with customer satisfaction—and it does, but only to a point. Often it merely *satisfices;* customers look for more. A 1998 study by Deloitte Touche showed that customers *want value more than quality* and that quality alone is simply not a significant differentiator for future success. Quality products today are *presumed.* Quality may not be the reason customers buy your products, but if quality is missing you're at a distinct disadvantage in the marketplace. Moreover, as products get more complex, consumers require more product friendliness and service—services that many companies fail to deliver.[4] So it's in your interest to consider a shift in strategy—from product quality to service excellence. Am I saying that product quality isn't important anymore? Absolutely not! I'm saying that if your product quality isn't at a high level, you're moribund. High quality is only your ticket to stay in the game. Your *real* opportunity lies in your choosing to provide superior—even *outstanding*—service excellence. It's how you win the game.

Easier said than done. In the early stages of new product planning, the customers themselves can be very useful to help you understand what they want. But once the product is developed, overreliance on customers' voices can be risky. Are you hearing from the whole choir of customer voices or just a few soloists? Will today's advisers also be tomorrow's customers—or will different product attitudes emerge to change things? How can you lead and stay ahead of your customers' expectations? Market research can be enormously helpful, but blind allegiance to it can be deadly. Heard the saga of the Edsel automobile back in the '50s? This automobile was designed as a compromise between two quite different concepts, with no market intelligence or customer profile inputs. As a result, it was the only auto in history that bombed even before it reached the dealers' showrooms.

So yes, solicit and listen to your customers' voices, but there are times when it takes visionary leadership to put the right bets on future products—even when a chorus of customers would lead you in a different direction. Underscore this message especially when you're dealing with breakthrough new products. If you had been a publisher ten years ago and asked your retail bookstore customers about what you could do better for them, you can bet they wouldn't have led you to creating Amazon.com. Ditto for Dell Computer. These ventures required the opportunities afforded by *disruptive* technologies, not the suggestions of complacent customers. Business success sometimes demands more. Knowledge of emerging technology and business trends, branding opportunities, promotion and other marketing strategies, and internal visionaries ultimately are critical keys to success.

6.3: The Goal: More Than Customer Loyalty, *Intimacy!*

Your goal is staunch loyalty from your customers. Loyalty increases sales, it grows your base, and it strengthens retention. It's the most cost-effective approach to profitable growth. But just how do you achieve greater levels of loyalty? You don't get there by focusing just on better customer service or quality or customer delight. These terms bespeak politeness and civility, but they don't carry much weight today. The term "customer satisfaction" is analogous to "higher profits" or "shareholder value." They sound nice but don't attach measurably to any particular business strategy.

Enter now the concept of customer *intimacy.* No, it's not just a punchier term for customer satisfaction or delight. It's a different and more powerful idea. Its goal is to deliver truly *valuable* results consistently to your customer. Unlike traditional customer satisfaction approaches, intimacy means building mutually dependent relationships that create measurable value. You don't just make your customer feel good about you; you take on specific responsibilities for your customer's success. When you do this—if you can do this—you build a powerful alliance. You're truly "family," and long-term loyalty is the result. If you're an industrial company, intimacy means capturing and using your customers' knowledge to personalize the way you deliver value in your products and services. It means measuring and tracking your performance with each individual customer. When Johnson Controls, the world's largest JIT provider of automotive seating systems, was asked to develop new seating systems for the Dodge Neon auto, it took total responsibility for *everything:* design, engineering, sourcing, and production. Both Chrysler and Johnson Controls looked at this long-term partnership as a customer-intimate relationship.

Industry consultant Fred Wiersema in 1998 polled more than 100 senior managers, looking for those U.S. companies that integrate outstanding service into their business philosophy and deliver superior results.[5] Based on his findings, here are the most customer-intimate companies:

Service Sector	Most Customer-Sensitive
Communications	MCI Communications
General merchandise	Nordstrom
Retail (home/hardware)	The Home Depot
Home delivery	Domino's Pizza
Transportation (service)	Delta Airlines
Chain restaurant	Starbucks Coffee Company
Automotive	Saturn Corporation
Retail catalog	Lands' End
Professional service	Temps & Company
Delivery (service)	Federal Express

It's not surprising that most of these companies are also leaders in their particular industries. Customer-intimate companies generally enjoy a profitability edge over their more conventional competitors—simply because they nurture their customers and minimize attrition. In this respect, there is a connection between business success and total quality management. Poor quality (poor attention to customers' needs) is a heavy, if invisible, tax a company puts on itself. Good quality is *expected*; those who practice it lessen their tax burden. And by the way, in the above survey the overwhelming consensus for the poorest customer-sensitive company was the U.S. Postal Service.

What's the road map for becoming a customer-intimate company? Wiersema has found three avenues. The first is problem-solving. Here you work with your customer as a consultant. You interact so that you *really* understand your customer's problem. Then you create a solution that meets the customer's needs, and you deliver that solution. Delivering on a commitment is the most fundamental stage of customer intimacy. It's more valuable than "service" or "satisfaction." This is *real* stuff! Your relationship now is that of close *friends*.

But you can go even further. Your next goal is to define and implement specific and total solutions that add *real* value. Your customer may not see the real problem. He or she may be looking for a rod and reel when what they really want is fish for dinner. When you take the opportunity to develop a total solution for your customer's real problem and to explain its real benefits—to him and to *his* customers—you take equal responsibility in its implementation. Education is an essential component of being customer-intimate.

For example, maybe your customer is plagued with high inventory costs. Some suppliers (but not *you*, of course) will simply roll over and say, "Too bad, but it's not my problem." But *you* decide to make it *your* problem because you want that customer—*forever*. You come up with a solution that makes sense with your customer's operations. Maybe it's the introduction of late-point product (LPPI) identification so that certain features can be added just prior to shipping, thereby reducing the need for inventorying products with every possible combination of features. Maybe you find a way for your customer's distributors to carry some of the inventory. Whatever you come up with, your responsibility is to implement a practical solution—and assist your customer in training the people who will implement it. She must know how and why this solution is important. She must be coached; you must lead. Now you're more than close friends; you're more like *cousins*.

The third stage of customer intimacy is partnering. Yeah, everyone talks about partnering; business partnerships abound. But here I'm talking about *real* partnering, in which you share the risks and rewards as collaborators in achieving your customer's goals. Using the example above, you do more than come up with a solution. You link your financial future together, perhaps by sharing the costs and sharing the gains. Now you've become *brothers!*

Customer intimacy is all about working in concert. You collaborate on creating new and better products and services. And one way to do this is to set up one or more sites where you and your customers—together—can interact on real or virtual product designs, features, and performance. Co-creation is an approach to product creation that is catching on, and conventional 3-D computational and graphics technologies can help it along. Whatever the approach, you must somehow synchronize your operations so both of you share the pain and the gain of improving operations and creating new and common futures.

Now, having extolled the benefits of customer intimacy, let's be practical. All companies—product or service—are not equally suited for customer-intimate relationships. For example, commodity-type businesses must concentrate heavily on price containment, must eliminate non-value-added features or services, and must deliver reliable and timely service. Customer loyalty is important, but in such industries loyalty is earned contract by contract and not necessarily by providing custom solutions.

Measuring Customer Intimacy

Customer intimacy can bring you significant leverage. And once you establish business intimacy with at least some of your customers, you'll eventually want to look over your shoulder and ask, "How well am I doing?" In other words, how can you measure your progress? Customer intimacy can bring you significant leverage, but you'll need some useful metrics. Here are a few to get you started:

- Customer retention rate (±1 percent change in retention has great leverage over your customer's bottom line!)
- Percent of your customer's total business that he or she gives you
- Rate of market share growth you're experiencing with your customer
- Your customer's performance against today's best-in-class benchmarks (quality, production cycle times, inventories, margins, market shares, and so on)

Try to steer your managers away from simply managing by maximizing sales and margins and minimizing customer complaints. Set your own compass for educating everyone in your company about the value and necessity of working toward customer-intimate relationships. Provide the training. Provide the process and the systems to make it happen. Measure your process. You'll be glad you did.

6.4: IDEAS FOR ACTION

1. Keep an eye on data-sifting software, such as Broadbase, Epiphany, Siebel Systems, and others. They may help you zero in on what your customers *really* want in your new product offerings.
2. Look into knowledge-based customer information software (CIS) that can help you capture and use customer attitudes toward your products and services. Equip your teams with the right tools and training to gather this information while in the office or on the road. Insist that teams use this tool and that they deliver useful ideas.
3. Give all your managers a one-day working seminar on how your company can begin practicing customer intimacy. Develop an initial strategy to pursue it.
4. Enlarge upon the examples in Section 6.3 about measuring customer intimacy and devise sensible measures that can help you improve your performance. Baseline your own current performance, but don't worry about benchmarking others'—there isn't much out there.

5. Pay close attention to your Web-based marketing strategy. Is it sending the right image? The right information about your company and the things you do particularly well? Are you eliciting feedback and responding quickly and completely?
6. Have your purchasing people look into the benefits of e-bidding for suppliers on the Internet.
7. Look into Internet possibilities for providing additional services to your customers: safety and other product-use issues, service and maintenance information, soliciting and sharing unusual uses of your products, and so on.

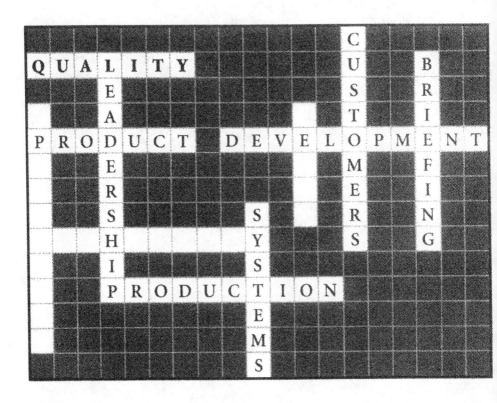

Chapter 7

Quality *Really* Counts!

In recent years we've come to understand that quality is something that must be built into a product or service, not merely added on. But even with the primitive waterwheels of long ago, quality was ensured because the master builders knew their creations required built-in quality if they were to be reliable. So they applied their knowledge of materials and construction to design durable stations that would withstand time and extreme natural forces. Purpose and plan were married to create a quality facility that would consistently serve both the stationmaster and the needs of villagers. The fact that so many waterwheels survive and operate today after centuries of service speaks to the quality those craftsmen built into their work. They were our earliest quality mentors.

In this chapter we'll look at today's tools of quality that drive not only product performance but also organizational improvement and customer loyalty. Understanding what waste and inefficient practices actually cost you is the starting point for cashing in on quality. From there I'll discuss setting appropriate quality objectives and goals and introduce some tried-and-true quality methods—including process mapping, benchmarking, Six Sigma, learning curves, and quality function deployment. I'll then outline the key issues of software quality and increasing quality of support functions.

7.1: YOUR QUALITY MISSION

In 1995 Jack Welch decreed that throughout all operations, GE was going to commit to reaching Six Sigma product quality by the year 2000. Six Sigma, developed by Motorola, measures the errors and defects produced through-out the entire process of making and delivering a product. It is a demanding standard—only 3.4 errors for every *million* opportunities to err. Most prod-uct makers commit errors in the hundreds—maybe even thousands—per million opportunities: error rates hundreds of times short of Six Sigma.

Welch was very aware of the costs GE would have to bear to accomplish the Six Sigma standard. For openers, *all* of GE's 275,000 people worldwide would be trained in new techniques for eliminating errors; a new culture would be created; a new, company-wide attitude would place the highest value on accuracy and error elimination. New process measurement sys-tems and measurement equipment would be needed; processes—both production and support—had to be tightened. Benchmarking and contin-uous improvement would become more pervasive than ever. And all this investment was made on faith that Six Sigma would ultimately reduce costs and improve customer loyalty. Going this route was a gutsy and coura-geous decision, but top managers had ample motivation: 40 percent of their bonus was tied directly to Six Sigma goals. And the payoff potential was huge, projected at 5.5 percent of *sales* by the year 2000.[1]

It has worked. The first year GE's costs associated with Six Sigma were $200 million, and the benefits realized were $150 million, or a 75 percent payback. In 1998 the payback was 270 percent! More than $600 million, was added to GE's bottom line in 1998 alone—all attributed to the Six Sigma effort. And this revenue doesn't even account for the intangible rewards, such as substantial increased consumer confidence and goodwill.

Other companies that have signed up for the rigorous discipline of Six Sigma quality also are finding great benefits. Among them are AlliedSignal (now Honeywell), Seagate Technology, and Bombardier.

Need more convincing? How about this? The publicly held winners of the Malcolm Baldrige National Quality Award—this nation's highest acco-lade for quality excellence—together have consistently outperformed the S&P 500 index by 250 percent. Why? Superior attention to quality! Year after year the Baldrige winners have shown that any U.S. business, large or small, service or manufacturing, in any sector of the economy can use the concepts embodied in the Baldrige Award quality criteria to improve the way it does business.

The message here is that quality pays, and especially so in new product development processes. But to realize these rewards you must establish and relentlessly pursue quantitative goals so that everyone knows what to shoot for. And for you to establish the right goals, you must have an understand-ing of quality principles. A whole lot of art and science exists in the quality field, but I'm going to cover only the key ideas here. As a backdrop, the following shows the quality visions of a few winners of the Baldrige Award.

A SAMPLE OF QUALITY VISIONS FROM MBNQA WINNERS

- "To achieve Six Sigma quality"—Granite Rock Company, 1992 winner
- "Growth through 100 percent customer satisfaction"—GTE, 1994 winner
- "Total Quality means doing the job right the first time, on time, all the time"—Trident, 1996 winner
- "To be the leader in quality and value of our products and services"—Eastman Chemical Company, 1993 winner
- "Continuous improvement; measure, measure, measure; total quality; Six Sigma objective; benchmark; eliminate waste and paper"—Dana Commercial Credit, 1996 winner
- "To achieve Total Quality performance in anticipating and meeting the requirements of our customers. Total Quality performance means understanding who the customer is, what their requirements are, and meeting those requirements *better than anyone else*, without error, on time, every time"—Corning, 1995 winner

---

A lot of executives out there will tell you their companies have "world-class" quality. Too often that boast is an empty one. As a professor friend of mine would often say, "All my students are above average." "World class" is a mantle the world *bestows on you* for consistent, extraordinary quality. You don't merely claim it. It is, instead, the quantitative results as measured by your customers and best-in-class industry quality standards. People who glibly talk about their world-class performance usually are not to be taken seriously. The *good* news is that any company that relentlessly pursues the principles discussed in this chapter and that delivers continually improved product and service quality to its customers will, as a consequence:

Enjoy higher margins.
Grow the top line faster.
Have more control over its destiny.

While others may prattle on about their world-class quality, you and your customers are better off sticking to disciplined, proven quality practices. The results will speak loudly.

7.2: GOOD QUALITY IS MONEY IN THE BANK

One of the cornerstones of the quality field is the notion of *cost of quality*. I've never really liked that term because it suggests that quality costs when, in fact, it *pays*. Yes, in the short term, human and work resources—costs— *are* required to reap the much larger rewards of good quality implementation. In the long run, quality always pays.

The American Society for Quality Control[2] identifies three cost categories associated with quality improvement: (1) *prevention* of poor quality; (2) *appraisal* of defects and errors through inspection, test, and audit activities; and (3) *failure* costs from purchased materials, manufacturing, delivery and poor product performance. Quality improvement involves reducing costs through improvements across all three categories. It begins with steps to make improvements in product design, purchasing, manufacturing, and operations support up to and including after-sales service. Early detection is a key element; adding further value to a defective product or service is the worst kind of waste because it represents ignorance.

Quality costs are real but rarely seen. Unlike budgets and P&L statements, quality costs aren't reported as such. The fat of poor quality is there, but it's marbled throughout the cost structure and can't easily be trimmed off with an accountant's knife. Some companies have developed cost-of-quality financial systems, but generally they've shed more doubt than light.

The fact is that the leading cause of declining profits is *waste in manufacturing processes and producing products that customers judge as poor quality*. Donald Fletcher, president of the George S. May International Company,[3] offers a practical "hit list" for you to attack as you evaluate your process quality. These are targets of opportunity for reducing the cost of quality:

Scrap—total cost of producing something you can't sell
Waste—material you buy that you can't use
Rework—doing it right the *second* time
Repair—making what's inferior acceptable
Re-inspection—costs of additional inspections
Shipping—and repackaging cost of returned goods
Warranty—for poor-quality products
Claims adjustments—for returned goods
Concessions—adjustments and compensation
Replacement—materials and inventory carrying costs
Additional overhead—such as purchasing
Goodwill—due to inferior quality

In Chapter 2, I told the story of Canon's triumph over Xerox in the office copier business. At the heart of this battle was the realization that just finding and correcting defects was no longer enough. Customers no longer were tolerating downtime and service delays with newly purchased equipment. Canon chose to break ranks with the standard order; they completely redefined their design process instead. And they committed to constantly improving that process. This quest led to lower overall production costs, reduced customer returns, and higher user satisfaction. Could the outcome be anything other than victory?

Poor quality is expensive. How expensive? And what's the payoff for purging poor quality? As a rule of thumb, a typical industrial company with conventional quality systems in place "spends" about 10 to 15 percent of top-line sales in producing poor quality. They don't see it, but it's really there! Although precise numbers and sources of costs are difficult to pinpoint, the upside benefits in developing good-quality practices are huge.

Here's just one example. It costs approximately 10 times as much to attract a new customer as to keep an existing one. Poor service is a silent business cancer. The customer simply goes quietly away—usually unnoticed by you—and then spreads the word to others. Losing one customer often means losing a family of existing and potential customers. On the other hand, you have a tenfold incentive to provide the best possible service to each and every customer. And in doing so, you recoup some of the 10 to 15 percent of sales that are doing absolutely nothing for you! (I find it fascinating that the venerable subject of economics doesn't even recognize quality as a cost element in business. Paul Samuelson's *Economics*, which has profoundly influenced the subject since it was first published in 1948 and which has gone through 15 subsequent editions and sold 4 million copies in 41 languages, doesn't even mention the word "quality."[4])

High-quality operations should be a hot priority not only for your operations and support functions but also throughout your entire supply chain, where excess costs lurk. Huge payoffs await those intent on improving their inventory strategy, logistics, purchasing methods, and supplier relationships. Taking out errors and inactive time up and down the chain puts money in your pocket *and* fosters greater customer loyalty. Debbie Fields, founder of Fields Cookies, put it succinctly: "*Good Enough, Isn't!*"

7.3: Think *Holistic* Quality

Quality means different things to different folks. Among the first few graphics that a speaker usually flashes when giving a talk about quality are summaries of the quality principles preached by the leading founders of the movement: Philip Crosby, Edwards Deming, and Joseph Juran. Table 7.1 provides a good synopsis of their main ideas.

Contemporary definitions of quality performance typically include satisfying the customer, being easy to do business with, delivering on time, delivering a product that works right, tolerating "zero defects," and just plain doing things efficiently and effectively. Certainly all these are hallmarks of "quality." Today's leaders and organizations within the quality movement have their own spins on what it is. But when you boil it all down, three distinctive and fundamental aspects of quality remain: *reducing defects, reducing cycle time*, and *fostering customer contentment.* Total quality, or *holistic quality*, must be seen in all three of these dimensions. Everything else—all the topics listed in Table 7.1—springs from these three basic aspects.

SOME FORMAL DEFINITIONS OF QUALITY

- "Conformance to requirements"—Philip Crosby
- "Fitness for use"—Joseph Juran
- "Performance, Features, Reliability Conformance, Durability, Serviceability, Aesthetics, Perceived Quality"—David Garvin
- "The totality of features and characteristics of a product or a service that bear on its ability to satisfy given needs"—American Society of Quality Control/American National Standards Institute

SOME CORPORATE DEFINITIONS OF QUALITY

- "Providing our external and internal customers with innovative products and services that fully satisfy their requirements"—Xerox Corporation
- "Satisfying our customer's needs with quality products and services that conform to mutually agreed upon requirements"—Nalco Chemical Company
- "To exceed our customers' expectations by continually improving our performance"—First National Bank of Chicago
- "Meeting the requirements of the customer, 100% of the time, on time every time"—Corning Inc.
- "Making products that meet the customer's needs and reasonable expectations"—Florida Power and Light
- "Quality is defined by customers"—Ford Motor Company

7.1   COMPARISONS AMONG THE QUALITY ICONS[5]

Topic	Crosby	Deming	Juran
Definition of quality	Conformance to requirements	A predictable level of uniformity and dependability at low cost and suited to the market	Fitness for use
Management responsibility	Responsible for quality	Responsible for 94% of quality problems	Less than 20% of quality problems are due to workers
Approach	Prevention, not inspection	Reduce variability by continuous improvement	Improve human elements
Performance standards	Zero defects	Multiple statistical-based scales; critical of "zero defects"	Avoid campaigns to do perfect work
Structure	14 steps to improvement	14 points for management	10 steps for improvement
SPC*	Rejects "acceptable quality level"	Approves SPC	Recommends SPC but warns about "tool-driven" approach
Improvement basis	Process	Continuous	Project
Teamwork	Teams, councils	Employee participation	Quality circles
Costs of quality	Free	No limit	There is an optimum

*SPC is statistical process control.

Reducing Defects

No customer wants to buy or lease a product or service that is defective. All of us have had these experiences: your car spends more time in the shop than in your garage; the "ready to assemble" furniture product is missing three necessary pieces of hardware; the incorrect billing statement takes three phone calls and a letter to correct. It's the little things that mean a lot to the customer. Good enough just *isn't!*

There are only two ways to deliver a product or service that is defect-free. The first (and best) way, of course, is not to make any errors in the first place. The alternative is for you to find 'em and fix 'em along the way—

before they get to your customer. It may seem that it's all the same: either way, the customer gets a product that is perfect. But it's *not* really the same. The extra effort for you to purge defects and errors from work in process costs time and money. And you might miss some defects. Yes, catching them as early in the process as possible is important because it is much less costly than finding them later on. But over the long run, errors inevitably translate as either higher costs or lower margins—neither of which is consistent with business competitiveness. It's a whole lot better not to make mistakes in the first place.

Reducing Cycle Time

However, reducing or eliminating defects is not the full story. *Time* is another key factor in delivering quality. Time shows up in many guises. Delivering promises on time is certainly one. Customers don't like surprises. If you say it will be there Tuesday afternoon, that's a *commitment*—a commitment that might be a cornerstone for your customer's plans and obligations to *his* customers. Time is too often squandered within business cycles. Indeed, it can be very enlightening to analyze a process or a project to determine the time *actually spent* in adding value and the time wasted when no value is added. Purging your inactive time makes good business sense. It brings in cash faster from your customers. It also reduces the opportunities for screw-ups. This concept is illustrated in Figure 7.1. The left figure shows how value is typically added over time. There are periods of additive work interspersed with dead times—indicated by the horizontal line. The idea, of course, is to reduce or eliminate those dead times. The figure on the right depicts exactly the same rates of additive or value-added work but without the dead times. The cycle time compression can be substantial indeed.

Time-based competitors are also better competitors. Taking the dead time out of product development and production processes *really* pays. But it may take a reengineering of entire processes—not just tinkering with it on the margin. That's how Motorola reduced the production time for its paging products from three weeks to less than two hours. Ditto Hewlett-Packard's test equipment products, from four weeks to five days.

Fostering Customer Contentment

Keeping your customers happy with your products and services *is* your business. Customers who are pleased keep buying from you and refer you to other potential customers. Moreover, good customers provide you with

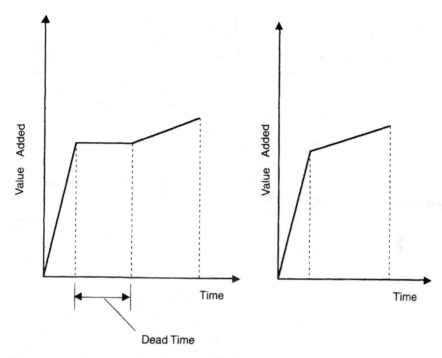

FIGURE 7.1   REDUCING CYCLE TIMES BY ELIMINATING DEAD TIMES

invaluable feedback that helps you deliver even better new and improved products or services. So it's important to understand that customer contentment (or satisfaction or delight or intimacy) is not merely a result of purging errors and cycle times from your internal operations. You can deliver error-free products or services, and you can improve your use of time and *still* not please your customers. Why? How about new products that fall short of your customers' needs? How about lack of service, friendliness, accountability, and courtesy? How about lack of going the extra mile by doing something special to please and surprise the customer in a jam? Some companies, such as Nordstrom, Singapore Airlines, and L.L. Bean, have grown strong as a direct result of doing the "little things" exceptionally well. Customer delight is the result of doing *everything* well—not just eliminating waste.

The Quality Map

Defects, time, and customer satisfaction are the three basic dimensions of quality. Think of quality as a stool with three legs. Take away any leg, and the stool is unstable and will fail to perform. In quality all three legs are required: elimination of errors, reduction of internal cycle time, and customer satisfaction.

One useful way to regard this three-pronged approach to quality is to use a device I call the Quality Map. This concept borrows from the familiar Myers-Briggs, or "spider diagram," model used in testing human personality assessments. The map helps to visualize these three dimensions. But unlike in the Myers-Briggs diagram, quality's "best" result occurs when each axis registers 100 percent, producing a perfect equilateral triangle. It's a good device for measuring an organization's overall quality performance against goals. The map includes quality's three fundamental dimensions—here labeled error (or defect) level, cycle-time efficiency, and level of customer delight. (Note: The axis representing the error or defect axis is represented as 100 percent *minus* the percentage defect level in order to suit the scale.) You can adjust the scales on the three axes as desired to present your information most clearly. For example, if your overall defect goal is 0.01 percent (100 parts per million, or ppm) and your actual performance is just half that good, you may want that axis to be logarithmic, running, say, from 50 to 500 ppm (0.005 to 0.05 percent). Other scales might be linear, as appropriate. The Quality Map is a useful visual tool for business reviews, strategic planning and setting quality goals.

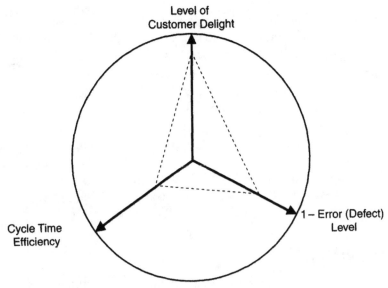

FIGURE 7.2   THE QUALITY MAP

7.4: Setting the Rights Goals and Objectives

I believe that the CEO should "own" quality. Quality is not a function in the sense that human resources, finance, sales, or engineering and production are functions; quality is *limitless*. Quality *is* your business. It touches every corner of every function within and outside the company. So ownership should be the responsibility of the chief executive. Sometimes a small committee of the most senior officers works—as in the case of Armstrong's Quality Leadership Team (a 1995 winner of the Baldrige Award). But even a committee at that level can be fraught with difficulties and needs active leadership.

Unfortunately often—*too* often—I find that the quality czars in large companies are midlevel managers. And when I talk with these folks, almost inevitably I find them filled with frustration. Great expectations are put on them. But despite all they know about quality, they have no real authority with the operating units. So they bury themselves in activity—staff meetings, newsletters, road shows, seminars, management summits, and such. This busy work is not a bad thing, but because they didn't have clout to do what really needs to be done, it's of little business consequence.

Midmanagement people are absolutely vital for the work of instilling a quality ethos across a company. They are the change agents. But they can effect change only with the active leadership and support of the CEO, or at least with a senior-level executive. Should the CEO be an expert in quality? Of course not, but he or she should:

- Set high yet achievable quality goals.
- Make quality performance a vital part of every executive meeting.
- Understand that, in the long run, quality is not a cost but an investment in future competitiveness and growth.
- Talk quality constantly, both internally and externally, and reinforce the company's commitment to continuous quality improvement.

With modest investments in time, most CEOs can pony up easily to the last three bullets. It's the first bullet that may require some homework. Let's have a closer look.

Setting and meeting goals—*quantitative* goals—is absolutely essential. Avoid setting fuzzy, feel-good goals, such as "the quality leader in our industry" or "world-class quality." Bragging doesn't improve or reduce the cost of quality. Rather, your quality leadership should pay attention to five basic principles:

1. Dissect the three dimensions of quality (errors, time, customer contentment) as they apply to your particular industry. Within each of these quality characteristics, what are the one or two most important quality measures for your company?
2. Establish an internal baseline performance for each of these quality measures, requiring a rigorous, quantitative examination. I'll cover baselining and benchmarking processes later in this chapter.
3. Apply the same methodology to consult with and benchmark those firms that you generally regard as "best in class" on one or more of the very same quality measures you're looking at. These companies can be competitors (yes, *competitors*), noncompetitors, or companies from very different industry sectors. There are preparations, protocols, reciprocal agreements, and other disciplinary elements involved in working with these companies—but your engineers and lawyers can fill in the details.
4. Narrow your information down to one concise quality policy statement and perhaps three quantitative goals as called for in the Quality Map.
5. Make sure you have the data collection systems and people to support the quality monitoring and reporting effort.

When you have all this information, you'll know what you're up against. Now think about establishing your overall quality goals. Bear in mind that in seeking best-in-class performance in new product creation—or in some other domain—you'll need to aim higher than today's top performers. Their benchmarks undoubtedly will be even better in the months and years to come. Quality is a moving target.

Quality Standards and Recognition

The ISO (International Standards Organization) and QS 9000 quality standards and the Malcolm Baldrige National Quality Award have had a very significant influence on improving productivity and competitiveness. ISO 9000 is an international standard for quality management and assurance, initiated in 1987. The QS standard extends ISO to suit the needs of the North American auto industry. The ISO/QS 9000 standards transcend total quality management in that they offer specific guidelines for quality management. They're preventative rather than remedial and are suitable for any size company. They address quality practices for companies that design, develop, produce, inspect, serve, and sell products. Their emphasis is on formal operating procedures and work instructions that will mini-mize errors and waste. They stress corrective actions and continuous improvement. These standards embrace the philosophy that a company must "say what they do, and do what they say." Certification requires an audit by an independent, accredited quality systems registrar. For now, ISO/QS 9000 carries no weight in prosecuting companies that don't meet minimum standards of quality. But that may change in the future as manu-facturers are pressuring the ISO to put teeth in their standards.

The Malcolm Baldrige NQA, by comparison, places greater emphasis on the vision of management, on the use of the company's human resources, and especially on customer satisfaction (which is not part of the ISO 9000 criteria). Many people consider the MB-NQA as the province of large com-panies. Not so. Among the winners in 1998 was Texas Nameplate, an iden-tification and information label producer having just 66 employees. Although similarities and overlaps exist between these two quality award systems, the ISO and QS 9000 certification is just the first step to achieving superior quality. Maybe, *maybe,* as the company earns true world-class quality, it later can compete successfully for the MB-NQA. Win or not, the benefits are worth the effort. CEOs and other business leaders overwhelm-ingly agree that it is highly valuable in stimulating quality improvements and competitiveness.

True excellence takes work. Even Motorola, the vaunted example of Six Sigma excellence, went through a difficult period of adjustment. Although Motorola had mastered defect and cycle time reduction, its customers were no longer tolerating its poor sales and service processes. Motorola was los-ing business. In 1998 new CEO Chris Galvin stepped in and ordered fun-damental change. Quality was to apply to *everything,* from R&D to sales and product service. That series of initiatives and training is credited with pulling the company out of a serious business slump.

Competitive Intelligence Assessment

Learning all you can about your competitors' products—and the earlier, the better—has become a cornerstone for developing quality products. It provides a path for product leadership. It helps you stay ahead of the com-petition by understanding the best features of your competitors' products so that you can gain advantage with yours.

This practice began years ago when engineers would routinely purchase competing products from the marketplace and tear them apart to look for new features, technologies, and signs of advances in production practices.

Over the years this practice of "reverse engineering" became more and more sophisticated, to the point that it was common to determine, through reverse engineering, exactly what the product cost, what new process technology was involved in creating it, and even who the various parts suppliers were. Every major auto maker, every PC manufacturer knows rather well what their competitors are doing—often even before the model is introduced into the market. Indeed, lawful espionage aimed at early knowledge of styling and industrial design is a high and valuable art.

Today reverse engineering has morphed into something even more sophisticated—competitive intelligence assessment (CIA). Although reverse engineering is still an important process, it's limited: it won't provide you with a solid knowledge of your competitors' products *before* they are manufactured. Imagine what you might be able to do if you knew ahead of market introduction just what the product actually would be? If you knew—even if it wasn't the certain knowledge that comes from reverse-engineering an extant product—you well might take a different approach with your own new product plans. This is the stuff of modern competitive intelligence assessment (and yeah, the initials fit).

How is CIA achieved? Some approaches involve illegal espionage and must certainly be avoided. Yet legal intelligence methods can provide valuable information for those who take this matter seriously. One perfectly legitimate method is to designate a few people to circulate in venues where competitors openly talk about or display new ideas. These people attend trade shows and listen to lectures and speeches. Are competitors beginning new relationships with universities or with other companies to explore new technologies? What are the trends and possible implications of their new patents? Have they hired senior people who represent different market or technology areas? Are merger and acquisition speculations in the press, and what might such events imply for their future products? Are new relationships with suppliers out of character with their present cadre of suppliers? And the list goes on and on.

CIA also provides you an early warning system for new competitors that may be positioning themselves to enter your markets. Often these are companies that share parts of your supply chain or companies that employ your same core technologies and processes. They may be offshore companies that serve local markets and have plans to "go global" by entering U.S. markets. The message here is to keep your eyes and ears open, ask lots of questions, and draw plausible inferences from sketchy information. Not everyone is cut out for this assignment, so choose your CIA disciples very carefully.

Here's another approach that's becoming commonplace. Every day, newspapers and other print media carry bits of news about your competitors. To harness this information, software can engage Internet search engines to ferret out periodically current information about companies that you choose to target. Mining the Web can bring intelligence riches. You'll find information chunks that need to be pieced together carefully if you are to develop useful conjectures. You might be surprised by the patterns that develop by doing a few simple things well. But it takes focus, and people have to be given the training and latitude to pursue and report intelligence effectively.

7.5: A Look at Some Powerful Quality Tools

Many tools and techniques are helpful in developing high-quality products and services. Of the many out there, here are five that I find among the most useful.

Process Mapping

Managers—especially senior managers and executives—understand process. Functions and tasks are the nuts and bolts of a business, but they need to be stitched together to be part of an operational process and contribute real value. Think, for example, of new product development. It consists of many functions: R&D, conceptual design, production processes, marketing information, and so on. But product development should be managed as an integrated *process.* Just as in manufacturing operations, you must manage the process, not the widgets. If you measure, control, and continuously improve the process, you *know* the widgets will come off the end of the line with high quality.

Process mapping is a powerful tool for identifying process problems. It may typically involve bringing the right people together and drawing on a large whiteboard all the significant activities and events that are part of the process. You link them with lines and arrows to indicate their precedent relationships. But it's usually not enough simply to draw diagrams of the *physical* processes. Most business processes also have information and maybe cash flow processes that overlay the physical processes. So these processes, too, need to be drawn and linked together. It takes time and insight to create a useful business map. However, when it's done, the team can use it to identify physical and informational disconnects, dead times, and other process problems. This enlightenment handily leads to redesigning the process to "tighten" it and correct the newly identified problems.

Process mapping is actually straightforward stuff. All it takes is the motivation to do it in detail and people who understand how various parts of the process *really* work—as distinguished from *should* work. The insight that springs from a good process map can be enormous. It's the first line of offense in your battle to trim fat, shorten cycle times, and improve customer satisfaction through great quality.

Benchmarking

If you want to be a quality leader, you must look outside your walls and see what the *best* are doing. That is the definition of benchmarking, and some companies—like Xerox and AT&T—have honed it to perfection. Much has been written about benchmarking; literally scores of books have appeared on the subject since about 1975.[6,7] Here's a brief introduction, a topic that, once introduced, quickly becomes self-evident.

The objective of benchmarking is to learn—to learn what the best practices are in new product development, manufacturing processes, supply chain management, technology applications, IT management, billing and collections, compensation and benefits, employee training, sales and marketing management—any aspect of your enterprise. You begin by deciding what function you want to benchmark, and why. What's a weak link in your organization? Does it impact your customers? How?

Once you've decided, organize a benchmarking team. Its initial charge is to measure—*quantitatively* measure—your own process's performance as of today. Use a number of measures, hard and soft. Seek metrics that are independent of the process but that reflect its capability and robustness. This first step is called "baselining." Think of it as your personal physical exam. It tells you, truthfully, how healthy you are right now.

The next step is to identify prospective benchmarking partners. If you manufacture plastic parts for auto engine compartments, you might look at auto suppliers that make similar kinds of parts. Yes, even if they are your competitors, you both stand to gain by benchmarking each other and sharing the results. But don't confine yourself to your own industry. How about companies in other market segments that excel at injection or blow molding—small companies as well as large ones, such as Mattel and Tupperware? Or if you want to implement a knowledge management process, look to IT consultants and some of the several benchmarking consortia that maintain benchmark databases. After you've scanned the horizon, your team does some more homework and narrows the field down to the few that they determine are the best benchmarking partners.

The partnering and benchmarking exercise itself should be thoroughly prepared and rigorously pursued. Nondisclosure documents must be prepared and signed; a detailed questionnaire should be prepared in advance so that upon its return from your benchmarking partners you can prepare the questions and identify the specific issues most important to you. Convey to your partners what specific measures you seek from them, which should be consistent with your own internal baseline data-gathering methods. Invite your partners' reactions to your data requirements. All this preparation is necessary so that the visit (typically a day or two) can proceed quickly and productively.

After you've completed the benchmarking visits, your team addresses the real issue: What is to be learned from studying the "best"? What changes should be considered? Why? What are the gaps between your baseline data and the benchmarks you developed earlier? These gaps can steer you to goal setting. When this research is done, you'll have embarked on a new path of better quality and productivity.

The above recipe for benchmarking is procedural. It requires careful preparation as to what to look for and measure, followed by a detailed on-site review of practices, reports, and recommendations to management. This approach is called *replication*. It says, "These folks are successful doing so and so, and if we copy their practices, we also can be successful." But be careful. If you benchmark a company that's beyond your level of practice, replication may not work for you. A child can't become an adolescent merely by acting like one; the child must grow into maturity. You'll be better off if you choose benchmarking partners that are within your grasp.

A second approach to your benchmarking is called *emulation*, as distinguished from replication. The difference is important. Emulation invites freshness and frees you to look closely and creatively at your own process—and what makes your particular process or application special— even unique. Don't blindly replicate someone else's benchmarking approach without fully appreciating your own requirements; it can result in measuring the wrong drivers of your particular process. Sometimes out-of-the-box thinking can really pay off.

As an example, consider the gravel trucking company GraniteXpress, which was looking for ways to reduce the time its drivers spent on paperwork before and following their deliveries. GraniteXpress found a solution well outside its particular business—by looking at how ATMs allow users to transfer funds (information) with the swipe of a card. By adapting some of the ATM's features to apply to its own particular business issue, Granite-Xpress cut truckers' turnaround time by more than half while also reducing administration errors. Had it fixed only on ways to streamline the paper process, this fresh-thinking firm would never have seen the much richer solution.

Six Sigma

In the early '80s Motorola sought—and found—a rational approach to quality standards for reducing defects. It was triggered in 1979 by a single comment from Art Sundry, then head of distribution for two-way radios, at a regular meeting of Motorola officers. Art had just returned from a visit to Japanese electronics companies. His comment: "There's a very important item that's not on the agenda: Our quality stinks!" At that time U.S. manufacturers bragged of their high-quality yields—in the range of 95 to 98 percent. Good, but not good enough. Leading Japanese manufacturers were aggressively improving the accuracy of their processes. Their quality yields were so high that they couldn't conveniently be stated in percent—but in parts per *million* (ppm). Thus, 99 percent is *ten thousand* parts in a million—10,000 ppm. At that time in Japan, quality leaders were typically producing at a few hundred, even a few score of ppm. Making an error was as rare as winning the lottery.

So Motorola engineers decided to develop an approach and a language for dealing with the very high yields that were becoming necessary for international competitiveness. That approach was Six Sigma. Soon thereafter, Allied Signal embraced Six Sigma, and it was off and running. I'll resist the urge to dip into the resulting methodology because it quickly gets into statistical jargon. The basic idea, however, is simple.

Recall the bell-shaped distribution curve you saw back in some statistics class. If you draw two vertical lines, one standard deviation ("sigma") to the right, and the other to the left of the distribution's center, the area enclosed is about 68 percent of all the area under the curve—and therefore 32 percent lies outside that enclosed area. Think of that 32 percent as waste, or errors. If you want to reduce that error rate, simply spread the vertical lines, say, to two standard deviations to the right, and two to the left of the center-line (a 4-sigma spread). The resulting waste falls from 32 percent to less

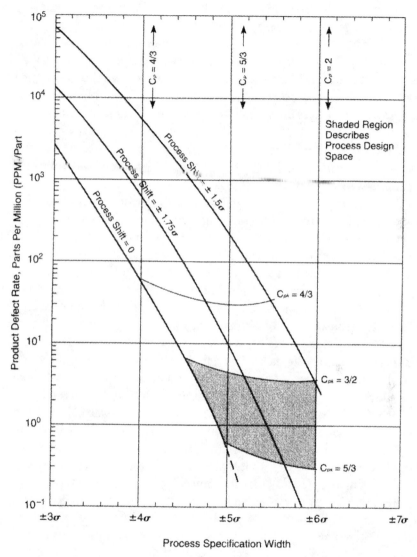

FIGURE 7.3   GRAPHIC OF SIX SIGMA[8]

than 5 percent. The wider you make the limits, the smaller the waste at the two tails of the distribution curve. If now you go out beyond two standard deviations to six, that is, a 12-sigma spread, what's left at the tails is virtually negligible—about 0.002 parts per million. Roughly speaking, that is the idea behind the Six Sigma approach to quality. The lesson is that if you can control your production processes so that they are repeatable within ±6 sigma, you are producing to a defect rate of 2 parts per *billion*.

I say "roughly speaking" because Motorola engineers introduced another factor. They realized that few processes were perfectly "centered." Most tended to drift off center a bit over time, so that the center of the bell curve was a little to the right or left of center. After studying many processes, the engineers found that the worst cases had processes that were off center by as much as 1.5 standard deviations. When you redraw the +6 sigma and the –6 sigma lines from this 1.5 sigma offset, it turns out that rather than producing at 0.002 ppm defect rates, it jumps way up to 3.4 ppm. But still very good. Think of it as fewer than two minutes in a *year* of time or a quarter inch in a *mile*. See Figure 7.3 on previous page.

One more important point. Controlling your product design tolerances and your production processes to deliver ±6-sigma quality is always a balance between adding cost and providing precision. Standard practice makes use of the idea of a "natural tolerance" or "design tolerance," assumed to be ±3 sigma (unless determined otherwise by actually calculating tolerance buildups). This leads to the notion of the "process capability index" c_p of 2, that is, ±6 sigma divided by the natural tolerance ±3 sigma. Statistical process control systems usually track the c_p index (striving at least for 2, or 6 sigma) rather than the sigma level directly. But the two measures are equivalent. [Processes that may drift off-center (and most do) are characterized by c_{pk}, which is $c_p(1-k)$ where k is the degree of process shift from center.]

And that is Six Sigma in a nutshell. Use it as a *management* tool, because it specifically provides a technical basis for measuring the cumulative defect rate of a particular workstation on the production line. It also gives you a methodology for telling you what the overall yield rate is of a process consisting of many people and many machines. Typically, industrial processes run at about ±3 sigma or a bit better. With effort you can advance to ±4, even ±5 sigma. And by "effort" I mean training and education of *all employees* who influence quality. Getting to Six Sigma—or beyond—takes a good deal of effort. But as I've been preaching throughout this chapter, that effort doesn't cost, it *pays!* Note also that Six Sigma addresses only defects—it doesn't *directly* touch the customer delight and cycle time dimensions discussed in the Quality Map. But Six Sigma is now generally recognized as the methodology of choice when going after defects.

Having just praised the pursuit of Six Sigma quality, let's get practical. First, Six Sigma provides a handy approach for improving quality in unit operations of all kinds. It's a tough standard and doesn't come overnight. Yet for highly complex systems that demand extraordinary reliability, Six

Sigma may in fact be a marginal standard. In some cases Six Sigma isn't even close to performance excellence.

Consider, for example, a system consisting of tens of thousands of components. Even if each component is within Six Sigma specification, the overall system may suffer poor reliability simply because of the likelihood that some component, somewhere, will fail to perform. Think of satellite communications systems and of the cost of repairing or replacing a satellite if just a single critical component fails. Such systems demand near perfect quality, perhaps Six Sigma and beyond. However, for most kinds of products, the extra cost to mount quality improvements beyond Six Sigma may not even register with your customer—or in your internal processes and operations. Here the defects are so rare as perhaps to be almost inconsequential.

Does that mean you declare victory on quality? Certainly not. It does mean, however, that you can shift attention from higher sigma levels to other quality factors that directly affect customer delight. Perhaps improving courtesy and accuracy at your help desk. Perhaps communicating to your customers about how they can reduce costs. These approaches may not be measurable on a sigma scale, but you can bet they have a huge effect on the way your customers perceive your "quality"!

Learning Curve

The learning curve is one of my favorite ways to measure—and forecast—quality. It's a specific and powerful tool with many practical applications. It was developed in the 1960s by the Boston Consulting Group. Basically, the learning curve looks at increasing quality through continued human experience, volume, or production.

It is useful in two general situations: process improvement (doing things better) and cost improvement (doing things more effectively). An example of the former is cycle time in production operations. If it takes "x" units of time to perform a particular operation now, the learning curve will show when at some point in the future, with more experience under your belt and using the same tools and procedures, you can expect to achieve a better cycle time standard.

The learning curve can also predict cost by answering the question, how much cost improvement can you expect at some point in the future by virtue of that added experience? That is, all other things being equal, the competitive marketplace will dictate that a product's cost should drop with time. You'll get better at doing what you do, and so will your competitors. Some cost reduction may come from economies of scale—better purchasing power as you produce more. But cost improvement must also come from your added experience in doing what you do. Just think of the dramatic drop in cellular phone prices in the first few years after their introduction. The experience curve provides a simple but sound methodology to forecast cost improvements.

As shown in Figure 7.4, the whole methodology rests on one simple truth: Any specific improvement in cycle time or in unit cost decreases linearly with *cumulative* volume or experience when represented in logarithmic coordinates. The key parameter here is beta (ß), the slope of the improvement line. The slope is characteristic of a particular process and will vary with particular situations. Its power is that it can be used to forecast, from current (cumulative) volumes, what production cycle times or incremental unit costs will be in the future. It's prognostic, and it's powerful stuff!

Learning/experience curves are very useful in such applications as:

- Cost improvements in new product launches
- Labor productivity improvement in assembly operations
- Analyzing economies of scale

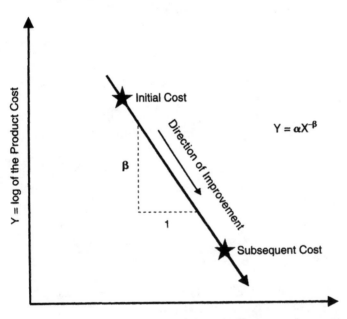

FIGURE 7.4   THE LEARNING/EXPERIENCE CURVE

- Benchmarking accumulated experience of a company or industry
- Cross-sectional comparisons of product lines or technologies
- Productivity enhancements due to improved materials, processes, or technologies
- Analyzing failure rates of new products under development

Quality Function Deployment

Quality function deployment (QFD) is a technique that originated in Mitsubishi's Kobe shipyards in the early 1970s. It has proven to be enormously useful in new product creation because of its structured methodology for evaluating the linkages between functionality and design features.[9] Here's how it works.

Suppose you want to design a product, new or derivative—let's say a handheld calculator. You begin by understanding the technical and user shortcomings of your current products or the enhancements you might include in a new model. You become thoroughly familiar with your competitors' products: design, features, performance, costs, and reliability. You then develop a concept based on the most important functionalities your customers want and expect. Suppose you conclude that the following are most important to your market: the unit doesn't slip when it's used on the table; the readout is crisp and easily read from a variety of angles; it has a relatively long battery life; it's easy to carry around.

You now turn to the technical design. Your engineers determine there are four attributes that are most important in addressing customer needs: total weight of the unit; rate of battery drain; pad adhesion; panel glare. As shown in Figure 7.5, now you can play the performance (customer) requirements off against the design (technical) attributes by means of a matrix to examine their interactions. Some intersections are null or meaningless, such as the influence of battery drain on the unit's adhesion to a table. Some may possibly be important, such as pad adhesion influence on the ease of readout. A stronger correlation is battery drain on the ease of readout. Even stronger correlates may occur, such as product weight on ease of carry. These various correlates can be quantified by assigning weighting factors, as indicated in the figure.

Look at each of the rows to evaluate which attributes demand the most design attention. For example, the first row is "scored" by calculating the product of the customer-importance factor and the correlation factor, then summing them across the row. In this case it's $(2 \times 3) + (2 \times 9)$, or 24.

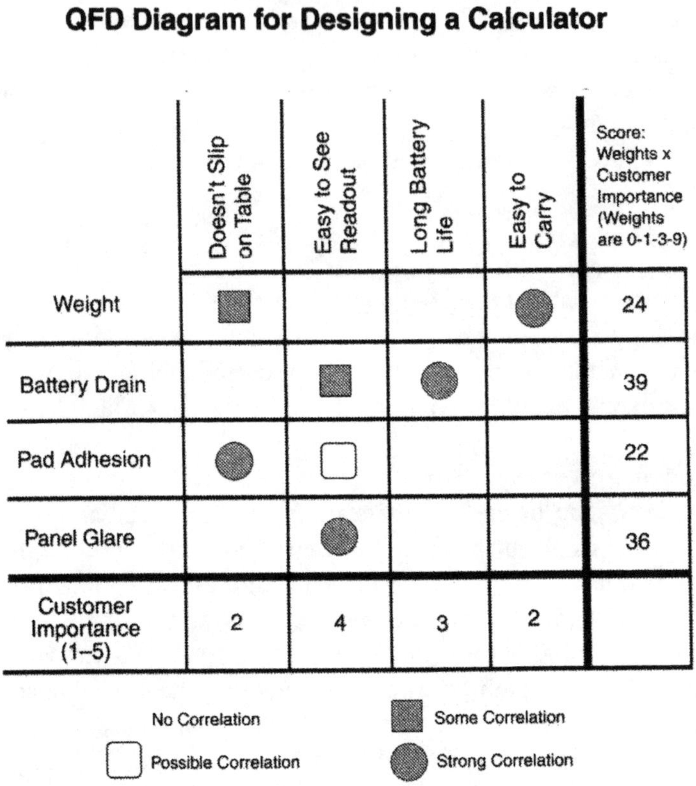

QFD Diagram for Designing a Calculator

	Doesn't Slip on Table	Easy to See Readout	Long Battery Life	Easy to Carry	Score: Weights x Customer Importance (Weights are 0-1-3-9)
Weight	▣			●	24
Battery Drain		▣	●		39
Pad Adhesion	●	☐			22
Panel Glare		●			36
Customer Importance (1–5)	2	4	3	2	

No Correlation		▣	Some Correlation
☐ Possible Correlation		●	Strong Correlation

FIGURE 7.5   QUALITY FUNCTION DEPLOYMENT FOR DESIGNING A CALCULATOR

Repeat this calculation for the remaining three rows, and you'll conclude that the second row, "Battery Drain," has the highest score and therefore requires the most design attention because it affects both ease of readout and battery life. Least important is pad adhesion. Such results give product designers explicit guidance about feature importance and about trade-offs among conflicting design attributes.

QFD is a potent tool that can be usefully applied to almost any new product (or service!) concept. And QFD has various enrichments that can reveal even more advantages—for example, by evaluating the interrelations of the design attributes themselves. But like any tool, it's only as useful as the insight that goes into it. Take care in choosing the customer/design attributes, and take care when developing the weighting scheme; it's always wise to experiment with this scheme to determine how sensitive the results are to the chosen weighting factors.

7.6: QUALITY IN SUPPORT OPERATIONS

Quality in an organization isn't exclusive to production-related processes. Every aspect of an enterprise should understand and practice the basics of quality as it affects its customers. The problem is, how to you put in practice the principles of TQM in, say, staff functions? What's the process look like? How do you measure it?

Perhaps you'll learn something from my experience with a human resources department in a large electronics company. HR's mission was to fill clerical positions within the division's various departments. They were getting more and more complaints from their internal customers, so they began working to identify and reduce their administrative error rates. Once the rate was successfully lowered, the team turned its attention to cycle-time performance. On average, the department needed about five weeks to complete a particular assignment. So, imbued with the spirit of continuous improvement, the team set a new goal: four weeks. But after successfully achieving that goal, they found no improvement in the complaint level from their internal customers; in fact, it appeared to be even higher. So they set a goal of three weeks—that ought to improve things! But as they approached that goal, they still heard a rising chorus of customer discontent. Customer interviews were clearly called for, and as they talked to their clients, they found the reasons for the growing conflict. Their customers didn't really care whether it took five weeks or four or even six. What they really wanted was the *right person for the job*. Time, within reason, was secondary. By doing their job ever faster, this service department was doing an ever poorer job of selecting the right people. The lesson is clear: first understand the customer's point of view *and then* set the right goals before you begin re-engineering your process. All quality-related activities must focus on customers—both internal and external.

Generally, this issue of quality in support operations has three sides. First is the *strategic* side. The strategic side deals with what kinds of services you deliver to your internal and to your external customers and how you deliver them. Perhaps you know their requirements already. *Perhaps.* But just in case, it can be very revealing to map your support processes, as outlined in Section 7.5. Mapping not only will reveal problems and opportunities of which you might not be aware but is also an excellent way to build teamwork and improve everyone's effectiveness. Too often staff associates get mired down in day-to-day demands and can't see the forest for the trees. They will welcome the insights uncovered by process mapping.

Second is the *technology* side. How good are your systems? Do you have good database management, networks, and security? Are your associates adequately and continually trained in the use of these systems so they can do their work efficiently and without technology anxiety? Do you have adequate systems support? Actively listen to your internal customers' concerns and suggestions. Productivity can really plummet when the technology infrastructure is unreliable.

Finally, quality in support operations needs constant attention on the *human* side. Therefore, create a workplace that embodies the very best in human behavior: honesty, integrity, truthfulness, openness, respect, care, and so on. With this kind of ethos, you invite a culture of friendliness and trust. This culture then extends naturally to your various customer constituencies. Now you have the basis for delivering *real* quality. Good internal and external communication lines enable you and your team to anticipate needs and to deliver commitments on time, every time. And it gives you feedback channels that help improve service continually. Isn't that what you expect from support operations?

7.7: IDEAS FOR ACTION

1. Establish a quality council chartered to develop plans, benchmarks, and metrics and to advise senior management on initiatives needed across all business functions.
2. Integrate quality principles and practices within your training and education programs.
3. Include a declaration of quality policy in your company's mission statement, and see that your performance measures up to that declaration.
4. Contact the Malcolm Baldrige National Quality Award office at the National Institute of Standards and Technology (NIST) in Gaithersburg, Maryland. They can provide you with a list of past winners, who in turn can arm you with information about their quality experience. It's a good way to start learning from the best.
5. Having a professional society lends legitimacy to any field of practice; contact the Society of Competitive Intelligence Professionals in Alexandria, Virginia, for further information.
6. Plan for and initiate a simple process for collecting and analyzing competitive intelligence about your most fierce competitors.

7. Partner with your suppliers to improve quality for everyone.
8. Mobilize your company to prepare for ISO or QS quality compliance. If you're past that challenge, consider performing an internal audit of your strengths as measured by the Baldrige (or equivalent state or regional award) criteria.
9. Arrange for your sales and marketing team and product creation teams to work together so that honest, accurate information from customers is reflected in new product concepts.
10. Make sure your R&D and design and development people are using modern tools that advance product quality—such as those discussed in Section 7.5.
11. Contact Motorola University for a training program that uses the "Black Belt" approach for learning the Six Sigma methodology.

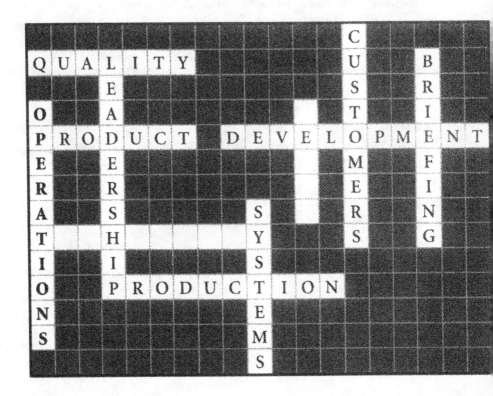

Chapter 8

Operations

If You Can't Measure It,
You Can't Manage It!

Waterwheel stationmasters were among the first operating engineers. For centuries they maintained their water-powered "factories"—the central community power station—so that it would reliably provide water and produce basic foodstuffs and materials. These operating engineers were responsible for keeping the village going. So they repaired and periodically upgraded their mills to ensure a flow of goods from the energy provided by the mill. They trained their laborers. They measured and managed the water flow, matching it to the work to be done. Just like today's industrial managers, those stationmasters were key to their communities' well-being.

In this chapter we'll look at the "operations" spoke of our New Product Creation Wheel. This spoke relates to industrial *processes,* and throughout this book I've underscored the importance of process design and process management. A key idea here is that unit activities within a process clearly are important, but without overall orchestration no process can reach its true potential. Recall the principle in systems engineering I described in Chapter 5 that says if you put all your efforts into improving unit activities *in isolation from the whole,* you fail to optimize the *overall* process. It applies to many aspects of life, including, of course, industrial processes. Up until the 1980s product developers and manufacturers paid very careful attention to the unit activities and processes so they would run efficiently. They performed their work and then threw it over the wall for someone else to pick up and run with. As a result, at the *overall* process level they tolerated long cycle times for project completion, delays in sharing information, errors and misunderstanding, excessive scrap in production, frustrated customers, and other symptoms of "suboptimal" performance. Manufacturers all tolerated them because, well, they just didn't really know any better.

Manufacturers are a good deal smarter today. They understand the importance of managing complexity in the overall process as well as in the details. They know that a key to competitiveness is continuous improved performance. Underpinning that continuous improvement is continuous measurement.

Today, of course, many more sophisticated options are available for managing industrial processes. The key is getting good information about them and using that information to improve process performance even further. Suppose companies could get accurate cost and operations information that truly reflected their business *processes* rather than simply counting the costs of production units. Wouldn't they be better equipped with actual production costs and pricing to make informed decisions? And wouldn't this information ripple through to the benefit of all business processes, systems, manufacturing strategies, sales and marketing, and ultimately end customers and new products? The answer is a resounding *yes*.

Today quality-driven operations, together with various financial measures of a firm's performance, lay down a sure path to intelligent decision-making. There's a wide array of tools and practices out there for accounting and financial analysis—far more than I can cover here. So allow me to hit a few highlights about what's really important: how you can *measure and evaluate* your company's production processes to drive better performance. Start by streamlining your internal processes—and begin with new product creation.

I'll give you a short overview of conventional income statements and balance sheets. Included are the notions of, and distinctions between, absorption and direct-cost accounting formats. Then I'll discuss activity-based costing (ABC) as a method to understand true product costs, showing you, along the way, how costing that's activity-based can be quite different from product costs determined by conventional accounting practices. It's important to have a working knowledge of ABC because it gives you the *origin* of certain costs—costs that can be reduced or even eliminated. With this knowledge you can take costs out of a product, allowing you to meet your "target costs" (see Chapter 2) and make you more competitive. I'll then present other measures of performance, including R&D, new product development, and production operations performance.

8.1: BACKGROUND: ELEMENTS OF PRODUCTION COSTING

The Limitations of Traditional Managerial Costing

Accounting is a centuries-old art, and one that is invaluable to the creation of valuable products. I've found that the terminology "managerial" and "financial" accounting confuses many good managers with little formal background in the art. They're very different disciplines. Managerial accounting deals with transactions and the flow of money within the firm. All managers with budgets and profit/loss responsibility must be familiar with the basic concepts of managerial accounting and the cornerstone concepts of income statements and profit and loss ledgers. Financial accounting, on the other hand, is concerned with the preparation of reports that are used by lenders, analysts, and others primarily outside the enterprise. This information rarely is used for managerial control and decision-making purposes. Therefore, I'll not discuss it.

Although lots of accounting methods are out there, what's important to you as an industrial manager is the managerial accounting used for the preparation of information and internal reports. They're the main source for assessing your current financial performance and trends. Managerial accounting—sometimes called cost accounting or, more generally, cost management—looks at overall profitability. With that information you can use proven methods to plan, measure, and disseminate necessary feedback to make fact-based decisions about costs, pricing, profitability, new product planning, and so on. However, cost accounting provides only historical data, not prospective information. Extrapolating even into the near future is risky, but often it's the best tool available.

Generally speaking, cost accounting is applied differently to job shop operations than to production process operations. The job shop is ruled by one-of-a-kind or small-run custom orders. Production process operations, on the other hand, involve a few product lines run at higher volumes and over longer time. Most of cost accounting's principles apply to production process operations, although some also apply to job shop and other kinds of manufacturing.

The accounting basis for traditional production process operations is the simple notion that costs are made up of fixed and variable components. Fixed, or "base," costs are those incurred regardless of production level. They include such categories as administrative and indirect salaries, space, depreciation, taxes and expensed supplies, and equipment. Variable costs, on the other hand, are those that are approximately directly proportional to volume. Each unit produced carries with it the cost of materials and direct labor for that unit. These variable costs are the real costs incurred in making one additional product unit, exclusive of the fixed costs. The total production cost is the sum of the fixed and variable costs for the production rates over the accounting period. However, some costs are both fixed and variable. Depreciation, for instance, regarded as a fixed cost, also has a wear-out component that is related to production rates and volumes. Administrative salaries—also usually considered a fixed cost—are often partly allocated to the product lines they support. Consequently, controllers' accounting systems break out costs into three components: fixed (e.g., managers' salaries), semivariable (e.g., operators' wages) and variable (e.g., materials). The first two categories are relatively insensitive to normal business swings, but variable costs often change rapidly. They are prime targets for continuous cost reduction programs.

Absorption and Direct Costing

The cost accounting used in traditional production environments is either of two types: *absorption* (or *full*) costing, or *direct* (or *marginal*) costing. Absorption costing allocates all fixed and variable overhead costs directly to products. Overhead is usually assigned to product groups or to administrative responsibility centers, which "absorb" all the production costs. Absorption costing is often preferred for *financial reporting* purposes because all fixed and variable costs are allocated to products, by business lines.

Direct-costing systems take a different view. Fixed outlays are lumped together into general overhead and are managed as such. Only variable costs are assigned to product groups. This model says that variable costs are the only true costs of production because fixed costs will be incurred regardless of the production output. Fixed costs are there simply by being in the business, whereas the supporting business processes encounter variable costs. Direct costing is useful for *management assessment* and control of operations and for short-term decision-making.

Businesses use both of these production-costing systems. Each suffers its own limitations. Absorption and direct costing are well-established industrial practices, the chief difference being the way they define and account for overhead or indirect costs and the way they assign inventory costs. Here are the premises that underpin these traditional accounting methods:

- Products at the business unit level consume all overhead costs; i.e., all overhead activities are volume-driven.
- Most factory overhead and fixed costs are matched to the yearly accounting calendar.
- Sales and marketing are not included in measuring product costs; they are part of general overhead and are allocated as such.
- There are no accurate means of attaching overhead to cost centers, so arbitrary measures are used, such as head count or factory size.

Limitations of Managerial Accounting

Absorption and direct costing are well-established industrial practices. As we've seen, their chief difference is in the arbitrary way they handle overhead and inventory costs. In fact, there are real drawbacks to both of these cost accounting methods, starting with the way labor and overhead costs are assigned. Typically, products at the business level are treated as consuming all overhead costs, so that overhead activities are regarded as being volume-driven, which of course is not the case. Traditional cost accounting practices have no accurate means for attaching overhead to cost centers; instead, arbitrary measures are used. Furthermore, standard practice is to allocate direct labor and overhead costs to products as they are produced, even though some units may later be reworked or scrapped for quality reasons. This practice not only can understate the "real" cost of the product but can send the wrong message to production workers that what "really" counts is volume, not quality.

Moreover, today some 95 percent of all manufacturers still allocate overhead by direct labor hours, despite efficiencies gained by automation, which significantly reduces the labor portion of total product cost. Typically, direct labor is usually about 10 to 20 percent of total product cost; the lion's share is in overhead. What really matters is the cost of individual product lines. Simple rules of thumb for determining overhead costs can easily mask the true costs of individual products. For example, channel and marketing costs are usually lumped into general overhead, despite their direct contributions to product lines. Yet these costs are real, and managers need to see and understand them for making decisions about new products and cost reductions.

And finally, traditional systems use, for convenience, the period of one year for calculating variable overhead costs. But in fact variable overheads frequently are driven by much longer market cycles. So the effect of these underlying market influences can easily be masked by the arbitrary annual time intervals used.

These assumptions reflect a view of production that was common in earlier eras: production was labor-intensive, profitability was driven by economies of scale, and product changes and product variety were much more limited than today. All that, of course, has changed. Today fast-paced technologies and global competition drive frequent product changes, economies of scope, high levels of automation, and knowledge workers displacing labor workers. Traditional approaches to product costing are therefore less effective as management control tools.

8.2: ACTIVITY-BASED COSTING AND MANAGEMENT

Enter activity-based costing. Robert Kaplan, a major framer of the concept, describes it as follows: "The theory behind ABC is that organizations perform activities that permit products to be designed, produced, distributed, sold and serviced. All these activities—engineering, manufacturing, logistics, marketing and sales, and administration—can now be traced to the products, product lines, and customers that create the demand for these activities. In this way, the activity costs can be accurately assigned to individual product costs."[1]

Doesn't this make perfect sense? Why, then, has it taken so long for ABC to be accepted and implemented? The one-word answer is technology. Until the late 1980s business information systems were not powerful enough to collect and assign all internal contributions properly to products and customers. It was just more expedient to assign costs to overhead and indirect accounts, even when such costs couldn't always be associated with specific end products.

How ABC Works: Putting Costs Where the Activities Are

ABC is catching on as a valuable management tool. It uses a fresh accounting framework, one that recognizes and eliminates non-value-added activities. And the ranks of the faithful are growing rapidly as managers see its usefulness in understanding just what product costs *really* are. Simply put, ABC is a better idea. It leads to a deeper understanding of actual product and distribution costs, so that you can make better product pricing and obsolescence decisions. Often a company will experiment with ABC to gain familiarity with the approach and, more particularly, to understand better the cost structure of some particular family of products. Some companies have developed ABC systems to supplement traditional absorption or direct-cost systems, and those that have stayed the course have gained ground. They've found that some product lines thought to be profitable weren't—and vice versa; they've been able to rationalize internal transfer pricing; and they've found activity-based management provides a clearer window into the company's cost structure.

Installing an ABC management system isn't easy, and getting people to trust and use it is even more challenging. Division controllers and plant managers have to see its value, which requires a great deal of internal examination and training, as well as a cultural readjustment. Companies contemplating ABC systems may find themselves better served by piloting a system at a business or product level before making the big leap to a company-wide "online" system. Some of the important preliminary steps to take before launching an ABC initiative are:[2]

- Secure top management commitment and involvement.
- Clearly define scope, goals, and objectives of the initiative.
- Establish a supportive culture, including intensive training for project members and general education for all.
- Focus on long-term improvement gains, not quick hits.

The basic structure of an ABC system consists of four steps: identifying the activities, identifying the cost drivers, defining the cost attachment points, and then attaching the costs. The first three steps require a thorough understanding of the company's internal systems and processes. Many factors may drive costs; some are complex and make ABC difficult to implement. However, ABC affords an opportunity for significant productivity improvements because it reveals the real cost drivers in product design, from part numbers and engineering change orders during design to complexity in product assembly operations. As for production, cost drivers include production throughput, process cycle times, product yields, and scrappage and in-process inventories. These and other components of the business simply aren't captured by conventional cost-accounting methods. Yet it's precisely these attributes—attributes reflecting the complexity of the business—that need to be related to the financial data elements for the ABC model to provide useful results. When seen through the eyes of ABC, they can reveal ways to simplify internal processes, reduce cycle times and enhance customer service and satisfaction. The effort to analyze activity costs can provide valuable management insight for streamlining internal processes, which can ultimately contribute to competitive advantage.

Here's a simple example from my own experiences with ABC. A small business unit of Schneider Electric (formerly the Square D Company) manufactured and sold a family of hardware components used by electric utilities. The unit prided itself on supplying customers promptly with any catalog or out-of-stock product. One particular component was ordered infrequently—about 500 units a year. Because most customers could wait several weeks or even months for delivery of this item, the company typically made only one or two runs of the product to cover that year's expected orders. By standard absorption practices, the product cost was fixed at $30 per unit. To this cost a markup of 50 percent was added, making the selling price $45 per unit.

Schneider Electric invited a consultant to review the company's overall cost-accounting practices. Among her observations was that making this "special" product took two people off their regular duties for two days while they scavenged for particular tools, molds, and fixtures and while they processed the parts. In addition, phone calls and correspondence flew back and forth, followed by special packaging and shipping. All of these costs—*real* costs to the company—were simply assigned to fixed factory overhead. Although the consultant found the direct labor and material costs as determined under absorption costing to be about right, it was the *real* indirect costs that was the shocker. The accountants booked the indirect costs for these few special items at $8 per unit, where on an activity basis the costs were actually $300 per unit. These understated indirect costs were—however unintentionally—spread over all the other standard products the business unit produced, making their real costs somewhat higher than management realized and therefore reducing profit margins.

This story had a happy ending for everyone. Realizing now the *real* cost content of these special units, plant management went to their customers, explained the situation, and secured agreement to price these special items more realistically at $450 per unit—ten times the former price. Moreover, two years later these customers had redesigned their product to accommodate the standard products the company offered, which allowed the company to obsolete this particular and other low-volume special products. But most important, this experience provided management with *real insight* into the true costs of its products. As a consequence, management could then make pricing adjustments on yet other product lines, which led to increased overall margins and profitability.

This anecdote brings me to the most important point about ABC. No matter the accounting system, the objective is to improve competitiveness. It's not *necessarily* to take out cost. Harvard's Wickham Skinner notes that manufacturers tend to follow predictable patterns in seeking ways to gain competitive advantage. He calls this pattern the "40-40-20 rule." About 40 percent of their competitive advantage stems from the way companies manage their workforce, their supply chain of parts, materials, and services, and their production facilities. Another 40 percent derives from their product development processes and their effective use of design tools, production equipment, technology, and work-flow processes. The remaining 20 percent—*and no more than about* 20 percent—comes from conventional accounting approaches to productivity improvement. In other words, focusing just on cost-cutting to improve "productivity" will only lead the company into decline. Rather, wise investments in product and process technology and related systems are far more effective to strengthen a company's competitive position. Cost-related productivity improvements are important, but their contribution to boosting competitiveness is quickly reached and has only marginal value thereafter. Whereas ABC can add valuable insight into a product's real cost structure, conventional cost accounting often fails to deliver the useful information that managers need to manage.

8.3: MEASURING YOUR PROCESSES

Sound cost-accounting methods, including ABC, are obviously essential for running industrial operations. They measure the sources and sinks of money flows. They provide the basis for decisions on capital projects and other investments. But they don't tell you about how your processes are performing. You need other means for measuring your key internal processes: R&D, new product development, and production processes. These are the *drivers* of business improvement. Performance improvements in these areas ultimately get reflected in the cost-accounting tallies in reaction to internal business improvements.

Your company may be able to survive without metrics for R&D, new product development, and production operations, but you'll never thrive without them. Measuring these operations tells you how well you're doing. They serve as benchmarks for continuous improvement and allow for comparison against the benchmarks of other companies. The metrics that I'll discuss here are among the better ones, but there are a great many others. I've cataloged well over a hundred that are useful in particular circumstances. You may already be tracking some metrics within your R&D, new product development, and production operations. That's good. As with most things in life, however, balance is important. You must develop and use a blend of performance measures, from the general, as in revenue per employee, to the very specific, as in the rolled yield of a particular production station. Most companies track a few key overall indicators of business performance but make the mistake of not following through with more specific measures. In this section I'll give you some proven metrics for R&D, for new product development, and for production operations. Then I'll wrap it up with an approach—from micro to macro—for measuring the entire enterprise.

Measuring the Unmeasurable: Your R&D Operations

Research and development is an investment. It represents a substantial stake—somewhere between 2 and 10 percent of your entire *sales*. Like any investment, it should be subject to measurement and management. Back in the old days of "blue sky," R&D's contribution to the enterprise was obvious but not measurable. No longer. As R&D gets closer to the customer, its effectiveness needs to be evaluated with the same rigor as sales and marketing, production, distribution, or any other delivery function.

In general, R&D measurements should be simple, objective, and should focus on significant outputs. Don't waste your time counting easy-to-measure things like the number of patents granted annually, speeches and published papers, or conferences attended. They have little or no value as useful metrics for R&D, and if you measure only these countable activities, guess what your R&D people will concentrate on? Instead, you want R&D to develop technologies that will be useful in selling your products and services, so focus on those things that, if consistently and accurately measured, can help you compete. Out of the many I've seen and used, here are seven measures that are at the top of my relevancy list. Note that they all are (or can be made) dimensionless ratios and therefore can be easily understood and compared with other companies' R&D.

Apply these metrics both within individual R&D teams and to the entire enterprise. The first year's numbers give you a baseline. (See the discussion of baselining and benchmarking in Chapter 7.) The figures for out-years give you a basis for evaluating whether you are improving the efficiency and effectiveness of your R&D investments. At the same time, keep score on how the competition is doing against these same metrics, making your

TABLE 8.1   MEASURING R&D PROCESS

1. *R&D Multiple:* Annual investment in R&D ÷ total sales. Alternatively, R&D ÷ (total sales − purchased materials). The R&D multiple is a measure of your R&D "intensity."

2. *Relative R&D Multiple:* The ratio of your company's R&D multiple (above) to that of your strongest competitors. This is a useful index when applied within an industry vertical.

3. *R&D Effectiveness Index:* The profit coming from new products in relation to the investment made in new product development. This index can be expressed either in dollars or percent of sales and is:

$$\text{Annual Revenue from New Products} \times (\text{Net Profit} + \text{R\&D Investment}) \div \text{R\&D Investment}$$

Index the quantities in this formula to the cost of money from a common datum. An index value of 1.0 indicates that new products are generating as much profit as the investment in R&D; more than 1.0 is even better; less than 1.0 tells you that your R&D engine isn't pulling its weight. An index of 1.25 or better is an outstanding performance.

4. *R&D Yield:* Gross profit contribution from sales of new or improved products that were enabled by lower cost-of-goods-sold from new or improved processes. R&D yield measures how much and how fast your R&D process investments are paying off in the marketplace.

5. *R&D Return:* The ratio of R&D yield (above) to your total R&D investment. R&D return measures how cost-effective your R&D investments are.

6. *New Sales Ratio:* The percent of overall sales and net income derived from R&D projects that have directly and significantly influenced new product creation in the past three and the past five years. The new sales ratio measures how efficient the linkage is between R&D and new product development.

7. *Patent Coverage:* Percent of current sales that are protected by patents and/or trade secrets, compared to three and five years ago. Patent coverage measurement is an index of your intellectual property coverage deriving from recent projects.

strongest competitors your benchmarks. Then compare your own baseline numbers with those of your benchmarks, and you'll know how best to change your R&D operations in the future, to put *you* on your industry's benchmark leader board.

The R&D multiple is the single most common index of R&D productivity. Of course, it doesn't *really* measure your productivity, just how much money you're throwing at R&D. But assuming your R&D operations are reasonably well chartered and led, it's a reasonable index of your R&D's overall health and commitment. Typical R&D multiples range widely by industry. For low-tech industries like basic materials and foodstuff production, the multiple usually is less than about 2 percent. At the other end, in the high-tech pharmaceutical and semiconductor industries, the multiple can reach 15 percent or more. For most midtech industries it's typically in the 3 to 5 percent range.

Let me illustrate R&D measurement as applied by some leading creators of valuable products. First let's look at London-based Glaxo-Wellcome (now part of SmithKline-Glaxo), the $8 billion pharmaceutical giant that competes against Bristol-Myers Squibb, Merck, and others. Glaxo-Wellcome has an R&D multiple of about 15 and has found even that isn't enough. Senior management upped the ante with a *threefold* increase in both R&D investments and in R&D productivity over the period 1996–2000. Incidentally, G-W outsources about 20 percent of its R&D budget to universities and other collaborators. This strategy lets them focus more on their core competencies and, at the same time, bring in fresh ideas from outside.

Procter & Gamble, the world's largest advertiser, is a company somewhere in the middle of the R&D scale. A major producer of soaps and beauty, personal, medicinal, and baby care products, P&G announced in April 1998 their intent to double their R&D spending to $2.4 billion, an R&D multiple of about 7. The rationale? P&G believes that any company wanting to be a leader in innovation has to be flexible enough to make rapid-fire changes in its products and management processes. P&G, for a time, more than lived up to its word: early 1999 saw an overall increase of more than 9 percent in corporate R&D spending.[3] Many analysts saw this increase in P&G's R&D spending as key to keeping or increasing profit margins—provided those increases were accompanied by increases in R&D productivity. But business conditions often dance to their own tune. More is not always better in funding R&D budgets. By mid-1999 P&G announced significant overall reductions in forces, suggesting in part that growth in R&D is best done in evolutionary steps.

Similarly, IBM, which in 1997 reduced its R&D spending from $6 billion to $5 billion, was applauded by Wall Street for its effort in creating new products that customers actually want! IBM began to distance itself from its heritage of pursuing "blue sky" technology dreams. The technology victims included people working in basic astrophysics, magnetic bubble memories, and gallium arsenide microprocessor technology. Winners were those enjoying IBM's increased investments in such product-related technologies as voice-recognition systems, Internet security software, data storage technology, and biometrics.[4]

Measuring Productivity of New Product Development Investments

Like R&D, the process of new product creation not only can be measured but should be, to ensure an even better return from investments.

Here again, many useful metrics are available for measuring the efficiency of a new product development process. What matters is that you select a few that make sense for your business environment and use them consistently to watch for year-to-year changes. As mentioned in Chapter 2, think of it as an annual physical. Your physician makes various tests of your body's efficiency: weight, pulse, lung capacity, stress tolerance, hearing, vision, and so on. No *single* test stands as a reliable indicator of your body's fitness. But by taking them together, an experienced practitioner can evaluate and determine whether you're more or less healthy than a year ago, what you can expect in the future, and how you to improve your health condition.

Table 8.2 provides some useful process metrics for new product development. Begin by using these suggestions, and always be on the hunt for others that apply to your specific business.

As much as I advocate taking a process view of new product development, let me caution you. Some folks think of production processes as usually being "in control," "well-tuned," with little variation. But NPD is vulnerable to the whims of the marketplace, and "in control" really means "control of risk." Unlike manufacturing processes, a good process here doesn't automatically ensure a good product. Recall from "Wrapping It Up—Measuring Your Process" in Chapter 2 the experience of Casio Computer, which struggled to cope with a huge market response to their new QV10 digital camera. This and the debacle of the Apple Newton communication product (also mentioned therein) remind us just how fickle new product introductions can be.

TABLE 8.2   MEASURING NEW PRODUCT DEVELOPMENT PROCESSES

1. *Process Throughput:* Number of new or improved products commercialized per year. Also, the number of new or improved product development projects in the pipeline, as a percent of last year's condition and as compared with comparable figures five years ago.

2. *Impact of Technology:* The technology share: The ratio of company-owned patents to all comparable patents owned by competitors. Also, the patent utilization: the percentage of the company's active patents that are actually incorporated into or used defensively for commercial products and processes.

3. *New Products' Impact on Sales, and the New Sales Ratio:* Sales (in $ and in %) from new or improved products released in the prior year and from the prior three years. Also, the new sales ratio: the current year's sales revenue from product developments commercialized in the five prior years, compared to the total current year's sales.

4. *New Products' Impact on Costs:* The cost savings ratio: The current year's savings in cost-of-goods-sold from product changes or process developments in the five prior years, in relation to the current year's gross profits.

5. *Cycle Efficiency of Project Management:* The break-even time: the time, in months, from project go-ahead to the recovery of the project's development investments by new profits from the product's sales. Also, the break-even-after-release: the time, in months, from manufacturing release to the recovery of the project investments in product *profits.*

Measuring Your Production Operations

In some ways measuring your overall production effectiveness is even more difficult than with R&D or new product development. It invites so many different measurements that it's like having a thorough physical exam, after which the physician gives you a 10-page report consisting of dozens of test results. The details are nice, but you *really* want an overall assessment of your health state. In production operations you have literally hundreds of process point measurements—relating to cycle times, repair and downtime, waste and rework, and the like. They're all important, of course, for gauging how well unit process equipment is working and how it can be improved. And to manage your processes, you need to measure them.

Table 8.3 provides a short list of high-level measures that will help you manage. They focus on processes and on quality. I recommend that you develop a system to track these measurements and report them monthly to managers and team leaders. Make them your focus for improvement goals.

TABLE 8.3 MEASURING PRODUCTION OPERATIONS PROCESSES

---

1. Book-to-bill ratio:
   ($ of production work booked and scheduled) ÷ $ of billed orders

2. Days of work-in-process (WIP) inventories

3. Back-order aging index:
   (avg. back order × avg. age) ÷ avg. production

4. Production cycle times

5. Percentage of operators who are cross-trained

6. Scrap and rework rates

7. C_{pk}—the "capability index" quality measure for each major unit processes and for the entire processes (see Chapter 7)

8. Cost of quality, as determined by your own measurement system

9. Year-to-date warranty costs as % of year-to-date production value
   (3-month rolling average)

A Model to Get You Started

Table 8.4 presents a measurement system for a production enterprise. It's based on five relatively independent categories: financial, business, quality, cycle time, and customer satisfaction, which I've listed down the left column. Across the top I've arranged three domains, or *drivers*, in increasing scope. The first is the smallest organizational level, the unit operations level. It might be, for example, a design group or a particular production line. The intermediate—or department—level might be the smallest organizational unit having profit and loss responsibility. Third is the overall business unit, plant, or sector level. The direction of the drivers is left to right, from unit operations, which drives departmental level performance, which in turn drives the business unit or plant level performance.

I've placed some examples of specific metrics that are appropriate for each cell in the matrix. These examples are useful performance measures for all points in the matrix. Yes, there are many other measures, and each enterprise should develop those metrics that make the most sense for its particular operations. In some cases supply chain management is a key determinate of good performance. For others it may be project management or geo-expansion or business diversification. The examples shown in the table, however, are examples of accepted "best performance" indices and will get you thinking further.

TABLE 8.4   EXAMPLES OF PERFORMANCE METRICS FOR THE ENTERPRISE

Metric Category	Unit Operations Level	Department Level	Enterprise or Plant Level
Financial Performance	(See Quality Performance)	Production performance to plan	RONA, EBIT, or EVA[1]; gross margin[2]; profit margin[3]
Business Performance	Productivity per employee	Finished goods inventory turns[4]	Sales per employee
Quality Performance	Schedule attainment; scrap rates, parts per million defectives	C_{pk}; AQL[5]; SPC[6]; hrs. training/worker; lost time accidents	ISO 9000 et al.; MBNQA[7] attainment; cost of quality; sigma level
Cycle Time Performance	Setup times; WIP turns	Total production cycle times; throughput÷WIP; pure work÷throughput cycle time	Inventory turns
Customer Satisfaction Performance	Completeness & accuracy of recording	Level of repeat business	Certified supplierships; customer satisfaction ratings

1. RONA (return on net assets) = net profit/net assets capitalization
EBIT (earnings before interest & taxes) = (pretax earnings + interest expense) ÷ sales
EVA (economic value added) = after-tax net income, plus land and plant equipment, less real cost of capital employed
2. Cost of goods sold ÷ sales
3. Gross profit ÷ sales
4. Cost of sales ÷ average finished goods inventory
5. Acceptable quality level
6. Statistical process control
7. Malcolm Baldrige National Quality Award or state-level equivalents

8.4: JUSTIFYING CAPITAL INVESTMENTS IN PRODUCT CREATION

One of the more vexing financial issues affecting R&D, product development, and production environments is justifying capital investments in new technologies. Technology advances always beckon for investment. They hold promise for greater productivity and faster internal cycles and transactions. They're often vital to new product and service lines. So it's natural for technology and operations champions to argue strongly about the benefits expected from investments in new design and prototyping tools, product data management and other information systems, flexible and agile production systems, and tools for virtual collaborations, not to mention new, more powerful, and effective research equipment.

Justification issues are also provoked when plans call for making basic changes in business processes. For example, introducing computer-integrated manufacturing (CIM) or flexible or agile production systems can change the very way in which the business works. It can affect internal organizations, people, and the skills they need. Also, such systems often require new market approaches because of tighter cycle times, greater product variety, and other factors.

In fact, it's difficult *not* to embrace the philosophy that making investments in new technologies—especially those that support core competencies—is absolutely necessary for continued competitiveness. It's self-evident, yet such investments often carry high costs—and sometimes risks. At what point does the "protechnology" argument give way to hard economic justification? And what, specifically, is the rational basis for making such decisions?

One emerging area where this issue is particularly felt is the environmental costs of new products and services. Manufacturers are being required by domestic and international standards to manufacture products that reduce interference with the environment and that are safely disposable or effectively reclaimed, recycled, and remade. Because of these standards, manufacturers must analyze product life cycles to identify energy requirements and the impacts they'll have on the environment. Here again, traditional accounting procedures fail to capture the true costs of new products launched under the new rules. They simply can't factor in the implications of these new *kinds* of technology—and their associated risks and benefits.

If a management team is faced with approving or rejecting a proposal involving a technology that is incremental—offering an improvement in *degree* over current practice but not an improvement in *kind*—the approach is relatively straightforward. The team analyzes the improved efficiency, productivity, labor impact, and other direct-cost implications expected of the proposed equipment, then makes a payback calculation: how many months will it take for the economic benefits from the new technology to offset its total cost. Comparing this payback time (or, equivalently, the "hurdle rate") with other investment proposals under consideration, the team decides on the proposal's economic value, weighing the expected gains against the decision *not* to adopt the new technology. In other words, the team must factor in what risks are assumed by *not* investing. This kind of analysis is unemotional and nonstrategic—merely a question of valuing a financial investment.

Of course, it's much more difficult when the new technology under consideration is different not in degree but in *kind*—as in the case of implementing a new process for production or for installing environmental remediation systems. In such cases a meaningful payback analysis may be impossible. The new equipment is attractive *because* it changes the basic capabilities of the company or organization. Although some brave souls can attempt payback analyses, these calculations require assumptions that aren't supported by prior experience and are therefore difficult to defend. Yet on a visceral level, the investment may make perfect sense.

Don't look to standard managerial accounting practices for simple answers to this knotty puzzle. The tools I described in Chapter 2 on portfolio analysis can be of help. But there is an answer that makes *common* sense. Kaplan[5] summarized this struggle between the need for accounting precision and for managerial judgment in making decisions about investments in new *kinds* of production technology: "Although intangible benefits may be difficult to quantify, there is no reason to value them at zero in a capital expenditure analysis. Zero is, after all, no less arbitrary than any other number. Conservative accountants who assign zero values to many intangible benefits prefer being precisely wrong to being vaguely right. Managers need not follow their example. Rather than attempt to put a dollar tag on benefits that by their nature are difficult to quantify, managers should reverse the process and estimate first how large these benefits must be in order to justify the proposed investment. Senior executives can be expected to judge that improved flexibility, rapid customer service, market adaptability, and options on new process technology may be worth $300,000 to $500,000 per year but not, say, $1 million. This may not be exact mathematics, but it does help put a meaningful price on computer-integrated manufacturing's (CIM's) intangible benefits."

8.5: IDEAS FOR ACTION

1. If you haven't done so already, become acquainted with the applications of activity-based costing to your business and how ABC can determine your true product and process costs.

2. Look into developing a system for capturing your cost of quality, as described in Chapter 7, to help you reduce these costs by making them visible.

3. Develop and continually improve the way you go about measuring the productivity of your R&D, new product development, and production processes. Use these metrics as a basis for annual adjustments in staff, facilities, and equipment decisions.

4. Taking the ideas in Table 8.5, develop a hierarchical system of performance metrics specific to your business; train all your associates in the purpose and use of these metrics.

5. Develop a decision support approach for accepting/rejecting proposals for substantial capital investments in new process equipment and facilities.

Chapter 9

Caveat Venditor—Beware of (Their) Lawyers!

Now we've come to perhaps the most overlooked spoke in our waterwheel metaphor—the "legal issues" spoke. It must be durable; otherwise, it can ruin your company as easily as inattention can bring down a water station. The New Product Creation Wheel can easily grind to a halt if this spoke fails to carry its load. Yet despite the importance of patents, trademarks, and other intellectual property tools, many organizations are not properly informed of its importance. Engineers particularly have a long history of belittling lawyers' contribution to the team for new product creation. Too often they're seen as thorns and obstacles to progress. This ignorance can be costly—even destructive. My own view, shaped over decades of experience, is it's hard to overstate the importance of the legal system to new product development. In some respects this chapter may well be the most valuable of this book because the subject is rarely included as part of the new product art. And it can cost you heavily if you fail to act appropriately or if, through ignorance, you don't comply with the basic principles and laws governing intellectual property.

Indeed, I've seen a lot of managers responsible for new product creation who have a blind spot when it comes to legal issues. Rarely do they have any training in this area; their knowledge of product liability and other important legal matters is spotty and often misguided. Most of their interactions with corporate attorneys are passive, dealing usually with the routine standards— confidentiality agreements, contracts, and perhaps patent applications. Yes, these formalities are important. But it's absolutely essential that managers be actively informed about a much wider arena of legal issues—both to craft sound business strategy and to avoid crippling liability exposure.

This chapter borrows significantly from my earlier book[1] and has been extensively revised. Here I'll summarize what you and your team need to know about the Big Three—intellectual property, products liability, and antitrust law—all of which play heavily in the process of developing valuable products. And if my language here seems a bit more formal and precise than in other chapters, it's simply because of the nature of the topic (and because my lawyers had to look at it!). So bear with me; the information you'll find here is crucial if you're to avoid running afoul of the law and, in fact, if you're to take advantage of what the law has to offer to assist your new product creation.

The overriding message of this chapter is that your attorneys are on *your* side. Yes, at times they may seem to be obstacles more than facilitators. Yes, they may take longer than you may feel is needed to draw and execute "routine" legal instruments. But they are there to help you avert problems— even disasters. Your lawyers, whether in house or not, are paid to worry about the *other* attorneys out there—lawyers who would sooner eat your lunch than seek accommodation. And the results from legal inattention ever more frequently shout at us from the media: "Jury awards hefty punitive damages against General Motors in fuel tank explosion case." "Punitive damages awarded in product liability action." "Willful patent infringement costs company $106M." "Felony charges leveled in antitrust violation." Now do I have your attention?

One more point. It's the folks in charge of new product creation who are responsible for taking the initiative with corporate counsel. Don't count on your attorneys to identify the issues that need special attention. Your attorneys are there to keep your company out of legal trouble and to advise you on forging effective legal strategies. But *you* need to bring the potential issues to *them*, especially regarding patents and licensing, product recalls, trade secret violations, and a host of related issues. Accordingly, you must be knowledgeable enough about such issues to know when to call on them. And if in doubt, call 'em anyway.

9.1: AN EXECUTIVE PRIMER ON INTELLECTUAL PROPERTY

What do you think of when someone speaks of "assets"? The business world usually thinks of assets as cash, securities, receivables, inventory, plant and equipment, and human resources. But another kind of assets—intellectual property—can be enormously valuable. Intellectual property may not be as tangible as some other assets, and it may be difficult to set specific monetary value on them. Nonetheless, they are valuable and command senior-management attention. The fact is that intellectual property rights are becoming even more important to industrial companies than the manufactured products themselves.[2]

What exactly is intellectual property? For our purposes intellectual property comes in four distinct categories—patents, copyrights, trademarks, and trade secrets—each of which may be licensed or otherwise transferred.

The ABCs of Patents

Patents are exclusive rights granted by the federal government to the inventor—in fact, a patent is a legal monopoly. In the greater scheme of things, however, a patent does more than offer protection; it stimulates creativity, innovation, and economic growth; it encourages the dissemination of information and competition; it enhances the standard of living.

The origins of U.S. patent law trace back to 15th-century Italy. One hundred years later Holland and Saxony in the 16th century issued a joint decree that afforded the first protection to inventors and their creations. This same safeguard was later fixed in the U.S. Constitution (Article 1, Section 8), which reads in part:

> The Congress shall have power To promote the Progress of Science and useful Arts, by securing for limited times to Authors and Inventors the exclusive Right to their respective Writings and Discoveries.

A patent provides the owner certain specified rights, namely, to prohibit others from making, using, offering to sell, and selling the invention for a specified time. In the United States patents are granted to inventors, not their employers or others. The patent and all rights thereunder can then be (and commonly are) assigned to an inventor's company because of specific clauses in employment contracts. In some foreign countries a patent may be issued either to the inventor(s) or to a company.

Patent law in the United States is concisely described by a 1942 Supreme Court opinion (*Ethyl Gasoline Corp.* v. *United States*) as conferring

> .... on the patentee a limited monopoly, the right or power to exclude all others from manufacturing, using, or selling his invention. The extent of that right is limited by the identification of his invention, as its boundaries are

marked by the specifications and claims of the patent. He may grant licenses to make, use, or vend, restricted in point of space and time, or with any other restriction upon the exercise of the granted privilege, save only that by attaching a condition to his license he may not enlarge his monopoly.

The U.S. patent system encourages dissemination of information concerning discoveries and inventions and spurs innovative competition that enhances the nation's well-being. The annual output of U.S. patents over the past decade has more than doubled. Data released in 1998 by the Council on Competitiveness show that numbers of patents by industry sector provide a good indication of sector innovation. Information technology, the fastest-growing sector, now accounts for about 15 percent of all U.S. patents issued annually. In that year the U.S. Patent and Trademark Office issued more than 150,000 patents. Patents are vital assets that can grow your company, and increasingly so.

The federal government's role is to confer exclusive rights to inventors. It also promotes innovation by publicly disclosing inventions once the patents are granted so that others may learn from these inventions to advance their own business interests, which, in turn, advance society's interests. However, critics of this system argue that advances in living standards attributed to the patent system are offset by the free exchange of ideas. It's an old debate and one not likely to be resolved anytime soon.

PATENTS IN THE UNITED STATES AND OTHER COUNTRIES

The United States is nearly unique among industrialized nations because of its "first-to-invent" approach. Under this approach, invention rights are granted to the inventor who is *first to invent*, regardless of whether the inventor was *first to file* an application for a patent. The inventor also need not commercialize the invention, as long as he or she is diligent in moving from conception to filing of a patent application. Most other industrialized nations employ a "first-to-file" approach, which grants protection to the inventor who first files for a patent, whether or not he or she was the first to invent.

Be aware of these differences. A U.S. inventor wishing multinational or "worldwide" protection should file as soon as possible in the United States, and then applications in most other countries will have the benefit of the U.S. filing date. The essence of the strategy is that although you might win as the first-to-invent party in this country, you could lose in a foreign country if a competitor files an application prior to your own U.S. filing date.

Significant efforts have recently been made to harmonize these disparate patent systems throughout the world. Eventually it will happen, but don't count on soon seeing a worldwide intellectual property system in which there is one examination and registration system, one rapid and cost-effective dispute resolution system, and one uniform, global enforcement. For now the reality is a polyglot of disparate patent systems, and a U.S. patent has no legal force in other countries. *Any* company can take a product or known technology patented only in the United States and manufacture and sell it in another country with impunity. Therefore, inventors (or the companies holding assignment rights) usually are driven to file for patent protection in multiple countries where the invention will likely be distributed to customers. It's the only way to protect your overseas markets. And it is very costly.

Another particularly interesting aspect of patent law usually done outside the United States is the practice of "patent flooding"—also known as minefield patents or picket patents. Patent flooding is a tactic whereby a company files many overlapping and narrowly differentiated patent applications covering a new product or process. This tactic is sometimes used to gain access to competitors' core technology by forcing cross-licensing agreements. These agreements occur when the "predator" company can surround the competitor's technology base so that it gives the competitor little room to expand. In effect, it forces negotiation. Flooding is also used to erect a fence around a core set of ideas in such a way that subsequent inventors are discouraged from inventing within the same technology area because of the risk of infringing, however trivially, on one or more of the first company's many patents. Patent flooding is particularly common in Japan and in some other countries because their system, unlike ours, permits patents having very narrow scopes of claims; patents are allowed that are based on very minor variations from existing patents. Keep these differences among different nations' patent systems in mind when seeking protection in other countries.

What Can Be Patented?

Just what can and can't be patented? Certainly products of "tangible" technology are patent eligible. The United States Patent Act[3] provides that "whoever invents or discovers any new and useful process, machine, manufacture, or composition of matter or any new and useful improvement thereof, may obtain a patent therefore, subject to the conditions and requirements of this title."

The act states that not only machines, manufactured articles, and compositions of matter but also production and other processes are eligible for patent protection. It is very broad, and it has been said that anything under the U.S. sun can be patented provided it meets two essential tests: the invention must be *novel* and *non-obvious.*

The patentability of original devices and processes is well established, but patent protection can now extend beyond the familiar. Mathematical algorithms, their computer execution, software, and even conventional and e-business processes are patentable, providing they meet certain standards.

However, having a patent doesn't automatically grant you the right to manufacture the invention free from possible infringement—the bane of many an invention and manufacturer. Suppose I own a patent for a Gadget. Suppose also that you file for, and are granted, a patent for a Widget—and that your Widget requires my Gadget in order to operate. Under such circumstances, you can't make, use, or distribute your Widget without my express permission. In this case you and I would most likely make an agreement under which I become a supplier of my Gadget (or license you to make it) so that you can incorporate it into your Widget, in return for royalties to me.

Two main kinds of U.S. patents are *utility patents* and *design patents.* Usually the term "patent" refers to a utility patent, which is granted for the invention of a new device or process that satisfies three essential criteria:

1. newness or novelty
2. usefulness or utility
3. non-obviousness

Of these criteria, the last—non-obviousness—is the most subjective. Legally, a utility patent may *not* be obtained "if the differences between the subject matter sought to be patented and the prior art are such that the subject matter as a whole would have been obvious at the time the invention was made to a person having ordinary skill in the art to which said subject matter pertains."

A design patent, in contrast, doesn't depend upon functionality. It can protect an invention based solely upon newness or novelty of "ornamental design." The legal term is "trade dress" and refers to trademark protection afforded since 1992 by the Supreme Court to protect products having "inherently distinctive" appearances. It provides no protection with respect to function or utility, which, of course, fall under patent law. A design patent is often more easily granted than is a utility patent. However, it can be less valuable in terms of commercial exploitation because design patents can often be easily sidestepped by other designs that are similar.

A recent example underscoring the value of a design patent is the suit filed in July 1999 by Apple Computer against Future Power, a computer maker backed by the Daewoo Group. Apple's new iMac desktop computer had created much excitement and won several design awards for its soft, rounded, and friendly look. In fact, this particular suit had nothing to do with functionality. Future Power's machine is quite different from the iMac. It runs on the Microsoft Windows 98 operating system and has a floppy drive. Rather, Apple took on Future Power because the latter closely replicated the former's style, its "look and feel" and its colors. The test of infringement in such situations is whether there is a risk of substantial confusion in the marketplace. At this writing, the case is yet to be settled, but it does define an area of patent law that is taking on more and more importance.[4]

SEEKING PATENT PROTECTION

An inventory must follow a formal process to secure patent protection. Typically, the first step involves a patent attorney (or patent agent) who reviews an invention in light of prior publications and patents covering devices of a similar nature and makes an assessment regarding patentability.

If the inventor chooses to go forward, the attorney (or agent) prepares the formal application. A key determinant of success here is the attorney's skill in the structure and wording of the claims, which ultimately determine whether a patent will be issued and, if so, the patent's scope of protection, that is the invention's potential for future commercial value. It usually takes a year or two—sometimes longer, depending on the scope and complexity of the patent application—before the Patent Office renders a final decision. However, throughout this period of examination, the Patent Office treats the patent application, its subject, and its contents as *confidential information* and may not reveal any part of it outside the office without the inventor's or attorney's specific authorization.

Eventually the patent examiner may issue an action indicating patentability of some or all of the claims. Usually the inventor and attorney have to modify the claims in light of the examiner's comments and then resubmit the application. A lot of time can be invested going through the process of seeking patent protection, and often differences of opinion crop up as to patentability. Of course, channels of appeal are available (up to and including the Supreme Court) if fundamental disagreements exist between the inventor and the examiner. Practically, however, time is money. If it appears that the process could drag on without prospect of meaningful protection, the inventor may abandon the patent process and pursue instead a trade secret approach. But more about this later.

In the United States a utility patent is normally granted for a term of 20 years from the filing date, some with extensions available for pharmaceutical and agrochemical products. Additionally, many countries—including the United States—require a periodic payment of fees subsequent to issuance to maintain the patent in force. These payments generally increase over time, so that patents in which the owner is no longer interested are likely to be dropped, thereby making the covered technology available to all, provided no other, more basic patents are maintained.

As mentioned earlier, in the United States when an invention is made by an employee utilizing the employer's facility and/or in relation to the work he or she performs for the employer, the employer generally acquires the rights to the invention. However, a company doesn't normally want to acquire rights to inventions made by its employees if such inventions don't relate in some direct way to organizational interests, markets, or the work that the employee performed for the employer. Most companies have specific clauses in their employment contracts by which the employee agrees to assign to the employer all rights in any invention conceived during the course of employment, provided such invention relates to the business interests of the employer.

The timing of patent applications can be an important element of business strategy. Once a patentable idea has been conceived, the inventor (or company, as assignee of intellectual property conceived by its employees) must move quickly to establish priority by filing a patent application and develop an action plan that addresses what filings, if any, are to be made in other countries. This plan should deal with such issues as how to exploit the foreign patent—by licensing a manufacturer? as a bargaining chip in swapping patent rights? by other means?—and how to prevent infringement in foreign countries. Here again, it's important to seek experienced legal counsel.

On the human side, company recognition of its inventors is an important motivator. Most organizations engaged in R&D motivate employees by providing rewards or recognition for employee patents. The rewards range from small lump-sum cash awards to a percentage of the royalties received from the licensing of the patent. Other organizations consider an employee's patents in evaluating overall performance for salary increase or promotion. A clear correlation exists between how a company recognizes and rewards the inventive work of its employees and that company's overall product development leadership.

To Patent or Not to Patent? Strategies for Exploiting Patents

As a practical matter, patents are not "free." Aside from the costs involved in securing them, carrying or maintaining patents often involves substantial and burdensome maintenance fees that must be paid periodically to the issuing governments. Therefore, most companies develop policies that determine which inventions should have patent protection. Is the patent to be kept for internal exploitation or for protection of an area of art, or will it be licensed to another company? In which countries should patent protection be sought, and why? How should the decision be made to abandon protection, for example by no longer paying the required maintenance fees? Is the invention really to be encouraged internally and therefore rewarded in some way, or are patent applications approved only in very special cases? These examples are matters for management policy, to be supported by sound legal advice.

Sooner or later, many companies are confronted with patent infringement issues. Patent infringement is understood as the unauthorized exercise of any rights granted to the inventor, such as unauthorized manufacture, use, or sale of the invention as defined by the claims. If these rights have been infringed, the inventor/company may file suit in federal court to recover damages as well as to obtain an injunction prohibiting future infringement. In deciding an infringement suit, the court may not only adjudicate the infringement question but may also consider the validity of the patent itself, because, as a defense, alleged infringers frequently claim invalidity of the patent. Legal fees alone for a patent infringement case can easily run $1 million or more.

The problems and policies surrounding the ownership and use of patents, the liabilities for their infringement, the licensing of patent rights, and the related problem of royalties present a complex and evolving area of civil law. Federal statutes dealing with patent problems are relatively few and tend to be directed at particular problem areas rather than at the subject as a whole.

Some companies, Black & Decker among them, have made patent strategy a centerpiece of their new product competitive game plan. They regard patents as silver bullets that can be used to disarm their competitors. They do this in two ways: First, they act defensively. They use a process that requires careful scrutiny of each new filing notice that features devices or mechanisms that might conceivably be used in a competitive product. They ferret out these claims and they challenge them, often successfully. They routinely file suit against others seeking patent protection. This strategy has proven to be quite valuable despite the cost involved. Such companies also act offensively. They're very careful in the manner in which they craft and word the claims of their own filings. They make sure that each patent filing contains claims that are as broad as are allowable. Patent strategy is an effective competitive tool for such companies and they invest heavily in it. However most companies do not have the discipline required to use patents strategically; perhaps they should.

Copyrights

Confusion sometimes arises over the terms copyright and trademark and how they differ from patents. A copyright is a set of rights granted by the federal government to an "author" (or composer, artist, and so on), whereby the author may exercise control over his or her own work and realize financial benefit from it. The copyright is designed to stimulate the creation and dissemination of creative work by providing recognition and reward to the author.

The United States Copyright Act defines what is protectable as "original works of authorship fixed in any tangible medium of expression, now known or later developed, from which they can be perceived, reproduced, or otherwise communicated, either directly or with the aid of a machine or device." Protection extends to written, pictorial, audio, and theatrical works, but not to ideas, processes, principles, and the like.

Whereas a patent can be granted only after meeting the criteria of novelty, utility, and non-obviousness, a copyright can be granted for *any original and expressive work* as long as it was done independently (that is, was not copied), whether or not similar works exist. It doesn't have to meet any kind of "quality" test. The creative expression of a copyrighted work must be in some tangible medium, such as paper, film, tape, or computer disk, from which the work can be perceived either directly—through the senses—or indirectly, as by means of a machine. Current U.S. copyright law grants protection from unauthorized reproduction to an originator of an artistic and literary work who has fixed that work in such tangible form of expression. Although the work doesn't have to be novel—as required in patent law—it must have some measure of originality. A copyright's owner has the exclusive rights to reproduce the work, to distribute it freely or by sale, rental, or lease, and to prepare derivative works based upon the copyrighted work. And copyrights are enduring; they generally exist for 70 years beyond the author's lifetime.

Unlike the lengthy process of securing a patent, a copyright is automatically vested as a legal right the *very moment* an original work is created. Copyright registration is not necessary for securing valid copyright rights. However, at times it's advisable to file an application for registration with the U.S. Copyright Office, which requires a filing fee and a copy of the work, whether published or not. This action will create a public record establishing the identity of the author(s) and the date of creation. This evidence can prove invaluable should a dispute as to authorship or originality arise. Also, a valid copyright registration is usually required before the copyright owner can enforce the rights in federal court.

An issue that relates to both copyrights and patents is the rights of ownership or possession of tangible property. In the case of tangible property, such as a machine or building, ownership includes the right of possession unless that right has specifically been transferred to another party, as by a lease. If the owner transfers the right of possession to another through sale or lease, one gains and the other loses that right of use.

The situation is fundamentally different, however, in the case of *intangible* property, such as information technology. Intellectual property in software may be transferred by sale or lease, but the original owner does not lose its copyrights. Unlike tangible property rights, intangible property rights "multiply" through reproduction. Such information, like tangible property, is protected by statutes covering rental and lease transactions and protects the owners of the information. But access security looms as a critical issue surrounding information technology because the proprietary information can so easily be duplicated and distributed. That is exactly the issue in the current debate about disseminating "free" music and other forms of art through the Internet, circumventing the rights of their creators to collect royalties.

Even though the criteria for granting a copyright registration are less stringent than for granting a patent, a copyright enjoys substantial and long protection. Just like a patent, a copyright is a monopoly but is somewhat more limited because it requires "copying" to establish infringement. And just like patent law, copyright law is constantly changing and the general law in this field varies somewhat from country to country. Never hesitate to call on your attorney for advice.

One more point on the subject of intangible property. Laws control sharing technical information and data with foreign nationals. The release of such information may require an "export of technical data license" under the Export Administration Regulations of the U.S. Department of Commerce (dual use) or the International Traffic in Arms Regulation of the Department of State (defense). Violations of these policies, whether willful or through ignorance, can result in civil penalties. And be aware that these laws apply not only to unrelated individuals or companies. If your company has operations in other countries, export of technical information laws apply *even within your company* if you share such information across national boundaries. So make sure you have sound legal advice before you begin such data sharing, even among colleagues.

SOFTWARE—COPYRIGHT OR PATENT?

If you're a software creator, you can go in two directions to protect your software code. On the one hand, you can make use of U.S. copyright, which affords protection against the literal copying of your software code: all copyrighted software is protected from unauthorized copying, thus protecting the owner's business interests in the software. Copyright can't, however, protect any of the underlying ideas or principles that support the software.

One important issue associated with copyrighted software is that of "derivative" works and improvements. A derivative work is any work that is substantially based on one or more preexisting works. Derivative works may also include the notion of improvements. Software improvements may take the form of error corrections (such as correcting "bugs" or general maintenance and improvements), additional features and enhancements, and substantial rewrites of the software that afford new features. Under federal copyright law, the owner of a preexisting copyrighted work has sole rights to prepare derivative works. For example, a customer who buys a software product may not, without permission of the licensor, legally enhance that product and then copyright and market the "new" software.

The second direction for protection is the patent. Since 1966 the U.S. Patent Office has made and enforced regulations for codifying standards for software patents. If your software is sufficiently new and inventive, it may qualify for patent protection *as well as* copyright protection. A well-drawn patent will provide significantly more protection than a copyright. For example, it will protect you from a developer who takes and implements your key and novel ideas, even if your code was not "copied" line by line. As a result of patent protection, many software developers are aggressively seeking both copyrights and patents for software code and embedded software devices.

Trademarks

A trademark, or "mark," is familiar to consumers in the form of company and brand names, slogans, and the like. The technical definition, which appears in the Trademark Act of 1946 (Section 45), "includes any word, name, symbol, or device, or any combination thereof adopted and used by a manufacturer or merchant to identify his goods and distinguish them from those manufactured or sold by others." The basic function of a trademark is to identify the origin of the product to which it is affixed. A trademark can take on several forms: real names (Midas), created names (Viagra), numbers (Channel 2), letters (ABC), slogans (When you care enough to send the very best), distinctive symbols (McDonalds' golden arches), visual forms (mascots of sports teams), product packaging (the Coca-Cola bottle) and even sounds ("This is CNN"). Its objective is to make it easy for a customer to identify the one product from among others so they can make certain judgments about its quality, value, source, or other attributes. In fact, a trademark is property—*valuable* property—and as such can legally be bought and sold. The primary distinction between a patent and a trademark is that a patent doesn't indicate origin but rather protects the inventor's rights to a new product or process, irrespective of origin. A trademark's purpose, on the other hand, is to protect origin. A recent example shows just how valuable a trademark can be. In 1998 German auto maker BMW bought the rights to the Rolls-Royce name for $66 million—considered a steal by industry analysts for one of the world's most known brand names.

Trademark registration confers a nationwide exclusive right for an individual or company to use the mark in connection with the goods or services claimed, subject to the limited rights of prior users. A registered trademark can also be recorded with the U.S. Customs Service to prevent the importation of goods bearing infringing marks. However, trademark registration isn't required to have legally protectable rights in the trademark. A company may enjoy protection for unregistered or "common law" trademarks merely because of their use and the ensuing consumer recognition of the marks. Also, the "mark" of a patent or trademark (or its patent number) should be physically attached to the product. If not, you may find it difficult to collect damages in the case of future infringement. As in all these matters, involve your patent experts whenever you're in doubt.

Trademark ownership can lead to some interesting and tough conflicts. In May 1998, just as Microsoft was preparing to unveil its Windows 98 operating system, the Patent and Trademark Office declared that the name Internet Explorer did not, in fact, belong to Microsoft but to SyNet, a defunct Chicago company that had begun using that moniker four years earlier. Microsoft argued that the name Internet Explorer is generic and therefore unprotectable, and it's simply part of the public domain. The battle of the barristers was settled shortly with all rights to the marks going to Microsoft after the company paid a substantial settlement to SyNet's owner.

A *service mark* is a kind of trademark but is used to identify the services—rather than goods—that a company provides. It may be a company name when used in the context of services offered. Thus AT&T, Ryder Truck Rental, and Manpower can be used interchangeably as trademarks or service marks, depending on the context of the message. To be protectable, a mark should be in use and must either be inherently distinctive or have acquired sufficient distinctiveness through use that consumers have come to associate the mark with a particular product line. The same federal protection associated with a trademark is afforded a service mark.

Like with patents and copyrights, trademarks enjoy legal protection. A trademark is a monopoly of sorts because it provides the owner with the exclusive right to use the mark in connection with the owner's goods. Its value is derived from its function as an assurance of the source or origin of the product bearing the mark, thereby both creating and maintaining a demand for the product.

Trade Secrets

Patents are the most common form of protection for technology's new products and processes. However, *trade secrets* offer another legitimate and effective means of market protection. A trade secret protects information on formulas, designs, systems, or compiled information, thus giving the firm or entrepreneur an opportunity to create an advantage over competitors who don't know the secret. Courts have held that a bona fide trade secret must involve information that exhibits a quantum of novelty and originality, generally unpublished, and provides a "competitive edge" over those who don't use it. Reasonable steps under the circumstances must also be taken to maintain the information as secret.

Within recent years trade secrets have enjoyed a certain degree of protection by the courts, although interpretations of trade secret law vary widely. In general, such law recognizes the organization's right to protect proprietary information from competitors, although this area of the law is still developing. In many cases the inventor has a choice whether to pursue a patent or handle the invention as a trade secret. There are times, however, when a trade secret does not qualify specifically as an invention, so trade secret protection is the only practical way to secure protection.

Regardless of the legal aspects, trade secrets can offer an attractive, practical alternative to patents and copyrights as a means of protecting proprietary information. In many cases an organization would rather avoid the time, expense, and risk involved in the more common patent procedures; consequently, it may choose instead to enshroud the project with secrecy and capitalize on it immediately, which denies competitors access to the information. After all, once a patent has been issued, the entire file accumulated during the pursuit of the patent becomes public, making all that information readily available to competitors.

As new products are developed and marketed ever faster, industrial spying has grown as well, so vigilance is essential for trade secrecy to work. Trade theft is a felonious civil or criminal offense, punishable by imprisonment. In fact, espionage technology has developed to the point where many executives are concerned about trade secret theft, and detective agencies are enjoying a growing business in safeguarding organizations from those who would steal proprietary technology. Generally, such efforts are aimed at protecting assets from outside forces, but most violations come from within—the result of carelessness or opportunistic indiscretion. Without doubt, what underlies trade secret theft is the strong technological orientation of contemporary society.

Further aggravating the security of trade secrets in R&D organizations is the lessening allegiance that technologists and executives have to their employers. The high mobility of such persons is related not only to current societal patterns but also to industrial instabilities caused by downsizing and mergers and acquisitions. R&D technologists and product developers are often parties to inside knowledge of inventions and other proprietary information; competing organizations then lure these favored individuals with offers of higher salaries and promotions.

Although a trade secret is generally considered to be a property right that's afforded some legal protection from fraudulent access by outside parties, it's quite legitimate to uncover a trade secret through the practice of *reverse engineering*. Reverse engineering, as you probably know, starts with a finished product or process and works backward in logical fashion to discover the underlying new technology. This practice is common within most industries. In the automotive industry, for example, manufacturers regularly purchase and tear down their competitors' vehicles to keep abreast of (and frequently adopt) the others' new technologies and practices and then infer the component/product costs.

Reverse engineering is part of the broader practice of competitive intelligence assessment (CIA). CIA, discussed in Chapter 7, uses any and all legitimate means to monitor and anticipate competitors' new product launches: keeping abreast of the published literature, gathering information and inferences from conferences and briefings, watching for hiring and organizational changes, and so on.

For many years employers have sought to control informational leakage to rival organizations by requiring new employees to sign nondisclosure or noncompete agreements as a condition of employment. With the implicit threat of legal action against the former employee and his or her new employer should proprietary information be leaked, these contracts probably prevent the loss of some trade secrets. Nevertheless, court interpretation of unfair competition can sometimes limit the protection that employee contracts provide. For instance, contracts don't obligate the former employee to forgo the exercise of inventive talents, even though they may be inspired by knowledge and experience gained during the performance of prior duties. In other words, the employee's skills developed in the course of employment are considered to belong to the employee and not to the former employer. Any noncompete agreement, to be enforceable, must be only for a "reasonable" period of time and for specific kinds of activity and may not unduly restrict a person from earning a living in his or her field. Ultimately, keeping good employees depends on treating them well: ethical and consistent leadership, competitive compensation, stock ownership, and job flexibility are important tools for employee retention.

9.2: Managing and Licensing Your Intellectual Property

Managing Your Intellectual Property Assets

Your arsenal of intellectual property is—or *should be*—a vital asset of your product creation process and, indeed, your entire company. In recent years the issue of intellectual property has moved from being defensively important to becoming offensively and strategically *vital*. Just like any valuable asset, intellectual property must be managed. The only issue is how.

For most companies that rely upon innovation, the answer is clear. Business managers and accountants can no longer effectively manage the innovation process by themselves. If your company counts on intellectual property to protect and advance its business, then it requires the active attention of senior management—backed up by modern information systems and patent attorneys. For example, many companies are beginning to use the developing tools of knowledge management to harness their own *tacit* knowledge—their deep insight about products and systems developed over years of trial-and-error experience. As we mentioned in Chapter 4, knowledge management is a new and promising frontier for leveraging a company's past experience to improve its future strategies.

Want another reason? Here's one that's sending chills up many a CEO's spine. Courts are now deciding that not only are novel ideas and devices protectable under patent and trademark law, but so are *business processes*. The implications of this shift could be staggering. If, in fact, a business process can be patented (providing it meets the usual standards of usefulness, novelty, and non-obviousness), then what's to stop any shop from developing novel business processes with the expectation of licensing them to established companies? And then what's to stop an established company from doing the same thing and licensing to other companies? Many small Internet startups are springing up to do just that. This issue ushers in an exciting new era of entrepreneurship in U.S. business.

Information technology is rapidly becoming tightly intertwined with business processes—processes that are built upon IT algorithms and systems and that provide a company with a valuable competitive tool. They're a form of intellectual property unique to the enterprise; therefore they are valuable. So why not patent a company's IT assets? Good question; perhaps you should! Here's another example that bears watching. At this writing, Wal-Mart is bringing action against Amazon.com, alleging theft of trade secrets. Wal-Mart accuses Amazon.com of deliberately hiring away 14 key

Wal-Mart IT professionals, thus providing Amazon.com with key information of Wal-Mart's distribution, logistics, merchandising, and data warehousing systems—all of which Wal-Mart regards as trade secrets.

Regardless of how this particular case is decided, a stream of similar suits is pouring into the courts, forcing decisions about the value of business processes as a form of intellectual capital. They raise tough questions: How do you protect your business processes from theft? How do you avoid unintentionally reinventing someone else's patented business practices? What if you knowingly reinvent an existing Internet-based process? What if, in the future, your core business process is inadvertently found to be the same as that of another company—which has already patented that process? Would that other company control your future? These are just examples of an enormously important body of issues that will be wrestled with for years to come.[5]

Here's another new twist. As mentioned earlier, software is patentable property. For years software has been regarded as an "intangible" asset, along with employee and institutional knowledge. Important, but not measurable. Now that's changing. Momentum is building to have financial statements reflect *all* costs and assets of a company, including a company's intangible assets. In fact, the Accounting Standards Executive Committee already requires that companies treat internal-use software as an asset on their balance sheets. One pioneer in this new reporting arena is the Swedish financial services company the Skandia Group. Since the early 1990s it has computed the value of intellectual property simply as the difference between a company's book value (tangible assets) and its market value. This difference is then regarded as the value of the company's intangible assets, or its intellectual capital.[6] Around the corner, expect additional reporting requirements placed on other kinds of intangible assets, such as knowledge, business processes, and intellectual wisdom.

The message here is clear. Your innovative capital is too valuable to leave entirely to middle managers. It is strategically vital; it is complex and ever changing; and it can bite you badly if you aren't on top of it. You would be wise to invest the appropriate time and talent to stay ahead of these issues.

Licensing Your Intellectual Property Assets

Intellectual property rights can be transferred outright or licensed to generate revenue for the owner of those rights. Maybe an organization can't manufacture its invention because of limited capabilities or because the invention is not compatible with existing product lines. To realize profit potential, the organization may sell or license those assets to another entity.

If an organization holds a patent on an invention and decides to manufacture and market it through a licensing agreement or series of agreements, it will recover at least part of the profit potential in royalties. Royalties are cash returns resulting from authorizing an outside organization, by license, to manufacture and sell the patented product. These income streams can be an important revenue source for large organizations, as well as for small companies with limited production capabilities. For example, Texas Instruments depends on royalties from patent licenses as part of its income. In 1997 TI made $1 billion in royalty fees; in fact, in some years it would have operated unprofitably but for such royalties.

The license agreement is a contract giving restricted (or unrestricted) exclusive (or nonexclusive) rights for a stated period of time to an outside firm to manufacture and sell an invention. Usually the license is granted in exchange for royalty payments, although other considerations and arrangements may be made. The license may be for any application of the technology covered by the patent, or it may be restricted to certain applications, such as specified products. It's vitally important to structure carefully the terms and conditions within the license agreement; they must not violate statutes such as antitrust laws. For example, a tying clause whereby the licensee is required to purchase other products from the patent holder may, in many cases, be held illegal.

Occasionally, however, a patented new product or process may have a future value that is likely to be more attractive to the company than its current value. In such cases the patent may be held until the time arrives when the technology covered by the patent is more marketable. Inventors linked to the biomedical and pharmaceutical industries use this strategy commonly.

9.3: THE FACTS CONCERNING PRODUCTS LIABILITY

An Overview of Products Liability

Of mounting concern to manufacturers and the public is liability incurred by society through the use or misuse of products. This aspect of civil law has undergone radical change, and it's important that technology managers understand how these changes in product liability might affect their own responsibilities. Although much attention is paid to consumer products, product liability questions arise often in connection with materials systems and other products of advanced technology that may not be considered a consumer product at all. This area of law is covered in part by the Uniform Commercial Code, adopted by nearly every state, and forms the basis for both product liability and warranties. This code deals with such matters as notice, damages, and warranties but does not address the question of negligence—a key element in many product liability disputes.

The history of manufacturers' product liability goes back some 4,000 years, to the kingdom of Babylon. There craftsmen who were found guilty of producing substandard wares were severely punished. However, under the principle of *caveat emptor* ("let the buyer beware"), a customer injured by a defective product was afforded no compensation. With the passage of centuries, the concept of consumer protection emerged and the notion of *caveat venditor* ("let the seller beware") began to appear in early English common law. Gradually the law developed various types of *implied warranties* making the manufacturer responsible for the product—that it's fit for the use intended—*merely because* the vendor is in that business. To remove the vagaries of the implied warranty, the express warranty (one that is stated orally or in writing) came into being. Today most express warranties are a combination of some type of promise of performance and a *guarantee*—that is, a promise of repair or refund for a defective product.

Product liability generally arises from a defect in design or manufacture or from a failure to give adequate warning about a danger that the designer, manufacturer, or seller should have foreseen. No single accepted legal definition of a defect or a defective product exists; most states and federal courts have their own unique guidelines for determining whether a product is defective. As an example of a legal definition, the Supreme Court of the state of Minnesota has generally defined a defect as "any condition not contemplated by the user which makes a product unreasonably dangerous to him; a product is not in a dangerous condition when it is safe for normal handling and consumption." This is a good "working" definition, but others range widely. Product developers ought to have an appreciation for what product liability really means and how it affects their design process.

To have a valid legal claim, the injured party must demonstrate that injury or damages resulted from negligence, under strict liability, or from breach of warranty. Under negligence, the claimant must establish, for example, that the defendant used a less than reasonable standard of care in the product's design or manufacture. Under strict liability, the claimant need only show that the product contained a defect, which was unreasonably dangerous, at the time it left the manufacturer. For a warranty claim, the claimant must show that a breach of an implied or express warranty caused the damage.

Litigation involving product liability has increased dramatically since the early 1960s and has become a major cost to industry and to society. In part this increase is due to the dollar value of the awards, which routinely are in six figures and much higher, and to the number and complexity of products and systems sold. One highly publicized case involved the death of a passenger in a 1985 Dodge Caravan when the minivan's rear-door latch allegedly failed in a low-speed crash. Although Chrysler vehemently denied any fault with the latch, a federal jury awarded the deceased's parents $250 million in punitive damages, plus actual damages. The jury found that Chrysler had withheld test studies that suggested the latch was inadequate and that the company had failed to take reasonable steps to improve the latch as subsequent test information suggested the possibility of safety shortcomings. Similar examples of hefty plaintiff awards are frequently in the news. In a recent case against GM, a jury in a state court in Los Angeles awarded a plaintiff, her children, and a friend $107 million in compensatory damages and $4.8 billion in punitive damages because a rear-end collision in 1993 resulted in her 1979 Malibu bursting into flames. Although this jury verdict may be reversed or reduced, this $4.9 billion award certainly warrants sober attention.

Courts presently are moving in the direction of holding a product defective in design if it's unfit for all uses *and abuses* that can reasonably be foreseen. In practice this attitude frequently goes hand in hand with the so-called *deep pockets* theory of tort liability: The party with the deepest pockets (that is, the most money) carries the burden of liability. However, the current trend in law is to hold that all damages suffered by the consumer or user are the responsibility of the organization that placed the product into channels of commerce. That is, those who profit are responsible.

Courts have increasingly sided against manufacturers in liability actions. As an example in 1998, the New York Court of Appeals ruled, in effect, that manufacturers can be held responsible even if a customer is injured as a result of disabling a safety device that is a part of the product. This landmark ruling involved a safety guard on a meat grinder that had been deliberately removed; the meat grinder then ravaged an operator's arm. The ruling essentially overturned a 1980 ruling that held that "a manufacturer is not liable for injuries caused by substantial alterations to the product by a third party that render the product defective or unsafe." The implications for product creators is starkly clear: You must design and manufacture so as to anticipate as many conceivable abuses and alterations of the product as possible. You must keep records of these design analyses, and you must go to lengths to attach warnings and safe-use messages to the product.[7]

Many states have enacted legislation providing for *comparative negligence*. This doctrine compares the negligence of the parties when negligence alone is the basis for recovery and when death or physical injury to persons or property is a consequence of that negligence. Under the principles of comparative negligence, any allowed damages are diminished in proportion to the amount of negligence attributable to the persons or party recovering the damages.

Creating New Products Defensively: Fault-Free Products

The best way to limit product liability litigation is to design and manufacture "fault-free" products and services. This strategy should even extend after the sale of the product or service and thereafter even beyond the product's useful life. Although this ideal standard may not always be achievable, a company can employ various methods to approach the fault-free standard.

The first step in addressing product liability exposure begins with the design of the product or system itself. In terms of product liability, the overriding design objective is to anticipate problems that might arise through reasonable use or foreseeable misuse. How might a child or adult reasonably misuse the product? What could happen if an inexperienced "handyman" tried to repair the product? What could go wrong if the product were stored improperly or exposed to the elements? A litany of such questions needs to be asked and addressed as part of the design process.

Design should be based upon accepted "best practices" and principles using verified performance data that can be reconstructed and supported at a future date. The responsibility lies squarely on the designer and on the design process to generate this kind of data and to generate permanent documentation of any data that supports those design decisions. Designers also have a responsibility to provide appropriate technical literature and safety labeling with the product, to educate the customer properly on the use and maintenance of the product or process, and to exercise diligent and timely recall practices. Another way to help avoid design problems is to maintain formal internal quality systems and to secure ISO (or QS 9000) registration from the International Standards Organization and other recognized standards bodies.

Strict adherence to standards is essential if the design is to meet minimum levels of acceptance. Standards exist in two forms: those that are generally accepted and those that are internally developed and applied. Generally accepted design standards include those that are promulgated by various professional and technical organizations: Underwriters Laboratories and its international counterparts, such as the CSA in Canada; the American Society of Mechanical Engineers; the Institute of Electrical and Electronic Engineers; the American Society of Testing and Materials; the Society of Automotive Engineers; and federal agencies that impose standards. Internally developed and implied standards are those that nearly all organizations and industry associations involved in the design of products that use new technology impose on themselves when accepted design criteria standards don't exist and the designer feels it's important to adhere to some rational standards.

For additional protection against product liability, a company can submit the design prototype to an independent testing laboratory for unbiased evaluation. Such action lends credibility to design claims and increases confidence in the design by exposing it to the critical eyes of objective, disinterested experts.

In addition to the design area, fault-free product creation is also affected by manufacturing. Therefore, a company should develop and regulate a good total-quality management system, as spelled out in Chapter 7. Such a system requires:

- Monitoring all stages of the production process in which value is added to the product.
- Both the product and the equipment used in the various stages of manufacture perform in accordance with established standards.
- Instrumentation and calibration devices used to check tolerance or performance be traceable to specification of the National Institute of Standards and Technology (NIST) or other accepted authority.
- Nondestructive inspection techniques such as ultrasonics or radiography be applied under strict adherence to standards of accepted good practice.
- Whenever the quality system discloses a problem, the company determine the root cause and then fix it.

But fault-free is the very highest standard, attained perhaps by very few. That's why a manufacturer should carry adequate liability insurance. The insurance policy should identify specifically who (individuals and/or organization) is insured thereunder and under what circumstances. As with all insurance policies, counsel must review the liability policy and then have it audited and updated regularly.

The federal government continues to write legislation that regulates products, services, and systems that the public uses. For instance, an important federal provision for consumer protection is the Magnuson-Moss Warranty Act. This act provides minimum disclosure standards for written consumer product warranties, defines minimum federal content standards for such warranties, and amends the Federal Trade Commission Act to improve consumer protection activities. Such legislation serves the dual purpose of protecting the public from faulty design or production and protecting industry from the sometimes fatally large sums awarded in damage suits. This second aspect is particularly important in high-technology industry, where exposure to lawsuits involving huge claims can and does impede technological progress by stifling innovative design.

Some believe that future legislation may well exempt producers of advanced technological systems, such as aerospace systems, from common-law recovery actions based on negligence, and will replace present laws with new ones that set definite limits on damage recovery. For example, many government R&D contracts now contain specific clauses that indemnify a contractor for any liability related to the product developed under contract. Clauses such as these tend to stimulate participation from R&D organizations that would otherwise decline to bid on certain contracts because of possible exposure to product liability litigation.

Individual Liability

Following recent trends in the medical and legal professions, a movement is afoot that holds individual technologists, design engineers, and quality specialists legally accountable for their work. Most vulnerable to liability suits are those practitioners who design systems that involve substantial capital investment and in which public safety is at stake. Structural engineers tend to carry the greatest burden because defectively designed buildings, bridges, and such put many citizens at risk. But the problem also confronts other engineering specialties, consulting firms, and research laboratories that design or provide advice to clients. Basic R&D

activities—in which applications are only potential and long-range—are largely immune.

A professional can be held accountable on the basis of two personal failings: negligence and/or incompetence. Of the two faults, *incompetence*— the lack of adequate qualifications or abilities to perform to accepted standards—is the easier to address. Nevertheless, it's difficult to prove incompetence in court except in the most blatant cases because the allegation is subjective and relative. Furthermore, internal approval of design work by a duly licensed and registered engineer virtually eliminates, in most cases, liability through incompetence. To an increasing extent, professional registration is being recognized as a definition of competence.

Negligence is more difficult to defend against. Negligence is often taken to mean anything short of the most exhaustive and exacting conformity to standards, whereas practical realities of time and cost nearly always demand some sacrifice in testing and analysis in favor of sound technical judgment. No one person can account for every specific contingency or potential anomaly in materials or for every accident of geological characteristics, environment, or other parameters with absolute assurance because nothing in life is absolutely assured. Nevertheless, in the majority of legal suits brought against engineers, some negligence has been proven to the satisfaction of the courts.

In some instances the engineer may be subject to prosecution under conditions where *strict liability* applies, which is a separate issue from the earlier mention of a company's exposure to product liability. "Strict" liability states that a professional should be held liable if the work is deficient; *there is no need to prove his or her negligence or intent.* The courts thus far have rejected strict liability in most cases involving engineering designers. However, recent trends in medical malpractice suits suggest that the door may one day be opened to strict-liability litigation in connection with technical design work.

The technologist or technology manager can defend against such claims in two general ways. The first is through more carefully worded contracts. Greater attention is being paid to current interpretations of traditional contract language. Construction engineers who are contractually required to "design and supervise" their projects and who, for reasons of cost, are limited in the amount of time they can spend in on-site supervision have been held liable for construction deficiencies that are normally considered to be the fault of the contractor. Thus, the trend has been toward replacing the wording "design and supervise" with "provide advice" to reduce the engineer's responsibility for such errors.

Other changing contract language is the "guarantee of performance." Here again, the engineer's or consultant's responsibility for backing the guarantee can be cushioned by giving the client assurance that the construction will meet specifications "to the best of the design professional's knowledge, information, and belief." In this way the client is called upon to share the burden of risk for the project with the contractor. Obviously, companies themselves remain responsible for cost-cutting actions that could be held unwise or dangerous if not justified by sound technical judgment.

The second defensive practice is to maintain thorough and orderly records, which applies not only to chronologies of technical data and calculations but also to memoranda and correspondence that can be used later to reconstruct the evolution of a project should the need arise. Where possible, a technologist should keep bound notebooks of technical results and should sign and date information when it's entered. Certified inspectors should calibrate instruments and test equipment at regular intervals, using instruments that are, in turn, traceable back to approved standards. These practices are required for ISO-9000 registrants.

Liability insurance, of course, is yet another option open to the private consultant. Unfortunately, carriers of individual professional liability insurance are few, and the costs quite high and rapidly escalating. Many individuals with potential exposure to liability litigation find that they either can't afford insurance or fail to meet eligibility criteria.

Managers of R&D enterprises whose businesses are potentially susceptible to litigation have a responsibility to inform and regularly train all staff members about such exposure, both personal and organizational. An organization needs to give serious consideration to setting up procedures or guidelines for the technical staff to reduce future legal risk. Frank discussion between management and staff will elevate overall understanding of the problem, help dispel misconceptions, and aid in creating a defensive practice posture. Meanwhile, as the entire issue of professional liability continues to develop, it's likely that the buyer of the services (usually the public at large) will assume a greater share of the risk, thus eventually lessening the burden on the profession.

Other Forms of Liability

Product liability associated with new and recalled products gets a lot of press. Ranging from children's toys to prescription drugs, product recalls are matters of strong public interest and concern. Consumers have little tolerance for a product that doesn't function as advertised, much less for a product that may create harm. However, other types of liability can also occur with products that may not cause physical injury but still corrupt a product's own integrity. Even here consumers are becoming more strident in their insistence that the product perform as advertised.

A very visible example is Intel's introduction, in 1994, of its new 64-bit Pentium microprocessor. At that time Intel was the world's largest producer of such devices, which were used largely for personal computers. The debacle that unfolded is instructive not so much because the product may have been lacking in design or testing, but because management failed to act swiftly and appropriately.

Just before the Pentium product was launched, a college professor experimenting with the product noticed that the division algorithm, which calculated quotients, had a flaw. Under a very rare and specific condition, dividing by a near-integer number could produce a completely incorrect result. He went public with his discovery. Intel responded by rationalizing that most applications were spreadsheet applications, which typically do not use floating-point divisions, and therefore computational problems generally would not occur. The company claimed its tests indicated that the "average" application would encounter an error only once in some 27,000 years of use (although IBM's tests put estimates at once every 24 days).

Intel decided to market the chip anyway, without even announcing the problem. Soon after launch, however, word was leaked widely in the press, and Intel then adopted a policy of replacing the flawed chip with a correct one *under the condition* that the applications intended by the particular user were such that the bad chip might provide faulty answers. Users angrily responded that such a policy was unfair; if they purchased a computer with a Pentium microprocessor, they had a right to a machine that would work correctly regardless of the intended applications. Ultimately, public opinion persuaded Intel to withdraw its caveat and simply exchange every flawed device with a corrected one at the request of any and all customers. Listening to and following the voices of Intel's customers averted what could have escalated to a product liability.

In general, manufacturers of component parts—like Intel—may be liable for problems arising from foreseeable uses of their products, including lost profits, and the consequences that may arise from incorrect designs. Intel failed to initiate a "crisis management" approach to the problem the minute it was found, which quickly turned into a public relations disaster. By deliberately taking a course that created concern and anxiety among its computer-maker customers (such as IBM, HP, Gateway, Dell, and Compaq), not to mention its end customers, Intel couldn't easily alter that course. However, because it soon acted decisively and correctly, Intel was able to recover from what might have been a debilitating loss of customer confidence and resulting sales and market share.

9.4: ANTITRUST LAW: WHAT YOU DON'T KNOW CAN (REALLY!) HURT YOU

All those involved in new product creation must understand the basics of antitrust regulations. Those who don't could find themselves in a stew like the following: Some of the officers of the Archer Daniel Midland Company, a major producer of basic foodstuffs, found themselves under federal indictment for alleged price fixing—agreeing with competitors to set price levels on certain worldwide products. In July 1999 two senior executives, Michael Andreas and Terrance Wilson, were sentenced to two-year prison sentences in addition to hefty fines. The cost to the company, its image, and its senior leadership, not to mention $100 million in fines, was huge. The tragedy is that such blunders can be avoided altogether if people are alert to the rules and implications of antitrust law and take them very, very seriously.

An early cornerstone of U.S. antitrust law is the Sherman Act of 1890, which prohibits all kinds of anticompetitive conspiracy agreements, price-fixing agreements between competitors, unlawful monopolies, and agreements that otherwise would unreasonably restrain trade. The purpose of this and subsequent antitrust laws is to promote consumer welfare through competition, by prohibiting conspiracies in restraint of trade, undue restrictions on purchasers, and other anticompetitive practices. The intent is to provide quality goods at the lowest possible cost. Some examples of practices that are illegal under the Sherman Act are bid rigging, allocation of sales territories, agreements on production levels among competitors, and other collusive practices. In the years since the Sherman Act, the federal government has enacted additional laws to extend and clarify protections against predatory and collusive practices. These laws include:

- The Federal Trade Commission Act of 1914, which prohibits unfair methods of competition and unfair or deceptive acts or practices.

- The Clayton Antitrust Act of 1914, which prevents exclusive dealing, tie-in arrangements, and mergers and acquisitions that diminish competition; this act thereby tied up certain loopholes in the Sherman Act and permits civil suits for up to treble damages for antitrust violations.
- The Robinson-Patman Act of 1936, which restrains companies from discriminating among their customers by price discounts, special terms or services, or other means.

In what surely was the most closely followed antitrust trial in anyone's memory, Microsoft aggressively defended its dominant position in the computer industry. The essence of the government's case was that Microsoft conspired to create a near-monopoly by tying its Web browser to its dominant Windows operating system software. And in a larger sense the federal government accused Microsoft of practicing a broad pattern of anticompetitive behavior—by using its clout to defend its monopoly of the PC software business. Bill Gates and his legal team made a simple argument: Microsoft had the right to develop its software in any way it wished to serve its customers. The operating system and the browser, Microsoft said, necessarily were so intertwined that they couldn't be unbundled without weakening Windows itself. And there were competitive threats, including Linux and Java, that Microsoft needed to blunt for their shareholders' interests. An expert testifying on behalf of the prosecution, however, argued there was no technical reason that Windows and the browser had to be intertwined and that he, in fact, had successfully unbundled the two with no operational penalty. In November 1999 a U.S. District Court judge issued his findings of fact that Microsoft was indeed guilty of anticompetitive behavior. The final resolution of this epic case may take years.

Compliance with the Federal Trade Commission—and Related Laws

The word "conspiracy" is one you don't want associated with your good name. A conspiracy is any kind of unlawful expressed agreement or implicit understanding between two or more companies or their employees. For example, two employees from competing companies might meet one day to discuss specific price increases and the next week actually increase their prices by that amount. Even though no explicit agreement might have been drawn up to raise prices, these employees and their companies might be found guilty of engaging in a price-fixing conspiracy simply on the evidence of their behavior. Furthermore, certain types of agreements, *per se* agreements, always and by definition violate the antitrust laws. Such agreements are *"per se* unlawful," that is, unlawful without any further proof than that some form of a proscribed agreement was reached. Other agreements that are not *per se* unlawful may be held illegal if they are found to promote anticompetitive ends. The bottom line is that conspiracy charges, if proven true, can separate you from your loved ones and your lifestyle for a very long time.

All companies, and officers and employees thereof, must be acutely aware of the risks attendant to violating antitrust laws, however unintended. In particular, employees in a position to deal with competitors or customers must be knowledgeable and sensitive to the following issues:

- No company may use its dominant market position to monopolize a market, control prices, or exclude competitors.
- Competitors may not even *discuss*, let alone agree on:

  Prices they charge for products or services, or the terms of sale
  Prices they pay for products or services
  Cooperation with each other by allocating customers, territories, or markets or by "rigging" bids
  Joining together in boycotting suppliers or customers to accomplish anticompetitive ends.

Conspiracies to restrain free competition are taken very seriously by the federal government. Indeed, individuals found guilty of violating federal antitrust laws are subject to imprisonment and large fines. Competition is the basis for a free-enterprise economic system, and antitrust violations subvert free enterprise by limiting competition. Conspiracies corrupt the system, thereby injuring producers, customers, and the public at large.

Your company should emphasize and continually reinforce the importance of scrupulous compliance with antitrust laws. Companies' interests are best served if they go beyond mere full compliance with the relevant antitrust and competition laws; in addition, they should consciously avoid any and all practices that may give even the perception of overstepping antitrust laws. Even though their practices may not be unlawful in and of themselves, by raising even a misperception of wrongdoing, they expose themselves to an unnecessary risk of litigation and loss of public goodwill.

Of course, antitrust law has many gray areas, and it's in these areas that businesspeople must be able to operate with some latitude, albeit carefully and with sound legal advice. Some common issues are:

- Mergers and acquisitions: M&As often must be cleared with the Department of Justice and/or the Federal Trade Commission to ensure they do not exceed anticompetitive guidelines. If the companies proceed despite opposition from the attorney general's office, they expose themselves to serious federal charges.
- Meeting competitive prices: Such practices are often permissible, but competitive and counteroffers must be documented to protect against charges of violating provisions of the Robinson-Patman Act.
- Unfair competition: The line separating vigorous from unfair competition is often vague. Reducing prices is generally legal, yet predatory pricing—reducing prices below profitability with the intent of driving a competitor out of business—and other practices will likely be held illegal.

The most certain way to avoid exposure to antitrust violations is to promote vigorous competition at all times. Any kind of explicit or implicit agreements with competitors are to be *absolutely* avoided. Company employees and agents must be sensitive to situations that can lead to forbidden behavior.

For example, it is very common for representatives of competing companies to come together in meetings of standards-setting organizations and professional societies and at trade shows and conventions. Especially during these times, they must be attentive not to discuss, even casually at the bar, such topics as prices or price multipliers, terms or conditions of sale, costs, profits or profit margins, market share, selection, rejection or termination of distributors, distribution policies or practices, bids or bid intentions, or sales territories. On the other hand, competitors can legally pool certain kinds of information to develop industry standards and conduct joint R&D programs and certain other forms of cooperation. Even here, however, it's wise to have an attorney involved to ensure no antitrust laws are being abrogated. Competing companies may also provide their industry association with sensitive information for it to compile industry-wide information on markets, sales, and so forth, so long as the association keeps the raw-source data proprietary.

Good practice dictates that the agenda for association meetings be written and distributed to everyone in advance and that meetings be restricted to proper topics. Here also the company's attorney should review the agenda before such a meeting, and the attorney ought to be kept constantly informed about trade association, industry, or special interest groups and get-togethers that company employees attend. As a matter of policy, a company ought to limit its membership and participation in association activities to that which are essential for legitimate business purposes.

The entire area of antitrust law is growing larger and more complex. Moreover, with the rapid expansion of international business, it's more important than ever for companies to take seriously any appearance they may give of compromising U.S. or other jurisdictional law.

9.5: IDEAS FOR ACTION

1. Place the responsibility of managing your intellectual property processes and assets directly in the hands of an officer-level executive who can use them to advance your company's strategic position.
2. Establish a continuing program whereby those responsible for new product creation are exposed to the relevant aspects of intellectual property, products liability, and antitrust law.
3. If you don't already have one, develop a patent strategy and related policies for your product lines. This strategy should address the annual level and scope of patent activity you require to make use of both offensive and defensive tactics that will maximize your scope of claims and to defeat those of competitors. Also, establish your position on foreign patenting and define the role of trade secrecy and licensing in your business. Identify your process for competitive products analysis.
4. Make sure you have the right level of legal capability (in house or outsourced; attorneys and agents) to service your ongoing needs, both corporately and in your business units.
5. Think about how to measure, year over year, your exploitation of investments in intellectual property and your costs of product liability. Use the concepts of "cost of quality" (Chapter 7) as an overall model, and benchmark patent practices among your industry leaders.
6. Develop a strategy to advance your business by licensing your intellectual property.
7. Evaluate whether your copyrights and trademarks are being adequately protected and enforced.
8. Make sure your engineers and product developers regularly chronicle and archive their technical work; a clear development record could be essential when and if litigation occurs.

9. Reward and recognize those who secure patents. Look to companies that highly value patent production and what kind of recognition they bestow.
10. Make intellectual property assessment a formal part of your product development process by requiring a legal review of the risks and opportunities in connection with product launch.
11. Promote the notion of fault-free products to all involved in new product creation.
12. Take the necessary steps to reduce trade secrecy leaks within your company.
13. Make sure your company is properly represented on standards-setting committees that are key to your principal product lines.

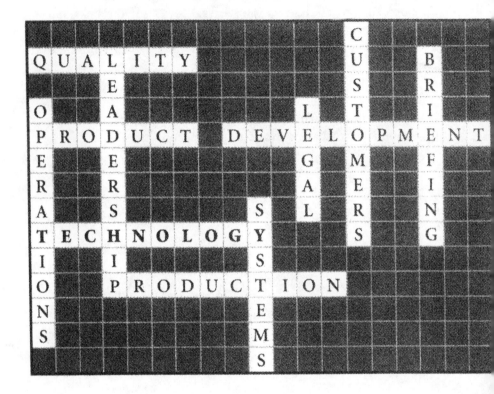

Chapter 10

Harnessing Your R&D and Emerging Technologies

Now we come to the final spoke in our metaphor of the waterwheel. There's a certain irony in using an ancient machine for discussing modern technologies and how they contribute to product creation. Surely if engineers were to build a large-scale waterwheel today, it would be quite different from those of our ancestors. It would be much more efficient in converting water power to other forms of energy. It would be more reliable because of modern built-in quality standards. It would be easier to repair and to adjust for variations in water conditions and the different kinds of work it is to perform. Undoubtedly it would be less labor-intensive to construct—more cost-effective. And it would look good—to our contemporary eye.

Of course, it was simpler in centuries past. Then village leaders saw the need for irrigation and for producing foodstuffs, found a nearby river, and put two and two together. Necessity being the mother of invention, those original civil engineers went about building machines that could harness water power to help control nature and feed growing populations. Today your R&D people are helping create valuable products by designing them to be produced more efficiently using modern tools and industrial technology. When R&D is done right, everyone wins. Your company reaps the direct rewards, sure, but indirectly so does the world.

The difference between ancient water-power machines and today's power-generating equipment can be compared with the space between today's product technology and your planning horizon. Today you're concerned with the gap between today's product and the competitive edge you might gain by adopting technologies just on the horizon. Similarly, our forefathers toiled to build machines that would harness water power to help them control nature's water supply, feed growing populations, and provide other necessities. Is it really so different today? In both eras we harness our industrial technologies to improve living standards and to secure our liberties.

In this chapter I'll look at two closely related matters: how R&D can be managed and made more effective and how to evaluate and place your bets on the technologies just ahead on the horizon, technologies that could—and surely will—shape your future products.

In early 1999 the *Wall Street Journal* published the results of a poll taken by some 1,000 scientists and other prominent techno-thinkers.[1] The purpose was to have these distinguished ladies and gentlemen determine the most important inventions of the past 2,000 years. The roster included such innovations as the mirror, space travel, the concepts of zero and the calculus, electricity, double-entry accounting, reading glasses, the steam engine, and the atomic bomb. It also included such unusual entries as board games, the philosophy of skepticism, distillation, and erasers. Who among those living in earlier times could possibly have envisioned their impact on the world? Now we stand in our ancestors' shoes. We know that today's advancements, ranging from molecular biology to space exploration, will surely reshape our future. We just can't see exactly how.

10.1: MANAGING R&D

Research and development is essential to any company whose destiny depends upon offering better products and services. And that's just about every industrial organization. The issue is not *whether* R&D but *how*—how to make R&D a flexible and responsive function. Whatever R&D's past mission was, it must now become actively engaged in building the business. How can it evolve to drive innovation throughout the entire organization? How can it forge intimate linkages with customers? How can it foster sustainable growth and competitive advantage? These far-reaching questions need answers. R&D's agenda must be broader and tougher than merely innovating and designing. In Chapter 8 I discussed how to *measure* your R&D processes; here we'll examine how to *manage* your R&D assets.

R&D is probably the most controversial link in the new product delivery chain. Although it's heralded as the means that creates America's industrial might and puts technology to work, it's also vilified as a kind of rudderless ship: slow, lacking focused goals, and needlessly expensive. To some extent all these characterizations are valid. But if R&D is a rudderless ship, it's too often because senior management doesn't have its hand on the tiller. R&D must be appropriately chartered, effectively led, and efficiently executed if it is to be an engine for growth and real, sustained benefits.[2] Only two issues should guide your research and development investments: *what* projects you should pursue and *how* you should manage the R&D your company needs.

R&D comes in both basic (or "pioneering") and applied flavors. Basic research is aimed at discovery and often results in inventions and utility patents. However, this type of basic R&D is risky and it's long-term. Few companies today truly engage in basic research; even those known for technological discovery all have definite business objectives for their R&D investments. Other than a few giants, such as Lucent's Bell Labs and IBM, few companies conduct basic research. Most of today's basic R&D is conducted within universities, in federal laboratories, or in various consortia wherein participating companies share costs and risks. And even here, projects are much more sharply focused and goal-oriented than in former times. The days of freewheeling scientific inquiry to support product creation are almost entirely gone. What's taken over is applied R&D—the clever application of known technology to a new product or process. Today's applied research, even when risky, produces more technology breakthroughs that did the basic research of yore.

Hewlett-Packard's H-P Labs well illustrates this trend toward more discipline in R&D programs. At one time the labs were credited with real breakthroughs, enabling the development of the first pocket calculator and ink-jet and laser printers. But over the past two decades scientists there have been laboring to make only incremental contributions. Recently, however, HP has taken steps to use its R&D assets for creating a science base that will provide a competitive advantage in the years ahead. It has targeted two key business areas for the future: digital photography and nano-technology—for building atomic-scale circuit elements that might lead to the much-hyped "ubiquitous computing" environment. This Web-based personal platform may one day integrate technology with our own person as we go about our daily routine. H-P Labs is seeking *breakthroughs* today that will enable such an environment tomorrow.[3]

So focused, applied research is the overwhelming reality. Here's how you can manage within this environment, harness technology effectively and profitably, and redirect a lethargic R&D to become a muscular process.

10.2: DEVELOPING YOUR CORE COMPETENCIES

Begin by paying close attention to your "core competencies"—those that are essential to your company's strength and competitiveness. Core competencies are very specific, well-drawn areas of vital skills and unusual competence—your company jewels. They enable your company to compete effectively in its principal markets. Both technical and nontechnical, core competencies may take the form of product technologies, design tools, manufacturing process art and technologies, and customer and market applications. All these dimensions, when integrated with internal business systems and distribution, are potentially the most valuable assets you have to sustain your position in a highly competitive market.

Properly managed, core competencies become the highway to your company's future. Some familiar examples of companies that have widely acknowledged core competencies are:

Technology —Canon, Hewlett-Packard, IBM, Xerox
Sales and marketing—Kmart, Sears
Customer care—Nordstrom, Caterpillar, Harley-Davidson
Quality—Motorola, AT&T, Ford, GE
New product development—3-M, Kodak, Sharp, Sony

There are three basic truths about core competencies. First, they ought not to be associated with any one particular business unit or product line. Real core competencies should apply to and influence *all* products and services of the enterprise. They enable future generations of products and services, and gaining or losing a core competence can have a very significant effect on a company's future. So protect them all.

Second, core competencies can't be shared or outsourced without undermining their essential value to your company. Think of them as your own trade secrets—indeed, they are. And third, companies that understand the importance of their core competencies often leverage them, through marketing messages, to separate themselves from their competitors. There are many such familiar messages: "Quality is Job #1," "All the News That's Fit to Print," "We Bring Good Things to Life." These are more than ordinary tag lines; they're powerful, subliminal messages that remind us about the distinctive value of a company's products and services—about, in other words, its core competencies.

In terms of technology, core competencies fall into three categories. These competencies are necessary to ensure a company's future, and allow companies to determine which technology investments are strategic, which are risky, and which are proprietary. It's helpful to understand their distinctions:[4]

Pacing Technologies: Those technologies that have the potential to change fundamentally the basis of competition but have not yet been reduced to practice. Pacing technologies may develop into key technologies (below). As examples, think digital wireless communication; think ultra-high-speed computing.

Key Technologies: Those that are most essential to competitive success because they offer valuable product differentiation possibilities. Sometimes called "dynamic," key technologies are vulnerable to quick obsolescence, potentially putting the enterprise at risk As examples, think low-cost polymer and sintered metal replacements for machined parts; think proprietary process technologies.

Base Technologies: Those that are needed regularly but offer little potential for competitive advantage because they are well known and widely used. As examples, think high-yield production technologies; think rapid order-to-delivery systems.

Gary Hamel and C. K. Prahalad[5] demonstrate how to think strategically about core competencies. Figure 10.1 looks at strategy in terms of markets, type, and the "maturity" of the particular core competencies involved. The horizontal axis identifies the nature of the market, from established to new or emerging. The vertical axis measures core competencies on a similar scale. Therefore, the lower-left quadrant shows how existing competencies might be exploited to protect or grow present markets. An example is sewing in the garment industry. By contrast, the upper-right quadrant brings attention to opportunities for developing new core competencies— those that might be vital to capturing market share in totally new product or service markets. Example: digital groupware products. The two "off-axis" quadrants address conditions wherein the nature of markets and competencies do not match. For example, in the lower right, the opportunity is to leverage existing competencies to apply to new, future markets— those that a company might, in fact, pioneer. Example: digital photography. The upper-left quadrant, on the other hand, asks what new competencies should be explored that might further protect or enlarge current market share. Example: online e-commerce publishing. This useful "two-by-two" mental image will help you think about R&D, technology, and market strategies.

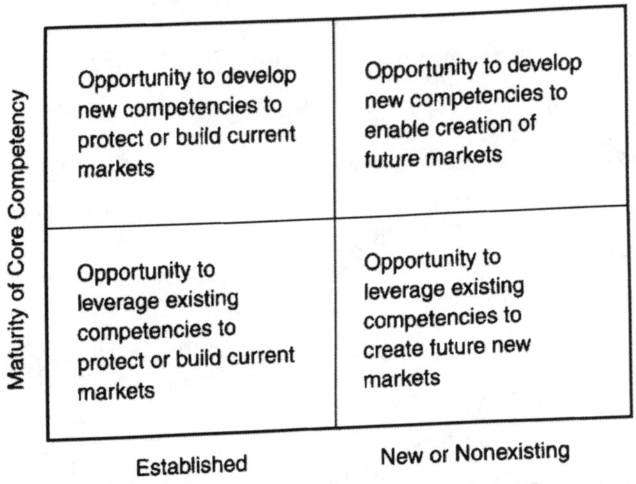

Opportunity to develop new competencies to protect or build current markets	Opportunity to develop new competencies to enable creation of future markets
Opportunity to leverage existing competencies to protect or build current markets	Opportunity to leverage existing competencies to create future new markets

Maturity of Core Competency

Established   New or Nonexisting

FIGURE 10.1   STRATEGIES FOR LEVERAGING CORE COMPETENCIES

Competitive intelligence, which few companies do really well, is a companion element to technology strategy. I'll refer you to Chapter 7 for details. However, some companies are elevating one aspect of competitive intelligence—the time-honored practice of "reverse engineering" (see Chapter 9)—to support product strategy proactively. They would do even better to broaden this approach by having internal processes that constantly monitor changes in what their competitors are doing—in their organization, acquisitions, leadership, investments for new technologies, new product lines, and so on. By knowing as much in advance as possible about the way your competitors conduct business, you can exploit that knowledge early and strategically. Competitive intelligence assessment may not be among your core competencies, but it certainly should be used and tied to your business strategy.

10.3: MAKING R&D WORK FOR YOU

How do you actually go about improving your R&D operations? It's instructive to see what top R&D leaders actually worry most about. The annual poll by the Industrial Research Institute showed in 1999 that the four top problem issues of their 275 member companies were:

1. How to manage R&D for business growth
2. How to focus and balance among long-term/short-term R&D objectives

3. How to integrate technology planning with business strategy
4. How to create and sustain innovation

These factors were of most concern also to Japan's leading industrial companies and heavily outweighed the many others on the list.

If these are the key questions, then what are the answers? Here is what I've found to be most effective. First, regardless of how R&D is organized across your company, have an involved, interested, and savvy senior executive oversee and "own" the entire R&D organization. Suppose this person is you—you become your company's R&D champion. You don't necessarily have to come from a background in R&D, and you *shouldn't* be an active "techy." Rather, you should function as friend, critic, mentor, and leader. Without that level of oversight, I can guarantee you're wasting a good share of your R&D multiple.

As the executive in charge of R&D, you'll understand that your unit's success depends on the following nine management factors.

1. Portfolio Management

Depending on the nature of your company, your oversight and ownership may include the management of your new product portfolio—spelled out in Chapter 2. Make sure you have a disciplined and competitive process for authorizing new R&D projects. Honestly estimate the expected payback or equivalent return from each authorized project and how risk plays into such estimates. How will your projects translate into new or existing products and services? The resulting portfolio should support the overall business strategy and should reflect a balance between "bottom-up" and "top-down" projects. And make sure tension occurs among competing internal interests: there should be competition for funding and a balance in the portfolio that reflects both the product and service technology requirements. Value your projects not just in terms of what is to be done, but where and by whom. Can the project benefit from participation by your suppliers, customers, or external partners? Who is responsible for taking the result of the project results to commercialization?

Another point about portfolio management: no matter how diverse, the projects in your new product development portfolio must have one thing in common—they must *all* be customer-friendly. Provide products and services that are as simple, safe, robust, and technically transparent to your customers as possible; strive to create "humane technologies." You may find this goal difficult to reach, especially with truly new technologies, but you must try. Recall in the early 20th century that auto owners needed to be mechanics to deal with the idiosyncrasies of fitful engines and flat tires. Early airlines needed nurses aloft to minister to passengers made nauseated from buffeting in small, low-altitude aircraft. The same can be said today for personal computers and other communications devices. Too many users need some kind of training to get real use from them, yet the overwhelming majority of new products are based upon well-known, marginally improved technologies. Your Aunt Nellie should be just as competent in using your products as your whiz-kid nephew.

Mindful of the need for humane technology in personal appliances, computers, and networks, Sun Microsystems and Microsoft are engaged in a leadership battle for domination of tomorrow's communications environment. Sun is betting on moving PC technology into consumer devices through intelligent networks. CEO Scott McNealy sees Java as becoming the common language medium that will provide seamless access to enormous stores of information and services—voice, video, text, and data—resident on its network. But Microsoft is attacking Sun's Achilles heel: that every device would have to have a Java platform—software that today requires significantly more memory than many consumer devices have. Instead, Microsoft's Bill Gates is betting on standardizing and using device interfaces so that special networks aren't needed. I'm betting that the most customer-friendly product will win in the end.

2. Corporate R&D

Planning and coordination must occur between the central or "corporate" R&D function, if any, and the R&D that individual business units fund directly. Indeed, corporate R&D can deliver real value and can contribute importantly to R&D productivity and yield measures. The corporate lab also is the ideal venue for skunk-works projects—those high-risk, high-reward projects that are best pursued in secrecy.

3. Boosterism

As mentioned earlier, R&D programs can be effective only if they are properly aligned with strategy, effectively led, and carefully organized to do what can't be efficiently done within individual business units. This underscores the need for an R&D advocate. Part of that role is to communicate R&D's challenges and successes to all interested constituencies—certainly including the CEO, the board, the stakeholders, and the shareholders.

4. Outside Partnering

As part of your portfolio management responsibility, look outside your company's walls and seek other sources of R&D expertise. The place to start is with your suppliers. Not only do suppliers have a vested interest in your company's future, but they often have technical resources that complement its needs. By partnering with them in the R&D arena, you create mutual dependencies that can further advance your relationships.

Other sources are out there as well. Increasingly, colleges and universities are reaching out to industrial and service sectors for research funding. These grant or contract R&D arrangements can be beneficial because they can bring up-to-date, highly focused technologies to bear on your requirement. But such arrangements need to be carefully evaluated, coordinated, and monitored if they are to fulfill your expectations. Partnering with selected schools that have solid technology assets can be very helpful—they are not only a technical resource but also a source of future employees. Moreover, industry and government consortia are additional sources for technology information and intelligence. And make sure your company is represented in those associations that ultimately have regulatory authority over your new products.

5. Project Funding

Next, pay attention to how your projects are chartered and funded. As discussed in Chapter 2, R&D projects should have to compete for funds. Their objectives should be clear and precise and include measurable objectives, goals, and timelines.

6. Board of Advisors

Consider creating an oversight function to review periodically and recommend measures to improve your R&D operations. I've seen it work effectively with external boards and with inside committees. The main objective of such a board is to advise on and recommend improvement processes and sometimes technologies. Also, such a body can play a role as advocate and buffer between you—the R&D head—and your direct report. As with any such initiative, I don't recommend it unless it's well planned, coordinated, and given the necessary time and attention.

7. Customer Face-Time

By *all* means, put every one of your R&D people in front of customers. No exceptions. And I don't mean occasionally—do it frequently. I recommend that initially 20 percent of each person's time be spent with customers, and then more! And I don't just mean just internal customers. Involve your R&D people with external customers, stakeholders in the R&D process, and stakeholders in your products. Coordination with internal customers is important, but external customers are your future.

8. Organization

Pay attention to the organizational dynamics of your R&D, both internal and external. Internally, if you have a central R&D lab, organize it around your core technologies and technical areas, not the markets you serve; it's the product development groups that ought to have first-line connections to your customers. Think through your needs for internal or corporate-sponsored R&D, as distinguished from R&D for direct product and process support. If your company is investing, say, 5 percent or more of sales in R&D, consider funneling a small portion of that investment into a corporate R&D program that supports your core technologies and that develops fertile ideas for your company's future. This program may be especially valuable if your company genuinely pursues a technology leadership strategy that ensures technology excellence across all business units. But if these conditions are not part of your culture and strategy, forget it; you'll be wasting resources.

Also, try creating communications for all your R&D associates. For instance, set up a special chat room on your intranet or hold an annual technology seminar where people can present ideas and accomplishments and—most important—become and stay connected. I've found mechanisms of this sort to be truly valuable. And honor those who create your patents. Motorola has an annual worldwide patent awards event—black tie, dinner, dancing—for all its patent winners and their guests, at which the CEO personally congratulates each employee and distributes the awards. Now *that* makes a statement!

Another point about internal organization. Along with your human resources executive, look carefully at the career paths for people in R&D. Although organizations have tried various kinds of "dual ladder" approaches, most have had mixed or poor results. However, it doesn't mean you shouldn't try. Better yet, provide an opportunity for those R&D people who want to move into other operations or staff functions. Don't overlook them.

9. Project Management

Finally, the strength of your R&D operations depends upon the project management skills of everyone, including you. In too many companies project management is just assumed as something that comes with experience. Not true. I urge that *all* people engaged in R&D be trained in the tools and leadership approaches of project management—from the ABCs for junior people and for narrowly focused scientists, to fairly comprehensive and continuing training for those in charge of managing substantial projects and programs.

I've recommended to some companies that they create a "Project Management Council" that will achieve two important goals. First, this insider council formally identifies project managers and elevates their status as leaders among peers. Second, it creates an ongoing dialogue among these leaders about challenges, new areas of knowledge, and improved coordination. Properly chartered and led, this council can bring many rewards to your new product creation programs. In fact, for some companies project management is regarded as a core competency.

10.4: Why You Should Scan Tomorrow's Technologies Today

Thus far this chapter has focused on leading your R&D programs and centers toward excellence. Here I'll complete the R&D picture by discussing the new technologies themselves. Some among them might play an important role in your company's competitive future. New technology may not *be* your business, but it's certainly an important component. Future requirements and opportunities will influence your business, so to anticipate their impacts today and capitalize upon their promise tomorrow, you need to be the driver, not the passenger.

But first, a disclaimer. Forecasting new technologies is risky business. Legendary filmmaker Samuel Goldwyn admonished "never prophesize, especially about the future." Sam was right: It's perilous to assess how technological innovations can influence—for good or bad—your business future. Technology advances are fraught with the many uncertainties that shape all future market needs. Therefore, developing technology-related strategy further out than the near term is speculative at best.

Expectations can be set too high. Remember when having domestic robots cleaning our homes was right around the corner? Ultimately, customers will set the product agenda, not necessarily what technology can deliver. History teaches repeatedly that most significant developments come about spontaneously through the chaotic combination of needs and technologies, not by deliberative evolution. And that same serendipity will continue to manage the future. Pundits can predict with some confidence just how much more powerful and cost-effective today's technologies will be tomorrow, but they really can't reliably foresee just what societies will do with them. Yet companies can and should stay on top of today's evolutionary technologies to take advantage of them.

Here's one technology forecast that is useful in framing new product opportunities. In 1999 engineers and scientists at Battelle Labs in Columbus, Ohio, came up with their top 10 technological challenges facing industry during the first decade of the new millennium:

1. Affordable home-based health care
2. Consumer-demand personalized products
3. Home-based technology use for work, education, entertainment
4. Environmental protection to manage resources
5. Human interfaces for technology-based products and services
6. Nutritional health for all the world's peoples
7. Mobile energy sources for rapid communications and for the automobile industry
8. Microsecurity—personal and community
9. Infrastructure renewal
10. Global business competition

This is a good list, reflective of society's general needs. However, you need to develop your own list, specific to your company. In the process you'll encounter visionaries who will tell you of blockbuster technologies that will propel your company to a better future. But beware of such prophets. Seers who forecast long-term innovations tend to be wrong, but by then nobody remembers. On the other hand, those who look at the near horizon are more likely to be right, to no one's surprise.

Looking at those specific technologies that likely will have very significant influence in molding your future valuable products means setting aside a wide assortment of technologies that, although important, will probably have only marginal influence on new product development. Rather, I'll mention only some specific technologies that hold potential for supporting better NPD. In particular I won't talk about genetics, brain technology, neurochips, biochemistry, environmentalism, and other areas of science and technology that surely will have profound effects on society in the decades ahead.

Moreover, I'll not indulge in any of the "gee whiz" technologies whose applications probably lie outside the application of new product development. That list is long—too long to cover completely. Instead, I'll limit the scope to those areas that are likely to be the bread-and-butter foundations for your products and services in the years ahead. This is a good list (if I do say so myself) and sets an agenda for broad-based thinking about creating future valuable products.

So much for my disclaimers. Here's my list of technology areas to watch that may have application to technology challenges and to your business:

The Landscape Before Us: Technologies You Need to Watch

Advanced Materials and Materials Sciences

- New kinds of electronic materials can now be engineered using super-computers in conjunction with lasers to lay down atoms in specific patterns. These thin-film deposition technologies (chemical vapor deposition and molecular beam epitaxy) will be able to create certain materials with properties "made to order."
- The economic law of superconducting is simple: the higher the temperature at which a material superconducts (flows with no energy losses), the more valuable the material. Bulk superconducting materials are now operating at temperatures above 75 deg. K (about −200 deg. C or about −325 deg. F) and will soon economically challenge conventional electrical distribution systems, possibly leading to reduced size and cost of motors and generators.
- New classes of polymers are being synthesized by rearranging carbon, oxygen, hydrogen, and nitrogen atoms to produce materials that can

conduct electricity, dissolve in sunlight, and carry light waves. One application: display screens that use polymer devices rather than conventional electronics. The result: screens that can be applied to curved surfaces or even rolled up when not in use.

- Photovoltaic cells hold great promise for many low-energy applications, ranging from sensors to lighting. These cells produce and can store direct electric current when exposed to sunlight. They require no fuel, are nonpolluting, and can last for decades.

Communications
- Networks of high-capacity, wireless data transmission from advanced satellites will play an ever-increasing and important role in making telephony available to all six billion citizens of this planet. It will also enhance business communications and geophysical relationships.
- Fiber optics are a hundredfold improvement over copper wire for transmitting information—along with having many other benefits: they're impervious to temperature extremes, corrosion, and electrical noise, and system upgrades can be made through the sender and receiving units, not the optical cable. Now wavelength division multiplexing (WDM) shows promise of greatly increased optical communications that can feed the world's insatiable appetite for bandwidth. Moreover, this technology can be achieved with the existing fiber-optic cable infrastructure across the land and under the sea. It will soon permit, for example, the widespread use of two-way voice/video communication.
- Personal communications appliances will evolve to perform a limited number of functions exceptionally well, in contrast to today's personal communicator device platforms, which do many things somewhat well. Getting there will require an infrastructure that can deliver services to customers using a variety of devices, such as cellular phones, PCs, personal assistants, and spontaneous videoconferencing. The development of "proxy" servers will allow for translating information from one format to another. The goal: freely accessing and exchanging voice, data, and video anywhere, anytime, with anyone.
- Interactive speech recognition that's indistinguishable from the human voice has long been just beyond our reach. But now it's just around the corner and soon will become a commodity product available for enhancing all sorts of new products.

Management Support Tools
- Knowledge management, presently little more than a consultant's buzzword, will become a powerful force in building tomorrow's organizations. KM offers enormous potential for capturing and retrieving tacit and explicit experience and applying it to build stronger company cultures and develop more effective relationships with customers. KM will truly revolutionize management systems and organizational efficiency.
- Modeling and simulating business processes could become much more powerful with further development of complexity theory (when chaotic systems organize themselves into well-ordered states—like bird flocks) and adaptive software agents (software icons imbued with basic decision-making abilities). Also, basic work now under way in understanding biological models that mimic the self-governing and learning techniques of complex organisms could show better ways of managing large, complex organizations. Developing business planning within this virtual world offers the possibility of more accurately predicting buying behavior, marketing effectiveness, and the consequences of implementing certain business strategies. It will free managers from traditional cut-and-try approaches based on econometrics and operations research. And it's already happening. One pioneer is the U.S. West and PricewaterhouseCoopers collaboration to predict customer and competitor behavior in response to various pricing and marketing programs. Another is Macy's program that improved its retail layouts to facilitate consumer clustering and more effective buying behavior.

Micro/Nano Technologies
- The field of micromechanics is advancing very rapidly and will enable new kinds of products that depend upon tiny mechanisms, such as accelerometers, force and pressure transducers, and surgical tools.
- The emerging science of nano-electronics holds out the possibility of placing *billions* of transistors on a signal chip, resulting in computers more powerful than today's by orders of magnitude. It might also lead to information storage devices of immense capacity—by "growing" chips and maybe even whole computers from individual atoms and molecules. Buzzword: *moletronics.*
- Nano-machines, the counterpart of nano-electronics, suggest incredibly small devices such as robots and assembly systems and consume minuscule quantities of energy.

- Nano-technologies involve designing and creating fundamental molecular clusters that have desirable electronic, mechanical, chemical, or biological properties. Such substances behave quite differently from molecules processed in bulk form and have the potential of creating entirely new kinds of products—and industries.

Advanced Computing

- Supercomputers, using massively parallel architectures and now operating at speeds as high as teraflops (trillions of floating point operations per second) will be available for a wide array of business modeling and technical projects. They will unleash the power of "chaos theory" to model complex systems as diverse as marketplace and buyer behavior, long-range weather forecasting, the spread of epidemic diseases around the world, and better ways to plan urban growth.
- Optical and copper wire will begin to replace aluminum in microprocessor and circuit interconnects, as they are smaller (line widths as small as 0.2 microns), run cooler, consume less power, and operate at faster clock speeds. These developments will lower costs as well; they hold the promise of countering Intel's late Gordon Moore's less-quoted "second law"—that chip labs get twice as expensive with each new generation of product.
- Highly compact optical data storage systems using lasers will greatly enhance the speed at which we will read information (data, text sound, and images).
- Encryption microchips and related technologies will serve society by protecting against fraudulent e-business transactions and by keeping privileged information from Internet interlopers. They will provide the electronic equivalent of personal signatures to authenticate buyers and sellers during online transactions. They will improve the security of networks and the computers attached to them. These technologies will push government policy regarding access and privacy.
- The role of the PC will certainly change because of its struggle to compete with the enormous capabilities that will become resident on the Internet. Rather, the PC likely will evolve as a network conductor, orchestrating software agents that deliver information.
- The ever-expanding demand for software will soon overcome the human ability to provide it; the solution lies in technology. One

authority, Paul Saffo (Director of the Institute for the Future, Menlo Park, California), suggests self-replicating software. His vision is platform-free software modules that could reside on a hyper-operating system within the Internet, that would design and assemble component packages to meet the user's specifications. Whatever the final answer, need compels the progress from custom, mind-crafted software to a mass-customization approach.

- More and more software services will reside on the Internet, giving any user vast access to tools, information, troubleshooting the network, recreational games, and so forth. Resident software will allow companies to outsource some management requirements to service providers on the net, or "netsourcing."
- Artificial intelligence will soon serve mainstream society in such areas as adaptive learning, recognizing, and identifying people and things, reasoning, and other functions attributed to natural intelligence.

Sensors
- Smart electronic and biosensors, now minuscule compared to their forerunners of the mid-1980s, already have become integrated directly into the point of use for such applications as air bags and antilock braking systems. Miniature electronic devices requiring far less power than conventional ones will make possible communications products that can function for long times on the smallest batteries. They will soon find wide applications in sports equipment, toys, military weaponry, and biomedical devices.
- Faster, more powerful digital signal processors (DSPs) will enable entirely new product families. Among them: noise cancellation technology—with latent markets ready to spring up to offer some measure of quiet in our ever-noisier society. Miniaturizing these devices will also improve such applications as mobile and tactile robots, more efficient numerical control machines, and auto/aircraft controls.

Production Systems
- The production environment of the future will be built upon representations of product data and process knowledge, drawn from geographically dispersed information bases. Intelligent software agents will create and integrate the specific production applications.

- The emergence of virtual products will allow customers to call up 3-D holograms to experience, via simulations, a personal interaction with the look, sound, and feel of automobiles and other complex products. Mass customization practices in cooperation with visual databases of CAD, CAM, CAE, and e-business will, in time, revolutionize the way many products are manufactured and marketed.
- The relatively new field of rapid prototyping will mature and extend into the production hardware domain, especially in the practice of mass customization.
- The apparel industry is poised for a revolution as computers now can laser-scan and map a customer's body, then simulate the colors and movement of various garments as the customer moves about naturally "wearing" them. This new dimension of virtual reality will eliminate the guesswork in choosing fabrics, styles, and colors and will then custom-cut and produce the garments and footwear.

Transportation

- The internal combustion engine that propels nearly every auto, truck, and bus on the planet is headed toward extinction. The future belongs to the science and technology of fuel cells. These "engines" produce electricity by the chemical combination of oxygen and either methanol or hydrogen. Oxygen-methanol emits carbon dioxide as a by-product, as does the conventional internal combustion engine, but only about half the amount. Oxygen-hydrogen fuel cells produce no CO_2—but hydrogen is expensive and is dangerously combustible.
- Long a dreamer's fantasy, the emergence of personal urban aircraft will lift us above the two-dimensional constraints of roads and freeways. Just think of the implications in the design, regulatory, and safety sectors of society.

The Internet: Tomorrow's Mega-Technology

The enormous promise of e-business isn't based on that preceding list of breakthrough technologies because it's even larger than the list. It's hard to overstate the commercial influence that the Internet will have for nearly everyone on planet Earth—probably the same impact that the mechanical lever and the steam engine had in their eras. It will change the balance of power between buyers and sellers. It will put information instantly in the hands of those who seek it. It will cater to every communications need. And in doing so, it will change the way people live and relate to one another.

The e-business industry soon will become a ubiquitous force in all aspects of work and play. Technologically, the backbone of this industry is fiber-optic cable having high-capacity, wide-bandwidth communications capacity. Through cable modem, this distribution system will provide an information pipeline bringing voice, video, text, and worldwide Web pages to everyone at speeds some 200 times faster than today's 56 kilobaud modem rates. And more powerful microprocessors will make these rates even faster in the near future—providing information fidelity on a par with our human senses. Memory and hard-disk storage capacities will likewise increase to supply the archival needs of this information-driven society. Local and long-distance telecom providers will make huge investments in this infrastructure, and the industry will further consolidate to provide the seamless system needed to satisfy the information appetite.

Wireless communication also will continue to have a major role in the new order. Just think of its transformational role in the world's underdeveloped regions that currently lack a cable infrastructure. Leaping instantly from the most primitive to the most advanced communications technology, these regions will forever change their cultures and value systems. Digital cellular telephony will take center stage in this evolving play. Satellite transmission is already functioning in many countries of the world through Motorola's Iridium project, the first among others sure to follow. It works by uploading signals to the nearest of the cluster of telecom satellites covering the globe, which then transmits those signals to others as needed and then downloads them to the local receiver. Although many technology obstacles need to be overcome to develop the traffic rates and bandwidths that provide the reliability and the fidelity to compete economically with cable systems, you can bet that such obstacles will be removed and that satellite telecom will be commonplace.

Along with the growth of these new information delivery systems will be a proportional growth in government regulation. This nation is already sensitized to the role of the federal government in regulating the telecom industry, but the best (worst?) is yet to come. Imagine the regulatory power the government could exercise over the burgeoning e-commerce industry. Yet this policing is necessary and appropriate. Data security, online privacy, intellectual property protection, and controversial content loom large over the e-commerce landscape, and tension likely will increase between government and industry groups over issues of regulating e-commerce—issues surrounding privacy and fraud. Businesses are already under mounting pressure from privacy advocates, government agencies, and Congress over the use of data gathered from online buyers. Many Web sites don't post specific privacy policies and subsequently sell the data they obtain to other companies. Some firms also track individual users as they move through a Web site, recording what they click on and what topics they search for.

As the e-business industry grows, so will major changes. Think back to the beginning of the auto industry. At one point, between 1904 and 1908, some 241 companies began operations in the United States alone. But within 20 years the industry consolidated to fewer than 10 successful companies. And the consolidation continues on a global scale even today. Expect that the nascent e-commerce business will follow a similar pattern. It will soon shift from domination by small, entrepreneurial companies to larger, established companies. This shift will then drive further growth of the infrastructure that enables e-commerce, which in turn will further accelerate the industry's growth (already doubling each year). But the fuel that will drive it depends upon ever-improving security, better existing and new services, and global commerce.

In the meantime, e-business will influence the future of current industries—in particular the print media. Metropolitan newspapers are now under siege because of lower readership. Sociologists say the reasons are many, among them users' impatience in finding what they want to read and overstimulation from long exposure to TV. Magazines of all sorts are "dumbing down" their content in efforts to keep readers' fleeting attention. Even the venerable Yellow Pages are threatened because of competition from the Internet, Web sites, and e-commerce.

Resale and service industries will also be affected by Internet-related services. Consumers can now deploy smart electronic agents known as "bots" (for "shopping ro*bots*") in the Web to search the commercial world for products and comparative prices. In their eagerness to offer customers exactly what they want, companies will be lured into providing more product options. Certainly mass customization has its place in the new order of things (see Chapter 2), but customization comes at a cost and, as the residential furniture industry has seen, you can be so eager to please customers that it drives your business into the ground.

Moreover, online shopping threatens to erode the strength of distribution channels by empowering buyers to end-run distributors and buy direct. Imposing widespread e-commerce and Web-based information access upon existing commercial methods will change these methods. Now add in such features as credit checking, customer-loyalty incentives, comparison-shopping services, and cross-marketing opportunities, and you have a revolution. As IBM's Wladawsky-Berger points out, a combinatorial explosion of agents will eventually float around in cyberspace in support of each commercial transaction. Yet it will take some years to develop the very high information bandwidths required to create virtual shopping.

Turning Technology Instincts into Product Concepts

If you own, manage, or otherwise have influence over your company's destiny, perhaps it's time to look critically at how you'll need to operate in the near future. In most respects, keep on doing what it is you do well. Work hard on the daily issues of total quality improvement, workforce training and empowerment, streamlining your R&D and new product development processes, tightening your supply and distribution chains, and of course, zealously winning and keeping your customers' loyalty. Continual improvement in these bread-and-butter issues will always pay off.

Beyond these quotidian tasks, however, you'll do well to craft a process that will challenge and refocus your strategies for the future, but be warned. The dizzying pace of technology change can get ahead of what markets want. It's called "technology push," and an example is personal computers: their capabilities have gotten ahead of what most users want and are comfortable using. The lesson is for you to keep an eye on these changes and think about how they likely will influence all aspects of your business. It's inevitable that you'll be doing some things differently in the immediate years ahead—like it or not. If you're technologically sophisticated, you'll find it easy to be "in tune" with new business patterns that technology will impose upon you. You're probably already tuned into some of the foregoing trends. But if you're not—like most managers—you have other ways to ride the right technology wave without remaking yourself into a neo-techie.

My first recommendation for turning technology into product concepts is to establish a process to track broad technology trends. Maintain vigilance over the rapidly changing technology landscape and make sure all your key people keep current on potential opportunities and threats. Don't just ask your chief engineer or technologist to be in charge. As a lone voice, he or she can't effectively preach to the unconverted.

A lot is at stake. History teaches that dominant players in an industry are often attacked and undermined by smaller competitors. The strategy is remarkably simple. Company A, an upstart or insignificant player, begins attacking giant Company B's low-end products with new technologies or technology innovations. Company B dismisses this minor annoyance and continues doing business as usual. But A gets a foot in the door because of superior product technology, pricing, or service. Once the door is open, Company A can continue choosing its attacks, setting the rules of engagement. Strategically successful growth begets more growth, and before Company B knows it, it's mortally affected.

Harvard's Clayton Christensen has described this phenomenon. Real examples abound. Highly efficient offshore minimills took 40 percent of the steel market from the giant U.S. mills, starting with the lowly rebar product line. Honda's success in the United States began in 1959 with the marketing of low-cost urban motorcycles in Los Angeles. Discount retail mega-stores seriously wounded mighty Sears, Roebuck's market dominance. Christensen warns of some potential future vulnerabilities. Think about digital cameras that would use cheap CMOS semiconductor technology (rather than costly charge-coupled device technology) to revolutionize photography. Think about Java and Linux program languages, with their independence from any specific operating system, as a means for changing the way software applications are delivered. And think about Internet telephony, which could well threaten established telcos such as AT&T, SBC, and their equipment suppliers, such as Lucent and Nortel. Beware of stealth attacks. How? By constantly monitoring emerging technology patterns and how they may affect your market.

To maintain that vigilance, consider the following ideas for harnessing R&D and emerging technologies—ideas that can work:

- Put the topic of technology trends on the agenda of every operating committee meeting. Expect all members to contribute to this dialogue; otherwise, some will only listen passively.
- Find and retain a *good* futurist who is familiar with your industry to brief your operating committee—and other groups—on changes that might affect your business. Select a person who is more down to earth than up in the sky.
- Create a "committee on futures" to come up with tactical recommendations for operating in the future. Its agenda should include system requirements, knowledge management, leveraging the Web

and e-commerce to your advantage, rethinking how new product candidates are proposed and selected, potential alliances, and so on. Include in this committee innovative people from all corners and levels of your business and encourage them to rock the boat.

- If you are to exploit the evolving technologies and changing market practices, you'll need managers who are comfortable working in the new environment. Make this a factor in your hiring, promotion, and succession planning.
- Most important, be critical of your business strategy and its linkage with the changing times. It's easy to create symbolic changes and point to them as proof that you are riding the right waves of the future. But it's much better to challenge and to measure your progress to ensure your competitive place in the future.

These steps are internal procedures. But what about business improvements with your suppliers and customers? Of course, you'll continue programs to reduce goods and payments cycle times; working with your suppliers to improve quality and dependability will always pay off. And if you haven't already, initiate some joint projects to implement e-business for handling all routine transactions.

But what else should you do with your supply chain to help carry you into the techno-environment of the future? My advice is to use and act upon newly gleaned information to make some supplier changes. It may be an opportunity in waiting. Historically, suppliers survived by cutting deals with their customers based on price. The game was simple: Customers beat up all their suppliers and kept only those left standing. But they didn't keep them for long because the next fight was just a year away. Then, sometime in the '80s, a fundamental shift occurred in supplier strategy—toward quality. Companies entered into multiyear supplier partnership agreements and linked success to training and to incremental price cuts. All parties enjoyed the benefits of the gain sharing realized by quality improvements. This enormously beneficial movement meant everyone stood to win. But that was then; the question now is, what's next?

I see the next step as building alliances with suppliers who are equipped to help you use and leverage the technology changes that lie ahead. It's more than just working more efficiently with your present partners, doing the same things you're doing today. You'll need partners who can support your transition into the new product families that will use these new technologies—partners who can help you provide the new services that will support those products. You probably don't have a sharp focus yet on what these future supply needs will be. But your vision must include it. I recommend that you continuously re-evaluate your supplier family and begin to place your long-term bets on those you think can support you down the road. Make this idea a task for your adviser groups. And always be vigilant of potential new suppliers who will help you meet your future needs.

You'll need to inform your supply partners of your changing technology inventory. Earlier in this chapter I described the three categories of core technologies to sustain a company in today's environment:

Pacing technologies—potential game changers, but not yet reduced to practice

Key technologies—essential for product differentiation, but can become obsolete by competitive forces

Base technologies—fundamental to your products, but don't offer competitive advantages.

The oncoming rush of new technologies will challenge your management of these knowledge-intensive competencies. They must be nourished by investments. They must also regularly be re-evaluated in light of your future product needs.

And what about your customers? Will the new wave of technologies alter the ways in which you relate to them? My answer is more no than yes. Generally, companies that embrace the principles of customer intimacy discussed in Chapter 6 will continue to do well. Shrink-wrap your products in ever-better services. Relate to your customers in the same way you'd like for your suppliers to relate to you. It's the *new* Golden Rule of business. Use it, and you'll succeed.

On the other hand, be a bit more cautious about being slave to the dictum "The customer is always right." Don't abandon it—just be cautious. Sometimes you *should* challenge your customer's wisdom. For one thing, be careful about being led into new product concepts that will yield you smaller margins. Look for alternative concepts to correct that approach. Weigh any product concept against newly developing technology: Is it the right approach? What are your competitors likely to do? And what about the market? Is your customer drawing you into a product targeted at a small market rather than an undeveloped, larger market?

These questions raise issues about training the decision-makers who have the power over new product creation. A race is on among companies of all sizes, and people of all levels within, to upgrade skills. At last count, over 1,600 corporate colleges and universities in the United States were chartered to provide the needed up-skilling. Even the venerable Dow Jones & Company has recently opened a university to focus on teaching investment principles. These and other companies see traditional universities not offering fast-cycle, tailored training and education that industry needs to compete. Training and education have finally found favor with companies of all stripes. Their leaders now are investing upward of 4 percent of total payroll in training and one trainer for every 100 employees.[6] These benchmarks are the kind all companies should look at. After all, your future depends in very large part upon your company's collective market wisdom and its technology savvy. Rest assured, these investments *do* pay back. Even average companies that modestly improve training programs see productivity gains of some 15 percent. Although few companies can approach the $800 million that GE invests each year on training and education, you still can't afford to sidestep this issue.

Then manage by asking questions. Should you outsource parts of your technology or keep it all in house? What about competitive intelligence? Training and education? Acquisitions and new alliances? Develop your information technology and human networks to share data, knowledge, and wisdom in real time. And then, of course, deal with the all-important issue of just who is going to be directly responsible for forging your technology strategy. This person (or executive team) should be adroit in building the critical connections between your research, product development, and market pieces.

You are now equipped with the best information available to manage your R&D operations and place your bets for your core and future technologies. Proceed with determination and vigor. You won't bat a thousand, but you will put in place the processes that will carry you to success. Your colleagues will follow your lead, and together you'll chart a more successful future for your company and all its stakeholders.

10.5: IDEAS FOR ACTION

1. Identify your core competencies—your special R&D and production competencies. Provide them with ongoing support at appropriate levels, and expect continuous improvement from them.

2. Consider outsourcing those technology competencies that you need but that don't contribute to your product distinctiveness. Look to partnerships with your suppliers.

3. Have senior management and one or more objective outside authorities review your R&D processes. Focus on two outcomes: creating a charter that meets your product creation requirements for the future, and setting ongoing measurements for your R&D processes and competitive benchmarks. Enlist your product and production people to develop suitable improvement goals.

4. Consider establishing an outside advisory board consisting of experienced technology executives and a futurist or two to work with your R&D managers. Give it a charter and specific expectations.

5. Have your R&D organization be accountable for a portfolio selection process, with ongoing justification and "kill" options for projects that don't have promise.

6. If your R&D operation is not integrally connected with your new product developers, fix it now; they must support a common agenda. One step in this direction is to set up a process that encourages R&D people to cycle through product development and production operations as part of their career planning.

7. Get as many of your technologists as possible in front of your customers, and frequently.

8. As in all business functions, provide suitable training and continuing education to keep your technologists current.

References

Chapter 1

1. *Wall Street Journal,* Aug. 9, 1999, p. A2.

Chapter 2

1. "Digital Rules: Technology and the New Economy," *Forbes,* August 10, 1998.
2. *Cathedral, Forge, and Waterwheel: Technology and Invention in the Middle Ages.* Frances and Joseph Gies. HarperCollins, 1994.
3. *Ancient Machines: From Wedges to Waterwheels.* Michael Woods and Mary B. Woods. Runestone Press (Minneapolis), 2000.
4. *Business Week,* June 29, 1998, pp. 62ff.
5. "Have You Looked at Your New Product Development Environment Lately?" by Philip H. Francis and John R. Greenwald, *Target,* the periodical of the Association for Manufacturing Excellence, vol. 13, no. 2 (April-May 1997), pp. 18–27.
6. *The Economist,* Feb. 21, 1998.
7. Francis and Greenwald, op. cit.
8. *Forbes,* March 10, 1997.
9. *Technotrends: How to Use Technology to Go Beyond Your Competition.* Daniel Burrus with Roger Gittines. HarperBusiness, 1994.
10. *Wall Street Journal,* June 23, 1998, p. A1.
11. *Harvard Management: Update,* May 1999, pp. 1ff.
12. *Wall Street Journal,* Nov. 11, 1998, p. B1.
13. *Newsweek,* April 20, 1998, p. 46.
14. "Planning for Product Platforms," by David Robertson and Karl Ulrich, *Sloan Management Review,* Summer 1998, pp. 19ff.

15. "Product Platforms in Software Development," by Marc H. Meyer and Robert Seliger, *Sloan Management Review*, Fall 1998, pp. 61–74.
16. ABC's *Nightline* news show, July 17, 1999.
17. *Mechanical Engineering* (ASME), April 1999, p. 56.
18. *Design News*, Dec. 21, 1998, p. 31.
19. "Key Drivers of Reduced Cycle Time," by A. K. Gupta and W. E. Souder, *Research*Technology Management*, July–Aug. 1998, p. 38.
20. "How Managers Can Succeed Through Speed," *Fortune*, Feb. 13, 1989, pp. 54–59.
21. *Product Development Performance*. Kim Clark and Takahiro Fujimoto. Harvard Business School Press, 1991.
22. "The Second Toyota Paradox: How Delaying Decisions Can Make Better Cars Faster," by Allen Ward, Jeffrey K. Liker, John J. Cristiano and Durwood K. Sobek II, *Sloan Management Review*, Spring 1995, pp. 43–61.
23. "SAP Stumbles in Creating a New Line," *Wall Street Journal*, June 23, 1999, p. A23.
24. *Manufacturing News*, April 20, 1998.
25. Clark and Fujimoto, op. cit.
26. "An Incremental Process for Software Implementation," by R. G. Fichman and S. A. Moses, *Sloan Management Review*, Winter 1999, pp. 39ff.
27. *The Economist*, Aug. 30, 1997, p. 49.

Chapter 2: General References

Managing Business Process Flows. R. Anupindi, S. Chopra, S. D. Deshmuhh, J. A. Van Mieghem, and E. Zemel. Simon & Schuster Custom Publishing, 1998.
Introduction to Supply Chain Management. Robert B. Handfield and Ernest L. Nichols, Jr. Prentice-Hall, 1999.
"Innovative Infrastructure for Agile Manufacturers," by J. D. Kasarda and D. A. Rondinelli, *Sloan Management Review*, Winter 1998, pp. 73ff.

Chapter 3

1. *Manufacturing News*, July 1, 1997, pp. 1ff.
2. *Manufacturing News*, Oct. 15, 1996.
3. *Wall Street Journal*, July 30, 1998.
4. *Manufacturing News*, Oct. 19, 1998.
5. *Upside*, Aug. 1998, pp. 94ff.
6. *Manufacturing News*, Jan. 5, 1998, pp. 1ff.
7. *Wall Street Journal*, Dec. 7, 1998, p. R30.
8. "Move 'Em or Wilt," *Word Trade*, March 1998, pp. 61ff.
9. *Wall Street Journal*, Nov. 16, 1998, p. B4.
10. *Manufacturing News*, August 5, 1996, pp. 1ff.
11. *Information Week*, Nov. 9, 1998, pp. 36–46.

12. *The Machine That Changed the World.* James P. Womack, Daniel Roos and Daniel Jones. Rawson, 1990.
13. *Product Development Performance.* Kim B. Clark and Takahiro Fujimoto. Harvard Business School Press, 1991.
14. "On the Couch," *Wall Street Journal,* Nov. 2, 1998.
15. *Manufacturing News,* April 2, 1998, pp. 3–4.
16. "Mass Customization: Implementing the Emerging Paradigm for Competitive Advantage," by Suresh Kotha, *Strategic Management Journal,* vol. 16 (1995), pp. 21–42.
17. "The Four Faces of Mass Customization," by James H. Gilmore and B. Joseph Pine II, *Harvard Business Review,* Jan.-Feb. 1997, pp. 91ff.

Chapter 4

1. "Cost Effective Information Technology," by Bill Rosser, *Executive Edge,* Sept. 1998, pp. 51–54.
2. *Manufacturing News,* Aug. 12, 1998, p. 2.
3. *Manufacturing News,* Jan. 5, 1999, p. 2.
4. *Manufacturing News,* Aug. 5, 1997.
5. *Wall Street Journal,* Jan. 6, 1999.
6. "ERP RIP?" *The Economist,* June 24, 1999, pp. 29ff.
7. *Insight,* Fall–Winter 1998, p. 16.
8. "PDM Moves to the Mainstream," by Ed Miller, *Mechanical Engineering,* Oct. 1998, pp. 74–79.
9. "Product Data Management: Beauty or the Beast?" *CIO Magazine,* May 1, 1998.
10. Ibid.
11. "Managing the Consultant," *Mechanical Engineering,* July 1981, p. 71.
12. "Enterprise Resource Planning (ERP)," by Robert A. Austin, Cedric X. Escalle, and Mark Cotteleer. Technology Note No. 699020. Harvard Business School, Feb. 1999, pp. 15–17.
13. Rosser, op. cit.
14. "What Is a Chief Knowledge Officer?" by Michael J. Earl and Jan A. Scott, *Sloan Management Review,* Winter 1999, pp. 29–38.

Chapter 5

1. *Leadership Secrets of Attila the Hun.* Warner Books, 1991.
2. *Sacred Hoops: Spiritual Lessons of a Hardwood Warrior.* Phil Jackson and Hugh Dellehanty. Hyperion Press, 1995.
3. *On Becoming a Leader.* Warren G. Bennis. Perseus Press, 1994.
4. Drawn from *Harvard Business Review,* Jan.-Feb. 1998, p. 194.
5. Taken from *Business Week,* Aug. 31, 1998, pp. 102ff.

6. *Wall Street Journal*, Sept. 8, 1997.
7. *Wall Street Journal*, Sept. 21, 1998, pp. 1ff.

Chapter 6

1. *Opening Digital Markets—Battle Plans and Business Strategies for Internet Commerce*. Walid Mougayar. McGraw-Hill, 1999.
2. *Mean Business: How I Save Companies and Make Good Companies Great*. Albert J. Dunlap and Bob Andelman. Simon & Schuster, 1997.
3. *Wall Street Journal*, June 22, 1998.
4. "Vision in Manufacturing," study by Deloitte Touche, New York, NY, 1998.
5. *Customer Intimacy: Pick Your Partners, Shape Your Culture, Win Together*. Fred Wiersema. Knowledge Exchange, 1996.

Chapter 7

1. "Revealed at Last: The Secret of Jack Welch's Success," *Forbes*, Jan. 26, 1998, p. 44.
2. *Principles of Quality Costs, American Society for Quality Control*. Milwaukee, 1986.
3. *Manufacturing News*, March 1998, p. 3.
4. "Play It Again, Samuelson," *The Economist*, Aug. 23, 1997.
5. *Total Quality Management*. John S. Oakland and Les Porter. Butterworth-Heinemann, 1995.
6. *Benchmarking: The Search for Industry Best Practices That Lead to Superior Performance*. Robert C. Camp. ASCQ Quality Press, 1989.
7. *Benchmarking for Best Practices: Winning Through Innovative Adaptation*. Christopher E. Bogan and Michael J. English. McGraw-Hill, 1994.
8. "Statistics of High Yield Manufacturing Processes," by Philip H. Francis, *Manufacturing Review* (ASME), vol. 1, no. 1 (March 1988), pp. 6–13.
9. "The House of Quality," by John R. Hauser and Donald Clausing, *Harvard Business Review*, May-June 1988, pp. 33–56.

Chapter 7: General References

Four Days with Dr. Deming: A Strategy for Modern Methods of Management. William J. Latzko and David M. Saunders. Addison-Wesley, 1995.
An Action Guide to Making Quality Happen. Robert Damelio and William Englehaupt. Quality Resources (The Kraus Organization Ltd.), New York, 1995.
A World of Quality; The Timeless Passport. Xerox Quality Solutions. ASQC Quality Press (Milwaukee), 1993.
Quality Planning and Analysis. 2nd Ed. J. M. Juran and Frank M. Gryna, Jr. McGraw-Hill, 1980.

Total Quality Management: Three Steps to Continuous Improvement. Arthur R. Tenner and Irving J. DeToro. Addison-Wesley, 1992.

Quality Management: Implementing the Best Ideas of the Masters. Bruce Brocka and M. Suzanne Brocka. Business One Irwin, 1992.

Taguchi Techniques for Quality Engineering. Phillip J. Ross. McGraw-Hill, 1988.

Developing Products in Half the Time. 2nd Ed. Preston G. Smith and Donald B. Reinertsen. John Wiley & Sons.

Chapter 8

1. "Must CIM Be Justified by Faith Alone?" by Robert S. Kaplan, *Harvard Business Review,* March 1986, pp. 87–95.
2. "What's Going Wrong with Activity-Based Costing?" by B. V. Balachandran and N. N. Thondavadi, *Corporate Controller,* Sept.-Oct. 1998, pp. 21–26.
3. From Battelle Memorial Institute, as reported in *Wall Street Journal,* Dec. 31, 1998, p. A2.
4. *Wall Street Journal,* Oct. 6, 1997, pp. A15ff.
5. "Relevance Lost: The Rise and Fall of Management Accounting," by H. Thomas Johnson and Robert S. Kaplan. *Harvard Business Review,* March 1987.

Chapter 8: General References

Principles of R&D Management. Philip H. Francis. American Management Associations, 1977.

Handbook of Cost Management. B. J. Brinker, editor. Warren, Gorham & Lamont, 1992.

Wickham Skinner, *Harvard Business Review,* July-Aug. 1986, pp. 55–59.

Mechanical Engineers' Handbook. Myer Kutz, editor. Wiley Interscience, 1986.

Fortune Magazine, Sept. 20, 1993.

World Class Manufacturing: The Next Decade. Richard J. Schonberger. The Free Press, 1996.

Chapter 9

1. *Principles of R&D Management.* Philip H. Francis. American Management Associations, 1977.
2. Larry Cohen, *Harvard Business Review,* Jan.-Feb. 1998, p. 185.
3. 35 United States Code 101.
4. *Wall Street Journal,* July 2, 1999, p. B4.
5. "Protecting Innovation," *Information Week,* Feb. 22, 1999, pp. 50–61.
6. Ibid.
7. *Loriano vs. Hobart Corp.,* 1998 WL 547071 N.Y.

Chapter 9: General References

"Japan's Dark Side of Time," by G. Stalk, Jr., and A. M. Webber, *Harvard Business Review,* 1993, pp. 93–102.

Wellsprings of Knowledge: Building and Sustaining the Sources of Innovation. Dorothy Leonard-Barton. Harvard Business School Press, 1998.

Chapter 10

1. *Wall Street Journal,* Jan. 4, 1999.
2. W. W. Lewis and L. H. Linden, *Sloan Management Review,* Summer 1990, pp. 76ff.
3. *Wall Street Journal,* Oct. 21, 1999, p. B6.
4. *Third Generation R&D: Managing the Link to Corporate Strategy.* Philip A. Roussel, Kamel N. Saad, and Tamara J. Erickson. Harvard Business School Press, 1991.
5. *Competing for the Future.* Gary Hamel and C. K. Prahalad. Harvard Business School Press, 1994.
6. "Training Expenditures Are a Good Indicator of Corporate Success," *Manufacturing News,* Feb. 19, 1999.

Chapter 10: General References

What Remains to Be Discovered: Mapping the Secrets of the Universe, the Origins of Life, and the Future of the Human Race. John Maddox. The Free Press, 1998.

The Inventor's Dilemma. Clayton M. Christensen. Harvard Business School Press, 1997.

"Aligning Technology with Business Strategy," by Arthur N. Chester, *Research* Technology Management,* Jan.-Feb. 1994, pp. 25–32.

Index

About the Author

PHILIP H. FRANCIS is a well-known engineer, manager, and author with some thirty-five years' professional experience. He began in research with McDonnell-Douglas and, upon completing his Ph.D. in applied mechanics, worked at the Southwest Research Institute in engineering research, where he published seventy articles in technical journals. During that time in San Antonio he also wrote the first professional book on the management of R&D organizations, edited two other technical books, and earned his MBA. From there he took an appointment as Professor and Chair at the Illinois Institute of Technology, where he developed an affinity to manufacturing and product development. After a brief time with the Industrial Technology Institute, Phil was appointed as Director of Advanced Manufacturing Technology at Motorola. While at Motorola, he also wrote the first article on the use of Six Sigma for quality improvement. Soon thereafter he was appointed Chief Technology officer at Schneider Electric (formerly the Square D Company). Following a brief stint at AT&T, Phil joined Mascon Information Technologies in Schaumburg, Illinois, as Managing Partner for Management Consulting.

A fellow of the ASME and recipient of its G. S. Larson Award for engineering excellence, Phil has served on the advisory boards of NIST, the Army Science Board, the Air Force Science Advisory Board, and some six universities.

This rich and varied set of experiences has afforded Phil a unique perspective on how new product development should be managed as *process*—and its essential dependencies upon R&D, manufacturing, and all other operations of the enterprise. Phil lives in Barrington Hills, Illinois, with his wife Diana, four children, and three grandchildren. In addition to writing, his hobbies include participating in track and field, appreciating fine wine, and admiring vintage sports cars. Phil can be reached at <philip@masconit.com>.

Printed in the United States
By Bookmasters